AMERICA'S NONPROFIT SECTOR

A Primer

Third Edition

Lester M. Salamon

with the assistance of
S. Wojciech Sokolowski and David Sturza

Library of Congress Cataloging-in-Publication Data
Salamon, Lester M.
 America's nonprofit sector : a primer / by Lester M. Salamon. — 3rd ed.
p. cm.
 Includes bibliographical references and index.
 ISBN 978-1-59542-360-3 (pbk. : alk. paper) 1. Charities—United
States. 2. Nonprofit organizations—United States. 3. Human services—
United States. 4. Public welfare—United States. I. Title.

HV91.S23 2011
361.7'630973—dc23
                                                    2011044159

ABOUT THE FOUNDATION CENTER

Established in 1956, the Foundation Center is the leading source of
information about philanthropy worldwide. Through data, analysis, and
training, it connects people who want to change the world to the resources
they need to succeed. The Center maintains the most comprehensive database
on U.S. and, increasingly, global grantmakers and their grants — a robust,
accessible knowledge bank for the sector. It also operates research, education,
and training programs designed to advance knowledge of philanthropy at
every level. Thousands of people visit the Center's web site each day and are
served in its five regional library/learning centers and its network of more
than 450 funding information centers located in public libraries, community
foundations, and educational institutions nationwide and around the world.
For more information, please visit foundationcenter.org or call (212) 620-4230.

The Foundation Center and author are grateful to the Charles Stewart Mott
Foundation for its support of this publication.

For Lynda, Noah, Genny, Matt, and Niki

With deep love and affection

Table of Contents

PART THREE. LOOKING TO THE FUTURE

List of Tables and Figures

CHAPTER 5

CHAPTER 6

CHAPTER 10

CHAPTER 11

CHAPTER 12

Foreword to Third Edition

by Reynold Levy

For more than 30 years, Lester Salamon has been the finest scholar and commentator on the nonprofit sector in America and around the world.

He has taught all within sight of his books, monographs, edited volumes, occasional papers, and scholarly journal articles more about the developed Third Sector in the United States and the burgeoning of NGOs outside of our borders than has any other scholar.

Thanks to Les, we know much about the inner dynamics of nonprofit health institutions, private primary and secondary schools, colleges and universities, and social service and performing arts organizations. We know the aggregate employment of 501(c)(3) organizations and the patterns of their earned and contributed income and of their assets.

Les has written meaningfully about the promise and the peril, the opportunity and the constraint, and the severe challenges that confront these precious pools of private initiative for the public good and of social capital.

Now comes the third and revised edition of *America's Nonprofit Sector: A Primer,* updating us on the immense contributions of the Third Sector to America's vitality and reminding us of the service choices we enjoy as citizens and of the contribution of nonprofit institutions to our nation's competitiveness.

The quality of Lester's scholarship is matched only by the continuity of his informed advocacy for these extraordinary institutions and social movements and all that they offer to the commonweal.

As an introduction to the nonprofit sector, this book is superb. As a reminder of the values advanced by the Third Sector and how it is changing, this update is of immense value.

If you are new to the subject matter, there is no better way to become familiar with it. If you are a veteran, *America's Nonprofit Sector: A Primer* will provide a terrific refresher course, bringing you up to speed.

In either case, and in any event, you will join me in utter admiration for the scholarly ingenuity and the evidence-based descriptions and explanations that animate this volume.

Lester Salamon is, himself, a nonprofit treasure. I have been privileged to learn much as his student and as an erstwhile colleague. So, too, will you.

Reynold Levy
President
Lincoln Center for the Performing Arts
New York City
September 14, 2011

Foreword to Second Edition

By John W. Gardner*

The nonprofit sector of American life is a wonder to behold. It includes an incredible range and variety of activities and institutions—from soup kitchens to the Metropolitan Museum of Art, from churches to hospitals, from the Girl Scouts to scientists studying DNA. It is an outlet for our community-serving impulses. It is the arena in which we fulfill our religious needs, serve our compassionate impulses, express our creativity in art and science, engage in citizen political action, and pursue our powerful urges toward education and health care. And much more.

Yet, until little more than 20 years ago, it was so comfortably taken for granted by the American people that no one had done much hard research on the sector.

When Brian O'Connell and I founded Independent Sector in 1980 to serve as an inclusive forum for the sector, it was apparent that we had to encourage the scholars of the nation to fill this unacceptable gap in our knowledge. And none responded more heroically than Lester Salamon. He has become the premier guide to the sector. He asks deeply relevant questions and answers them with hard data and keen analysis.

In this book he tells a story the reader won't find anywhere else. It is a critically important story for the understanding of our society.

*Foreword to second edition, November 1998.

Acknowledgments

Capturing the size, composition, financing, and role of America's nonprofit sector in solid empirical terms, as this volume attempts to do, is no task for the faint of heart. America's nonprofit sector is an enormous and richly diverse set of institutions, ranging from small soup kitchens and homeless shelters to enormous hospital complexes and far-flung research universities. Its functions, too, are wonderfully varied, embracing not only service activities, but also purely expressive and advocacy ones, for this sector is the home not only of soup kitchens and hospitals but also of orchestras and operas, religious congregations and recreation clubs, advocacy organizations for and ones against virtually every imaginable cause.

As if this were not sufficient to deter the kind of overview attempted here, the data sources through which to view this richly diverse set of institutions are themselves fragmented and confusing, despite some notable improvements. Official government data sources still define the sector differently in different fields of nonprofit activity. Official data on nonprofit revenues treat some forms of government payments as market sales, obscuring the true impact of government funding on the sector's fiscal health. Widely used estimates of private giving contain considerable double counting. As a result, different data sources yield widely different estimates of the same parameters of the same institutions. Piecing together an accurate picture of the underlying reality thus requires a great deal of patience and a great tolerance for ambiguity.

Luckily, my journey through this jumble of statistics was helped enormously in this revision by two very skillful associates. For the basic nonprofit financial and government spending data reported in Chapters 3-5, I benefited greatly from the assistance of Dr. S. Wojciech Sokolowski, who tapped into a variety of Bureau of Economic Analysis, Internal Revenue Service, and Census Bureau sources. For the remaining chapters I had the able assistance of Mr. David Sturza, who chased down and reconciled literally dozens of data sources on the numerous separate components of the U.S. nonprofit universe and its relation to government and business. To both of them I express my gratitude and my admiration.

Thanks are also due to editorial supervisor Teri Wade and Foundation Center production manager Christine Innamorato for invaluable assistance in keeping this project on track and for making it as clear and attractive as possible.

Finally, I am indebted to the Charles Stewart Mott Foundation for crucial support that made it possible for us to make this new edition available to the many students of the nonprofit sector in the U.S. and abroad who have come to rely on it for a basic introduction to this important sector.

Needless to say, none of these organizations or individuals bears any responsibility for any shortcomings this work may still contain or any views or interpretations it may reflect. That responsibility is mine alone.

The nonprofit sector has long been the invisible subcontinent on the landscape of our society, buried in our economic statistics, ignored in academic curricula, and frequently misrepresented for ideological reasons in our political debates. This book, like its two preceding editions, is designed to rescue this set of institutions from the obscurity and misunderstanding to which it has long been consigned, to lay out the contours of this set of institutions in as clear and precise a way as possible, and thereby to provide policymakers, the press, nonprofit managers, students, and citizens at large an accessible guide to this sector and its important work. If it accomplishes this objective in some small measure, it will have served its purpose well.

Lester M. Salamon
Annapolis, Maryland
November 2011

1

Introduction

Modern societies, whatever their politics, have found it necessary to make special provisions to protect individuals against the vagaries of economic misfortune, old age, and disability; to secure basic human rights; to preserve and promote cherished social and cultural values; and to provide institutional vehicles through which individuals can join together to bring important matters to public attention and voice their support for policies they favor or oppose.

Because of growing social and economic complexity, what could be handled at an earlier time, however imperfectly, by a combination of self-reliance, spontaneous neighborliness, ad hoc coalitions, and family ties has required more structured responses in modern times.

The nature of these responses varies, however, from place to place. In some countries, governments have guaranteed their citizens a minimum income and a minimum level of health care, housing, access to culture, and other necessities of life. In others, private corporations or private charitable institutions shoulder a far larger share of the responsibility for coping with human needs. And in still others, perhaps the most numerous, complex, mixed systems of aid have emerged, combining elements of public and private finance and provision, collective and individual responsibility.

In few countries is the system of aid more complicated and confusing, however, than in the United States. Reflecting a deep-seated tradition of individualism and an ingrained hostility to centralized institutions, Americans have resisted the worldwide movement toward predominantly governmental approaches to social welfare provision, adding new governmental protections only with great reluctance and then structuring them in ways that preserve a substantial private role. While it may no longer be true, as it was when the Frenchman Alexis de Tocqueville visited America in 1835, that "Wherever at the head of some undertaking you see the government in France, or a man of rank in England, in the United States you will be sure to find an association,"[1] the fact remains that nonprofit organizations continue to play a vital role in American life even as government social protections have expanded.

America has an intricate "mixed economy" of welfare that blends public and private action in ways that few people truly understand.

The result is an intricate "mixed economy" of welfare that blends public and private action in ways that few people truly understand. In fact, the resulting system is not a system at all, but an ad hoc collection of compromises between the realities of economic necessity and the pressures of ideology and political tradition.

One of the more important features of this American approach to social welfare provision is the considerable role it leaves to private, nonprofit organizations, to nongovernmental institutions that nevertheless serve essentially public, as opposed to private, economic goals. Moreover, these organizations do not serve only social welfare ends; they play many other roles as well—as vehicles for cultural or religious expression, as mechanisms for policy advocacy, as instruments for social cohesion, and more.

Of all the components of American society, however, this is one of the most commonly misunderstood and about which the least is known.

The purpose of this "primer" is to fill this sizable gap in knowledge about America's nonprofit sector and the role it plays in American life. To do so, however, it is necessary not only to examine the scope, scale, and structure of the nonprofit sector, but also to put this set of organizations into context in relation to government and private businesses operating in the same fields. More specifically, this primer seeks to answer questions such as the following:

- What are nonprofit organizations, what features do they have in common, and why do they exist?

- What different types of nonprofit organizations are there, and what is the scale of each major type?

- Where do nonprofit organizations get their funds? And what share of these funds actually comes from philanthropy, from private charitable contributions?

- How extensive is government activity in the fields in which nonprofit organizations are active? Is it true, as many people believe, that government spending has "crowded out" nonprofit activity in these fields, or is it more the case that it has "crowded" nonprofits "in"?

- What do nonprofit organizations do, and how significant a role do they play in the various fields in which they are involved? For example:

  - What share of all hospital beds are in nonprofit hospitals as compared to government hospitals or private, for-profit hospitals?

  - What proportion of all home health facilities are nonprofits as opposed to for-profits?

  - What share of all colleges and universities are nonprofits, and what proportion of all college students are enrolled in nonprofit institutions as opposed to public (governmental) ones?

  - What have been the recent trends in all these dimensions of the nonprofit role in American life? Are nonprofits generally gaining ground or losing it? What implications does this have for the quality of life in this country?

Of all the components of American society, the nonprofit sector is one of the most commonly misunderstood and the one about which the least is known.

To answer these and related questions, the discussion that follows falls into three major sections containing twelve chapters beyond this introduction. The four chapters that comprise Part One provide a broad overview of the nonprofit sector and its role in American life. The first chapter in this section (Chapter 2) defines more precisely what nonprofit organizations are, identifies what features they have in common, and outlines what the basic rationale for this set of organizations is. Chapter 3 examines the differences that nevertheless exist among the entities that make up the American nonprofit sector and looks in detail at the "public-benefit portion" that is the major focus of the balance of the book. In Chapter 4, attention turns to the governmental and business roles in the fields where nonprofits are active and the relationship between governmental activity and the activity of the nonprofit sector. Chapter 5 puts current realities into historical perspective by reviewing the evolution of government and the nonprofit sector and the recent trends to which they have been exposed.

Against this backdrop, Part Two looks more closely at the scale and role of the major subcomponents of the public-benefit nonprofit sector— health, education, social services, arts and culture, religion, advocacy, and international aid. For each, an attempt is made to identify the role of the nonprofit sector; to compare it to the roles played by government and private, for-profit firms; to document the sources nonprofits draw on to support their activities; and to highlight recent trends.

Part Three then rounds out the discussion in three ways. First, it puts American realities into context by examining the overall scope, composition, and financing of nonprofit organizations elsewhere in the world. Second, it reviews some of the key trends and challenges that American nonprofit organizations are facing at the present time. Finally, it draws some general conclusions that flow from this work.

Clearly, no work of this scale can offer a full evaluation of the nonprofit sector and its contributions to American life. The conscious purpose here, therefore, is primarily descriptive, to portray the major components of this complex sector, to show how they fit into the larger mosaic of societal institutions, and to do so in as accessible and non-technical a fashion as possible.

Nonprofit organizations not only serve social welfare ends; they are vehicles for cultural or religious expression, mechanisms for policy advocacy, instruments for social cohesion, and more.

Even this modest objective poses serious challenges, however, and the challenges have not grown easier over time even though this is the third edition of this work.[2] No single data source compiles systematic information on all the various facets of the nonprofit sector or of the social welfare system of which it is a significant part. Some highly useful data sources available earlier have been discontinued. Thus, for example, the U.S. Social Security Administration used to publish an annual estimate of government social welfare expenditures broken down between national and state/local government, but that series has been discontinued. What is more, various data sources covering similar aspects of the same field often provide widely varying estimates because of subtle differences in definitions and coverage. For example, total spending by hospitals as reported in the Health Care Financing Administration's "national health expenditures" series is hard to reconcile with the independent estimates provided at five-year intervals in the U.S. Census Bureau's *Economic Census* or the annual surveys conducted by the American Hospital Association.[3] Assembling a full picture of the scope of nonprofit activity and how it compares to the scope of government and business activity in each of the major subfields is therefore a Herculean task, requiring careful sifting of dozens of different data sources and reconciliation of hundreds of definitional and empirical anomalies.

Though complicated, however, such an effort is well worth undertaking, and not just for descriptive or academic reasons. In addition:

- It can better equip both policymakers and the citizenry at large to understand a system that has long seemed to defy comprehension;

- It can clarify the role of the long-overlooked nonprofit sector and thereby boost this sector's visibility and credibility;

- It can introduce non-Americans to the important role that nonprofit organizations play in our social and political life;

- It can debunk some of the myths and misconceptions that continue to confuse public understanding of this important sector;

- It can thus enable all concerned to make more sensible policy choices and comprehend the serious challenges that this set of institutions currently confronts.

These, at any rate, are some of the objectives we seek.

ENDNOTES

1. Alexis de Tocqueville, *Democracy in America: The Henry Reeve Text,* Vol. II (New York: Vintage Books, 1945 [1835]), 114.

2. Other accounts provide useful information on the American nonprofit sector, but none of these systematically compares the nonprofit sector to other components of our mixed economy both in general and in particular subfields. See, for example: Waldemar A. Nielsen, *The Endangered Sector* (New York: Columbia University Press, 1979); Michael O'Neill, *The Third America: The Emergence of the Nonprofit Sector in the United States* (San Francisco: Jossey-Bass Publishers, 1989); and successive editions of *The Nonprofit Almanac,* most recently published by The Urban Institute Press. See, for example: Kennard T. Wing, Thomas H. Pollak, and Amy Blackwood, *The Nonprofit Almanac* (Washington, DC: The Urban Institute Press, 2008).

3. The *Economic Census,* for example, includes public (governmental) institutions in its data on "tax-exempt" hospitals, whereas the American Hospital Association differentiates between nonprofit and government entities.

PART ONE
Overview

2

What Is the Nonprofit Sector and Why Do We Have It?

Nothing, in my opinion, is more deserving of our attention than the intellectual and moral associations of America.

—Alexis de Tocqueville, 1835

Few aspects of American society are as poorly understood or as obscured by mythology as the thousands of day care centers, clinics, hospitals, higher education institutions, civic action groups, advocacy organizations, museums, symphonies, and related organizations that comprise America's private, nonprofit sector.

More than a century and a half ago, the Frenchman Alexis de Tocqueville identified this sector as one of the most distinctive and critical features of American life. Yet, despite a steady diet of charitable appeals, most Americans know precious little about this sector or what it does. Indeed, to judge from press accounts and national policy debates, not to mention college curricula, it would seem as if the nonprofit sector largely disappeared from the American scene around the time of the Great Depression of the 1930s, as attention came to focus instead on the role of government and market enterprises.

In fact, however, in this, the third century of the American democratic experiment, the private, nonprofit sector remains at least as potent a component of American life as it was when Tocqueville observed it more than a century and a half ago. This sector contains some of the most

9

prestigious and important institutions in American society—Harvard University, the Metropolitan Museum of Art, and the NAACP, to name just a few (see Table 2.1). More than that, it engages the activities and enlists the support of literally millions of citizens, providing a mechanism for self-help, for assistance to those in need, and for the pursuit of a wide array of other interests and beliefs. Indeed, more than 70 million people work for American nonprofit organizations either as paid employees or part-time volunteers, well over half as many people as turned out to vote for president in the historically high-turnout 2008 election.[1] Finally, this sector has helped give rise to a characteristically, though hardly exclusively, American version of the modern welfare state, though it is a version that few Americans seem to recognize or understand. The heart of this pattern is a widespread partnership between government and nonprofit groups in which government supplies much of the funding but nonprofit organizations deliver much of the assistance.[2] For all of these reasons, it is as impossible to comprehend American society and American public policy today without a clear understanding of the nonprofit sector as it was in the time of Tocqueville.

TABLE 2.1: Sample Nonprofit Organizations

American Cancer Society	Girl Scouts of America
American Enterprise Institute	Harvard University
American Red Cross	Metropolitan Museum of Art
Audubon Society	Montefiore Hospital
Boy Scouts of America	National Association for the Advancement of Colored
The Brookings Institution	People (NAACP)
Catholic Relief Services	New York Philharmonic
C.A.R.E.	Planned Parenthood
Environmental Defense Fund	Princeton University
Folger Theater	Rockefeller Foundation

What Is the Nonprofit Sector?

But what is this "nonprofit sector"? What do the organizations that are part of this sector have in common? Why do we have such organizations? What purpose do they serve?

A DIVERSE SECTOR

Unfortunately, the answers to these questions are somewhat complicated because of the great diversity of this sector. U.S. tax laws contain no fewer than thirty-nine separate sections under which organizations can claim exemption from federal income taxes as nonprofit organizations.[3]

Mutual insurance companies, certain cooperatives, labor unions, business associations, and charitable and educational institutions are all included (see Table 2.2).

TABLE 2.2: Types of Tax-Exempt Organizations Under U.S. Law

Tax Code Section	Type of Tax-Exempt Organization
220(e)	Medical Savings Accounts (MSAs)
401(a)	Qualified pension plans
408(e)	Individual Retirement Arrangements (IRAs)
501(c)(1)	Corporations organized under Act of Congress
501(c)(2)	Title-holding corporations
501(c)(3)	Religious, educational, charitable, scientific, etc.
501(c)(4)	Civic leagues, social welfare organizations
501(c)(5)	Labor, agricultural organizations
501(c)(6)	Business leagues
501(c)(7)	Social and recreational clubs
501(c)(8)	Fraternal beneficiary societies
501(c)(9)	Voluntary employees' beneficiary associations
501(c)(10)	Domestic fraternal societies
501(c)(11)	Teachers' retirement fund
501(c)(12)	Benevolent associations
501(c)(13)	Cemetery companies
501(c)(14)	State-chartered credit unions and mutuals
501(c)(15)	Mutual insurance companies
501(c)(16)	Corporations to finance crop operations
501(c)(17)	Supplemental unemployment benefit trusts
501(c)(18)	Employee pension trusts (pre-1959)
501(c)(19)	Veterans organizations
501(c)(21)	Black lung benefit trusts
501(c)(22)	Withdrawal liability payment funds
501(c)(23)	Pre-1880 veterans organizations
501(c)(24)	Retirement funds
501(c)(25)	Title-holding corporations or trusts
501(c)(26)	State-sponsored high-risk health insurance organizations
501(c)(27)	State-sponsored workers' compensation reinsurance organizations
501(d)	Apostolic and religious organizations
501(e)	Cooperative hospital service organizations
501(f)	Cooperative services organizations of educational organizations
501(k)	Child-care organizations
501(n)	Charitable risk pools
521	Farmers' cooperatives
527	Political organizations
529	Qualified state-sponsored tuition programs

The best known, however, are the "religious, charitable, and educational" organizations eligible for tax exemption under Section 501(c)(3) of the Internal Revenue Code, the so-called "501(c)(3) organizations." Even this narrower group embraces a wide assortment of institutions, however, including:

- small, one-room soup kitchens for the homeless;

- massive hospital complexes;

- museums, art galleries, and symphony orchestras;

- day care centers;

- prestigious universities;

- foster care and adoption agencies; and

- advocacy and civic action groups bringing pressure on government and businesses to clean the environment, protect children, promote civil rights, or pursue a thousand other causes.

It is as impossible to comprehend American society and American public policy today without a clear understanding of the nonprofit sector as it was in the time of Tocqueville.

THE TERMINOLOGICAL TANGLE

Complicating understanding of this sector further is the diverse, and somewhat confusing, terminology used to depict it. A great many such terms are used—nonprofit sector, charities, independent sector, voluntary sector, tax-exempt sector, and, more recently, civil society sector, "social economy," and "social ventures." Each of these terms emphasizes one aspect of the reality represented by these organizations at the expense of downplaying, or overlooking, other aspects. Each is therefore at least partly misleading. For example:

- *Charities,* or *charitable sector,* emphasizes the help these organizations give to the poor and the support they receive from private, charitable donations. But as we shall see, help to the poor is by no means the only function of these organizations, and private charitable contributions do not constitute the only, or even the major, source of their revenue.

- *Independent sector* emphasizes the important role these organizations play as a "third force" outside of the realm of government and private business. But as we shall see, these organizations are far from independent of government and business. To the contrary, they are intimately interrelated with them.

- *Voluntary sector* emphasizes the significant input that volunteers make to the management and operation of this sector. But as we shall see, once account is taken of the number of hours volunteers actually work, it becomes clear that most of the activity of these organizations is carried out by paid employees.

- *Tax-exempt sector* emphasizes the fact that under U.S. tax law the organizations in this sector are exempt from the national income tax and from most state and local property taxes. But this term begs the question of what characteristics qualify organizations for this treatment in the first place. In addition, because the income earned and the purchases made by employees of these organizations are taxed just like those of other workers, it is not true that these organizations generate no tax revenue. Finally, units of government are also "tax exempt," creating another source of possible confusion.

- *Civil society sector,* the term that gained particular currency during the popular uprisings that overthrew the Communist regimes in Central and Eastern Europe in the late 1990s and that is still widely used internationally, emphasizes the citizen base of these organizations and the role these organizations play as vehicles for citizen engagement. But in the United States, nonprofit organizations are by no means all membership associations, and advocacy activity often takes a back seat to service delivery as the focus of their energies.

- *Social economy* is a term used widely in some parts of Western Europe to refer to the broad array of organizations whose primary purpose is to serve the common needs of stakeholders rather than to maximize shareholder profits. However, this term embraces not only nonprofit organizations but also cooperatives, mutual insurance companies, and other financial institutions that have a decidedly commercial character and that distribute profits to their shareholders.[4]

- *Social venture* is a relatively recent term used to depict a particular class of organizations that utilize market-type approaches to pursue social objectives. Some of these are organized legally as nonprofit organizations, some as for-profits, and still others as a new hybrid legal form known as an L3C, or low-profit, limited liability corporation.[5]

- Even *nonprofit sector,* the term most widely used in the United States, is not without its problems. As we shall see, it is not the case that these organizations are prohibited from earning profits. What is prohibited is the distribution of any profit they may earn to their officers or directors.

A CRUCIAL DISTINCTION: PHILANTHROPY VERSUS THE NONPROFIT SECTOR

A further source of confusion in this field arises from the widespread practice of equating "the nonprofit sector" with "philanthropy." In fact, however, these two terms, while related, are quite different:

- The *nonprofit sector* consists of a broad set of organizations that share a number of common characteristics that earn them special privileges, such as exemption from most federal, state, and local taxes. Included are thousands of day care centers, private hospitals, universities, research institutes, community development organizations, soup kitchens, foster care facilities, social service agencies, employment and training centers, museums, art galleries, symphonies, zoos, business and professional associations, religious congregations, advocacy organizations, and many more.

- *Philanthropy,* by contrast, refers to one of many sources of support such organizations can receive, namely voluntary gifts of time or valuables (money, securities, property) provided by private individuals or organizations. To be sure, some nonprofit organizations have the generation or distribution of such philanthropic contributions as their principal line of activity. But as we will see, these are not the only types of nonprofit organizations, and philanthropy is not the only, or even the major, source of nonprofit support.

A source of confusion arises from the widespread practice of equating "the nonprofit sector" with "philanthropy." In fact, while they are related, they are also quite different.

FIVE DEFINING CHARACTERISTICS

What, then, do the organizations that comprise the "nonprofit sector" have in common? What are the defining characteristics of this sector?

Broadly speaking, five characteristics seem most fundamental (see Table 2.3), while a sixth is present by implication.[6] In particular, as we will use the term here, the nonprofit sector refers to a collection of entities that are:

TABLE 2.3: Five Defining Characteristics of the Nonprofit Sector

The nonprofit sector is a collection of entities that are:

1. organizations
2. private, as opposed to governmental
3. non-profit-distributing
4. self-governing
5. noncompulsory

- *Organizations,* that is, they are institutionalized to some extent. Purely ad hoc, informal, and temporary gatherings of people are not considered part of the nonprofit sector, even though they may be quite important in people's lives. At the same time, under American law it is not necessary for an organization to be formally incorporated, or even to secure formal recognition by the Internal Revenue Service, in order to function as a nonprofit organization. Typically, however, nonprofit organizations secure legal standing as corporations under state laws. This corporate status makes the organization a legal person and largely frees the officers from personal financial responsibility for the organization's commitments. Confirmation of their *tax-exempt* status is then secured through registration with the Internal Revenue Service, an organ of the federal, or national, government.

- *Private,* that is, they are institutionally separate from government. Nonprofit organizations are neither part of the governmental apparatus nor governed by boards dominated by government officials. Nonprofit organizations can, however, receive government financial support, even very significant government support. What is more, government participation on nonprofit boards is not unheard of, as was the case with Yale University, for example, until the 1870s.[7] But what is important is that nonprofit organizations be fundamentally private institutions in basic structure and governance.

- *Non-profit-distributing,* that is, they cannot distribute any profits they might earn to their directors, managers, or other stakeholders. Nonprofit organizations may accumulate profits in a given year; that is, their revenue can exceed their expenditures. But the profits must be plowed back into the basic mission of the agency, not distributed to the organizations' stakeholders. This differentiates nonprofit organizations from the other component of the private sector—private businesses.

- *Self-governing,* that is, they are fundamentally in control of their own activities. Nonprofit organizations have their own internal procedures for governance and are not controlled by outside entities. Indeed, they have the ultimate power to vote themselves out of existence.

- *Non-compulsory,* that is, participation in them is not a function of birth or required by law or official sanction. Rather, it involves some meaningful element of free choice. Voluntary service on the governing boards of such organizations is one manifestation of this criterion, but staffing of the organization solely, or chiefly, by volunteers is not required.

In a complex society such as ours, the right to free expression has little effective meaning unless it is joined to the right of free association, so that individuals can merge their individual voices and thereby make them effective.

A sixth crucial characteristic that is often associated with nonprofit organizations but that is difficult to use as part of a general definition of these organizations is that of serving the "public good" or being "of public benefit." The problem with treating this concept as part of the definition is that notions of the "public good" are highly subjective, and people can and do differ in what they embrace in the term. In the United States, the interpretation of public purpose is fairly broad and follows British "common law" usage, which has relied on more than four hundred years of legal interpretation of the term "charitable," initially incorporated in the Elizabethan Statute of Charitable Uses in 1601, as the touchstone for exemption from taxation and hence as the definition of valid public purpose. As summarized in the late nineteenth century, this line of cases established four broad meanings of the concept of "charitable": relief of poverty, advancement of education, advancement of religion, and other purposes beneficial to the community.[8] In addition to the broad umbrella term "charitable," the U.S. Internal Revenue Code identifies over forty more specific purposes that are viewed as being sufficiently imbued with public purpose to qualify organizations primarily engaged in them for exemption from corporate income taxes. Quite apart from these specific elaborations of exempt purposes, moreover, at least two of the five defining characteristics of nonprofit organizations identified above function as "proxies" for the concept of "public purpose" without having to spell out what public purposes are or to rely on changing legislative enactments. After all, if people choose to participate voluntarily in a class of organizations from which they are barred from receiving profits, it must be because they see some broader public purpose being served by the organizations. Including a particular "public benefit" criterion in the definition is, therefore, not only potentially misleading but also redundant.

The Rationale: Why Do We Have a Nonprofit Sector?

Why does the nonprofit sector exist in the United States, or any other country? Why did such organizations come into existence, and why do we give these organizations special tax and other advantages? Clearly no single explanation can suffice to answer these questions. To the contrary, at least five lines of argument have been advanced to explain the existence of nonprofit organizations.

MODERNIZATION

In the first place, the emergence and growth of nonprofit organizations, of institutions that people join voluntarily, has been traced to the process of modernization, to industrialization and urbanization. Traditional societies relied on families, tribes, and kinship relationships into which people were born to provide support and protection against the vagaries of nature or of other humans. As long as society was relatively simple, people essentially lived with their kin, and kin networks provided sufficient protection against most dangers, there was little need, and little opportunity, for individuals to join together in broader groupings based on voluntary association. As economies became more complex and populations more dispersed, however, these traditional institutions could no longer provide sufficient protection, and people found it necessary to join in voluntary groupings, often building them, however, on the base of the pre-existing tribal and kinship networks.[9]

MARKET FAILURE

In addition to modernization theories that attribute the development of nonprofit organizations to the growing complexity of social and economic life, a second set of theories points to the limitations that even modern social institutions exhibit to explain the emergence of a nonprofit sector. Especially noteworthy here are certain inherent limitations of the market, what classical economic theory refers to as *market failures*. According to this line of theory, the market system works quite well for supplying *private goods*, the things we consume individually, such as shoes, cars, clothing, and food. But it has difficulty responding to demands for *public* or *collective goods*, that is, those things that can only be consumed collectively, such as clean air, national defense, or safe neighborhoods. What sets these so-called *public goods* apart is the serious "free-rider" problem that attends their production because, once they are produced, everyone can benefit from them even if they have not shared in the cost. Therefore, each individual has an incentive to let his or her neighbors bear the cost of these public goods, knowing full well that he or she can nevertheless still share in the benefits. Since everybody has the same incentive, however, the inevitable result of relying solely on the market to produce such collective goods is that far less of them will be produced than people really want, creating an unsatisfied demand for collective goods.

According to the "market failure" theory, nonprofit organizations exist to meet citizen demands for "collective" goods and services that both markets and governments have trouble meeting in diverse societies.

In classical economic theory, it is this unsatisfied demand for collective goods that provides the ultimate economic rationale for government, since government can overcome the free-rider problem by compelling all citizens to share in the cost of desired collective goods. But students of the nonprofit sector have pointed out that government itself has inherent limitations in supplying collective goods, even in a democracy. According to one line of argument, this is particularly true in circumstances where religious, ethnic, or racial diversity makes it difficult for citizens to come to agreement on the range of collective goods they want, thus making it impossible to generate the majority support needed to trigger a governmental response in a democracy.[10] Ideological and economic disputes can also lead to government inaction. To meet the unsatisfied demands for collective goods in such situations, another mechanism is needed, and nonprofit organizations provide such a mechanism. These organizations allow groups of individuals to pool their resources voluntarily to produce collective goods they mutually desire or find it important to provide but cannot convince a sufficient majority of their countrymen, or those in positions of power, to support. Indeed, support for reliance on such organizations has at times been used as a rationale to avoid extending governmental protections and the taxation and regulation it can bring with it.[11]

TRUST

A third explanation for the existence of nonprofit organizations emphasizes another limitation of the market: its reliance on a robust flow of information between buyers and sellers of goods and services. Where such information is not available and information "asymmetries" exist, the market cannot adequately transmit clues from buyers to sellers, and buyers can easily be duped. Yet this is precisely the situation in circumstances where the purchasers of goods or services are not the same as the consumers of these goods or services, as is the case, for example, with nursing home care, where the consumers are often elderly people with limited consumer choice or ability to discriminate among products, and the purchasers are their children. In such situations, the normal operations of the market, which require that consumers base their decisions on their opinions about the cost and quality of the goods or services that they purchase, simply cannot operate. Economists refer to this as *contract failure*.[12] In such situations, purchasers look for some substitute for the pure operation of the market. According to this theory, nonprofit organizations offer such a substitute because the "nondistribution constraint," or prohibition on the distribution of profits, under which they operate makes them more trustworthy than for-profit firms, whose profit-maximizing objective may cause them to cut corners on unsuspecting consumers.

PLURALISM/FREEDOM AND STAKEHOLDER THEORIES

A fourth explanation for the existence of nonprofit organizations has less to do with the services these organizations provide than with the flexibility and freedom they afford and the expression they can give to a variety of social, political, religious, cultural, occupational, ethnic, and other perspectives. This feature of nonprofit organizations resonates especially strongly with America's ideology of individualism. In fact, so strong is this impulse in the American psyche that politicians, especially on the right, have used this feature of the nonprofit sector as a rationale for opposing extensions of governmental social and environmental protections, arguing that voluntary action through nonprofit organizations can handle the problems instead, often overlooking in the process the extent to which nonprofit organizations have had to turn to governmental support to sustain many of their critical service functions.[13]

Nevertheless, nonprofit organizations do facilitate the exercise of individual initiative for the public good just as private businesses facilitate the exercise of individual initiative for the private good.

This line of argument connects as well to what some theorists of the nonprofit sector refer to as the "supply-side" or "stakeholder" theory of the nonprofit sector.[14] The central argument of this theory is that a need for nonprofit organizations is not sufficient to ensure that such organizations are created. At least as important, and perhaps more so, is a supply of individuals who take the initiative to form such organizations. Such individuals can be motivated by religious or other moral convictions, by ideological concerns, by a desire to win adherents to a religious or other cause, by dissatisfaction with the existing range of services for those about whom they care, by a sense of justice, by professional interests, by a desire for creative expression, or by any of a host of other considerations. Whatever the motivation, where individuals with such motivations are in plentiful supply, as they appear to be in the United States, the likelihood is great that substantial numbers of nonprofit organizations will be formed.

"Government operations tend to be everywhere alike. With individuals and voluntary associations, on the contrary, there are varied experiments, and endless diversity of experience." —John Stuart Mill, On Liberty

---

Reflecting this, it should come as no surprise that most of the major reform movements that have animated American life over the past century or more have taken form within the nonprofit sector—the abolitionist movement, the women's suffrage movement, and the more recent movements for civil rights, environmental protection, workplace safety, child welfare, women's rights, and libertarianism.

What is more, this line of theory also helps explain why nonprofit organizations often survive and prosper even after government enters a field. As John Stuart Mill pointed out in his classic treatise, *On Liberty*, "Government operations tend to be everywhere alike. With individuals and voluntary associations, on the contrary, there are varied experiments, and endless diversity of experience."[15] This consideration has led Americans to be willing to sacrifice the efficiency that might come from unitary government action for the greater flexibility that more pluralistic approaches afford.

One manifestation of this is America's federal structure of government, with its extensive sharing of responsibilities among national, state, and local governments. But another, as we shall see, is a widespread pattern of reliance on nonprofit organizations to deliver government-funded services, especially in fields that nonprofit organizations entered before a government role was established. This same pattern of government-nonprofit cooperation is evident in many other countries as well.[16]

SOLIDARITY

Finally, the nonprofit sector is a response to the need for some mechanism through which to foster sentiments of solidarity. This is particularly important in individualistic societies like the United States, as Alexis de Tocqueville pointed out in his seminal essay over 150 years ago. In fact, it was this facet of the nonprofit sector, and not the sector's promotion of liberty, that Tocqueville had principally in mind when he argued that "In democratic countries the science of association is the mother of science; the progress of all the rest depends upon the progress it has made." The reason, Tocqueville observed, is that:

> ...among democratic nations...all the citizens are independent and feeble; they can do hardly anything by themselves, and none of them can oblige his fellow men to lend him their assistance. They all, therefore, become powerless if they do not learn voluntarily to help one another.[17]

Voluntary associations are critical in democratic societies to create artificially what the equality of conditions makes it extremely difficult to create naturally, namely, a capacity for joint action. It is for this reason that Tocqueville argues that "If men living in democratic countries had no right and no inclination to associate for political purposes, their independence would be in great jeopardy, but they might long preserve their wealth and their cultivation; whereas if they never acquired the habit of forming associations in ordinary life, civilization itself would be endangered."[18]

The Stakes: Why We Need the Nonprofit Sector

These explanations of the existence of nonprofit organizations help to clarify the contributions that these organizations can make and the stakes that American society consequently has in them. Broadly speaking, these contributions take five major forms:

OVISION

-- place, nonprofit organizations perform an important service function. This function has been particularly important in the United States due to the ideological hostility to government involvement in some quarters and the features of the political system that make it easy to veto expansions of government service provision. The nonprofit sector has thus functioned as a first line of defense, a flexible mechanism through which people concerned about a social or economic problem can begin to respond immediately without having to convince a majority of their fellow citizens that the problem deserves a more general, governmental response. As noted earlier, moreover, the nonprofit sector also provides a vehicle through which publicly financed services, once established, can themselves be delivered in a more flexible way, and specialized demands—for example, for culture and arts or other collective goods—can be pursued. In short, nonprofit organizations perform an important service function by:

- addressing unmet needs;

- fostering innovation;

- providing "collective goods" that only a portion of a community wishes to support; and

- adapting publicly funded general policies and programs to local circumstances and needs.

ADVOCACY AND PROBLEM IDENTIFICATION

In addition to solving problems themselves, nonprofit organizations also play a vital role as mechanisms for mobilizing broader public attention to societal problems and needs. In a complex society such as ours, the right to free expression has little effective meaning unless it is joined to the right of free association, so that individuals can merge their individual voices and thereby make them effective. Nonprofit organizations are among the principal vehicles for doing this. By making it possible to identify significant social and political concerns, to give voice to under-represented people and points of view, and to integrate these perspectives into social and political life, these organizations function as a kind of social safety valve that has helped to preserve American democracy and maintain a degree of social peace in the midst of massive, and often dramatic, social dislocations.

THE EXPRESSIVE FUNCTION

Political and policy concerns are not the only ones to which the nonprofit sector gives expression. Rather, this set of institutions provides the vehicles through which an enormous variety of other sentiments and impulses— artistic, religious, cultural, ethnic, occupational, social, economic, recreational—also find expression. Opera companies, symphonies, soccer clubs, churches, synagogues, fraternal societies, book clubs, professional associations, trade associations, and Girl Scouts are just some of the manifestations of this expressive function. Through them, nonprofit organizations enrich human existence and contribute to the social and cultural vitality of American life.

The nonprofit sector has functioned as a flexible mechanism through which people concerned about a social or economic problem can respond immediately without having to convince a majority of their fellow citizens.

SOCIAL CAPITAL

Nonprofit organizations also play a vital role in creating and sustaining what scholars have come to refer to as "social capital," that is, those bonds of trust and reciprocity that seem to be pivotal for a democratic society and a market economy to function effectively, but that the American ethic of individualism would otherwise make it difficult to sustain.[19] Alexis de Tocqueville understood this point well when he wrote in *Democracy in America* in 1835:

> Feelings and opinions are recruited, the heart is enlarged, and the human mind is developed, only by the reciprocal influence of men upon one another.... these influences are almost null in democratic countries; they must therefore be artificially created and this can only be accomplished by associations.[20]

The perpetuation of a vital nonprofit sector is thus essential to the development and sustenance of a sense of community, which is required to uphold contracts and make it possible for both a market system and a democratic polity to operate.

VALUE GUARDIAN

Finally, well beyond these operational roles, the nonprofit sector also functions as a "value guardian" in American society, exemplifying and embodying a fundamental national value emphasizing individual initiative in the public good. Nonprofit organizations thus give institutional expression to two seemingly contradictory principles that are both important parts of American national character—the principle of *individualism*, the notion that people should have the freedom to act, in their individual, private capacity, on matters that concern them; and the principle of *solidarity*, the notion that people have responsibilities not only to themselves but to their fellow human beings and to the communities of which they are part. Just as private economic enterprises serve as vehicles for promoting individual initiative for the private good, nonprofit organizations provide a mechanism for promoting such initiative in the pursuit of public purposes. In the process, they foster pluralism, diversity, and freedom. As such, they give expression to what has long been regarded as a central dimension of the American experience—the protection of a sphere of private action through which individuals can take the initiative, express their individuality, and exercise freedom of thought and action.

Conclusion

In short, there is a vitally important set of institutions in American society that, despite many differences, nevertheless share certain common features. It consists of organizations that are private, self-governing, non-profit-distributing, and noncompulsory. Together they comprise what we will call the *nonprofit sector*.

The existence of this set of organizations is partly a function of social and economic development. But it also reflects certain inherent limitations of the market in responding to public problems, the need that a democratic society has for some way to promote cooperation among equal individuals, and the value Americans attach to pluralism and freedom.

The rationale for the existence of a nonprofit sector is not peculiar to American society, of course. The same arguments apply to other societies as well. But there is no denying that these organizations have come to play a particularly important role in the American setting. While there is reason to question whether American nonprofit organizations always live up to the expectations that these theories assign to them, it seems clear that the existence of such a set of institutions has come to be viewed in this country as a critical component of community life, a convenient and fulfilling way to meet community needs, and a crucial prerequisite of a true "civil society."

ENDNOTES

1. In 2007, an estimated 60.8 million Americans reported volunteering for nonprofit organizations and another 11.1 million were employed by such organizations. By comparison, 129.4 million people voted in the 2008 presidential election. See: Corporation for National and Community Service, Office of Research and Policy Development. *Volunteering in America 2010: National, State, and City Information.* Issue Brief (Washington, DC: Corporation for National and Community Service, June 2010); Wing, Pollak, and Blackwood, *The Nonprofit Almanac* (2008), Table 2.13; cnn.com/ELECTION/2008/results/president/.

2. For other examples of countries that have built extensive reliance on the nonprofit sector into their publicly funded social welfare systems, see Chapter 13 below and the chapters on Germany and the Netherlands in Benjamin Gidron, Ralph Kramer, and Lester M. Salamon, eds., *Government and the Third Sector: Emerging Relationships in Welfare States* (San Francisco: Jossey-Bass, 1992); and Lester M. Salamon, S. Wojciech Sokolowski, and Associates, *Global Civil Society: Dimensions of the Nonprofit Sector, Vol. III* (Sterling, VA: Kumarian Press, 2011).

3. Several of these types, while legally recognized, are almost nonexistent in practice. This includes §501(c)(22) multi-employer pension plans; §501(c)(23) veterans associations founded prior to 1880; and §501(c)(24) trusts described in section 4049 of the federal pension act, ERISA.

4. On the definition of "social economy," see: Jacques DeFourny, Patrick Develtere, and Bénédicte Fonteneau. "L'économie sociale au Nord et au Sud," New Social Practices 13:2 (December 2000), 216-219; and José Luis Monzon and Rafael Chaves, "The European Social Economy: Concept and Dimensions of the Third Sector," *Annals of Public and Cooperative Economics* 79:3/4 (2008).

5. See, for example: Alex Nichols, "Introduction," in *Social Entrepreneurship: New Models of Sustainable Social Change*, ed. Alex Nichols (Oxford: Oxford University Press, 2006), 1–36; Mark Hrywna, "The L3C Status: Groups Explore Structure that Limits Liability for Program-related Investing," *The NonProfit Times*, September 1, 2009, accessed at: nptimes.com/09Sep/npt-090901-3.html.

6. This definition draws on the work of the Johns Hopkins Comparative Nonprofit Sector Project and was incorporated into the official United Nations System of National Accounts, which guides international economic data-gathering and reporting. For further detail see: Lester M. Salamon and Helmut K. Anheier, "In Search of the Nonprofit Sector: The Problem of Definition," *Voluntas*, Vol. 3, No. 2 (1992), 125–151; and United Nations Statistics Division, *Handbook on Nonprofit Institutions in the System of National Accounts*, Series F, No. 91 (New York: United Nations, 2003), 17–20.

7. John S. Whitehead, *The Separation of College and State: Columbia, Dartmouth, Harvard and Yale, 1776–1876* (New Haven, CT: Yale University Press, 1973).

8. The term "charitable" is enshrined in Section 501(c)(3) of the Internal Revenue Code, which identifies as "exempt purposes" activities that are "charitable, religious, educational, scientific, literary, testing for public safety, fostering national or international amateur sports competition, and preventing cruelty to children or animals." According to the Internal Revenue Service, the term *charitable* here is "used in its generally accepted legal sense and includes relief of the poor, the distressed, or the underprivileged; advancement of religion; advancement of education or science; erecting or maintaining public buildings, monuments, or works; lessening the burdens of government; lessening neighborhood tensions; eliminating prejudice and discrimination; defending human and civil rights secured by law; and combating community deterioration and juvenile delinquency." See: www.irs.gov, accessed August 14, 2010; on the common law definition

of "charitable," see Jeremy Kendall and Martin Knapp, "The United Kingdom," in Lester M. Salamon and Helmut K. Anheier, *Defining the Nonprofit Sector: A Cross-National Analysis* (Manchester, U.K.: Manchester University Press, 1996): 257.

9. See, for example, Michael Bratton, "Review: Beyond the State: Civil Society and Associational Life in Africa," *World Politics* 41:3 (1989).

10. This line of argument has been applied to the nonprofit sector most explicitly in Burton Weisbrod, *The Voluntary Nonprofit Sector* (Lexington, MA: Lexington Books, 1978).

11. See, for example, Lester M. Salamon, "Of Market Failure, Voluntary Failure, and Third-Party Government: Toward a Theory of Government-Nonprofit Relations in the Modern Welfare State," *Journal of Voluntary Action Research* 16:1–2 (January–June 1987), 29–49.

12. This line of argument has been developed most explicitly in Henry Hansmann, "The Role of Nonprofit Enterprise," *Yale Law Journal 89* (1990), 835–901.

13. The classic expression of this point of view was provided in President Ronald Reagan's pronouncement that "We have let government take away the things that were once ours to do voluntarily." For an analysis of this perspective and its consequences, see: Lester M. Salamon and Alan J. Abramson, "The Nonprofit Sector," in *The Reagan Experiment*, eds. John L. Palmer and Isabel V. Sawhill (Washington, DC: The Urban Institute Press, 1982), 219–243.

14. For a discussion of this "supply-side theory," see: Estelle James, "The Nonprofit Sector in Comparative Perspective," in *The Nonprofit Sector: A Research Handbook*, ed. Walter W. Powell (New Haven: Yale University Press, 1987), 397–415; Avner Ben-Ner and Theresa van Hoomissen, "Nonprofit Organizations in the Mixed Economy: A Demand and Supply Analysis," in *The Nonprofit Sector in the Mixed Economy*, eds. Avner Ben-Ner and Benedeto Gui (Ann Arbor: The University of Michigan Press, 1993); Michael Krashinsky, "Stakeholder Theories of the Nonprofit Sector: One Cut at the Economic Literature," Voluntas 8:2 (1997): 149–161.

15. John Stuart Mill, *On Liberty*, quoted in Bruce R. Hopkins, *The Law of Tax-Exempt Organizations*, 5th ed. (New York: John Wiley and Sons, 1987), 7.

16. For a fuller explication of this pattern in the American setting, see: Lester M. Salamon, *Partners in Public Service: Government-Nonprofit Relations in the Modern Welfare State* (Baltimore: Johns Hopkins University Press, 1995). For evidence of the similar pattern operating in Europe, see: Ralph Kramer, *Voluntary Agencies in the Welfare State* (Berkeley: University of California Press, 1981); Lester M. Salamon, S. Wojciech Sokolowski, and Associates, *Global Civil Society: Dimensions of the Nonprofit Sector, Vol. II* (Bloomfield, CT: Kumarian Press, 2004); Jennifer Wolch, *The Shadow State* (New York: The Foundation Center, 1990).

17. Alexis de Tocqueville, *Democracy in America: The Henry Reeve Text, Vol. II* (New York: Vintage Books, 1945 [1835]), 115, 118.

18. Tocqueville, *Democracy in America*, 115–116.

19. See, for example: James S. Coleman, *Foundations of Social Theory* (Cambridge, MA: Harvard University Press, 1990), 300–321; Robert Putnam, *Making Democracy Work: Civic Traditions in Modern Italy* (Princeton: Princeton University Press, 1993), 83–116, 163–185.

20. Tocqueville, *Democracy in America*, 117.

3

Scope and Structure: The Anatomy of America's Nonprofit Sector

To say that nonprofit organizations share certain common characteristics and a common rationale is not, of course, to suggest that all nonprofit organizations are identical. To the contrary, the complexity and diversity of this sector are among the major factors that have diverted attention from it over much of its history. Indeed, nonprofit organizations are so diverse and so specialized that some observers question whether it is appropriate to consider this group of institutions a "sector" at all—a point that could be raised about the "business sector" as well, of course.

Complicating things further is the fact that significant portions of the nonprofit sector are largely informal in character and therefore difficult to capture in empirical terms. This reflects the fact that under American law, organizations are not required to incorporate, or even to seek formal recognition by the tax authorities, in order to function as tax-exempt nonprofit organizations. This organizational fluidity is, in fact, one of the prized features of this sector, enabling groups of people to meet together to pursue common purposes without having to seek official approval or even acknowledgment. At the same time, however, it makes it exceedingly difficult to gauge the size of this sector with any real precision.[1]

While recognizing these problems, this chapter seeks to make some sense of the vast array of institutions that comprise the American nonprofit sector by examining the basic anatomy or architecture of this sector and the scope and scale of some of its constituent parts. In the process, the chapter seeks to strip away some of the confusion and misperception that too often characterize popular understanding of what the nonprofit sector really is and how it functions in American life.

To do so, we first examine the overall scale of this sector and then look in more detail at some of the sector's major components, focusing particularly on what we refer to as "public-benefit organizations," the portion of this sector that most people have in mind when they refer to the "nonprofit sector." The chapter concludes by comparing the U.S. nonprofit sector to its counterparts in other countries. Given the limitations of available data, our focus is inevitably on the more formal and institutionalized organizations, although, as we will see, the line between these and the rest of this sector is far from clear.

Included within the American nonprofit sector are two very different categories of organizations: primarily member-serving organizations and primarily public-serving organizations.

Overview: Basic Contours

Americans are accustomed to thinking of the nonprofit sector as a quaint collection of soup kitchens, homeless shelters, day care centers, and related operations that may produce enormous social good but do not constitute a significant component of the national economy. While it is true that the vast majority of American nonprofit organizations are quite small, however, with annual revenues below $25,000, the sector as a whole is enormous both in numbers and in economic weight. In particular:

• As reflected in Table 3.1, there were nearly 2 million identifiable nonprofit organizations in the United States as of 2009. This includes the slightly more than 1.5 million organizations formally registered on the Internal Revenue Service's Exempt Organization Master File (EOMF), and an estimated nearly 500,000 organizations not included in the EOMF but visible through other information sources.[2] To be sure, because the Internal Revenue Service has lacked a systematic method for purging inactive organizations from its Master File, it is hard to determine what portion of these organizations are truly still active. As one indication, however, only one-sixth of them, about 332,000 organizations, filed the Form 990 financial information schedule that U.S. law requires of all tax-exempt organizations with expenditures of $25,000 or more.[3]

TABLE 3.1: America's Nonprofit Sector: An Overview

Dimension	Amount
Number of organizations (2009)	1,968,158
Revenues (2007)	$1.963 trillion
Paid employees (2007)	13.5 million
Volunteers (2007)	61.9 million
converted to full-time-equivalent workers	4.5 million

Sources: See Chapter 3, endnotes 2,3,4,5.

- Even so, these organizations represent a significant segment of the national economy. As of 2007, for example, they had revenues of $1.963 trillion, which, for the sake of comparison, was roughly 12.6 percent of the entire U.S. gross national product. Indeed, if the U.S. nonprofit sector were itself a country, its revenues would exceed those of most countries in the world, including Australia, Brazil, Canada, India, and Russia.[4]

- These organizations are also an important source of employment, both paid and volunteer. Nearly 13.5 million workers were employed by U.S. nonprofit organizations as of 2007. This represents 10 percent of the entire U.S. labor force and makes the nonprofit paid workforce the third-largest of any U.S. industry, behind only retail trade and manufacturing but ahead of such industries as construction (7.6 million), finance and insurance (6 million), and transportation (4.2 million), as shown in Figure 3.1. In addition, as Table 3.1 shows, nonprofit organizations attract the efforts of numerous volunteers. Thus, as of 2007, approximately 62 million people volunteered to and through nonprofit organizations. Because volunteers typically work less than full time, this translates into the equivalent of another 4.5 million full-time workers, bringing the total "workforce" of the U.S. nonprofit sector to approximately 18 million workers. With the volunteer workers included, the U.S. nonprofit sector has a larger workforce than any "industry" in the nation—larger than construction, larger than finance and insurance, even larger than retail trade and all branches of manufacturing, as shown in Figure 3.1.[5]

If the U.S. nonprofit sector were a country, its revenues would exceed those of most countries in the world.

FIGURE 3.1: Employment in the Nonprofit Sector versus Selected
Industries, 2006 (millions)

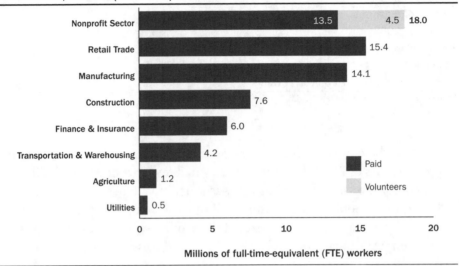

Millions of full-time-equivalent (FTE) workers

Source: See Chapter 3, endnote 5.

FIGURE 3.2: Anatomy of the U.S. Nonprofit Sector

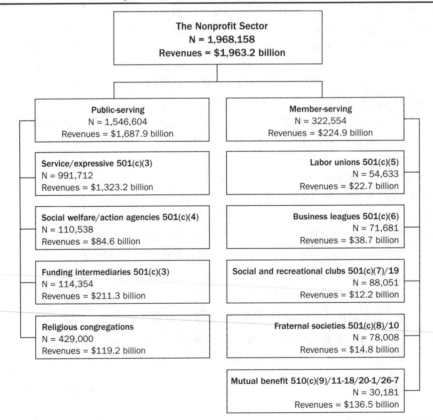

Source: See Chapter 3, endnote 7.

A Basic Division: Public-Serving versus Member-Serving Organizations

Included within these figures, however, are organizations that differ along many different dimensions. One of the most useful of these dimensions focuses on the question of whom the organizations primarily serve. In addition to being conceptually important, this distinction is also enshrined in U.S. law. More specifically, two broad classes of nonprofit organizations can be distinguished along this dimension: primarily *member-serving* organizations and primarily *public-serving* organizations.

MEMBER-SERVING ORGANIZATIONS

Member-serving organizations aim primarily at providing benefits to their members rather than to the public at large, although they may often provide some benefits to broader segments of the public. As reflected in Figure 3.2, member-serving organizations include, for the most part, organizations exempt from income tax under Sections 501(c)(5) through 501(c)(27) of the U.S. Internal Revenue Code. They include labor unions, business and professional associations (for example, chambers of commerce, the Automobile Manufacturers Association, the American Bankers Association, the National Association of Homebuilders, the American Medical Association), social and recreational clubs, and a variety of fraternal or mutual benefit organizations such as veterans organizations, mutual insurance companies, cemetery companies, credit unions, and cooperative telephone companies. Approximately 323,000 of these organizations were officially registered with the Internal Revenue Service as of 2009, but a far larger number likely exist more informally. Those on which financial data are available reported revenues of $225 billion as of 2007.[6] As noted in Figure 3.3, although accounting for about 18 percent of all registered nonprofit organizations, these organizations account for only 12 percent of total nonprofit revenue.[7]

Public-serving organizations comprise the largest portion of the nonprofit sector in financial terms. And within this component, the largest group by far are the service and expressive organizations.

FIGURE 3.3: Revenue Shares of Major Components of U.S.
Nonprofit Sector, 2007

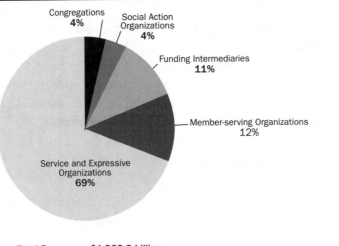

Congregations
4%

Social Action
Organizations
4%

Funding Intermediaries
11%

Member-serving Organizations
12%

Service and Expressive
Organizations
69%

Total Revenue = $1,963.2 billion

Source: See Chapter 3, endnotes 3 and 4.

PUBLIC-SERVING ORGANIZATIONS

The second category of nonprofit organizations is primarily public-serving
in character. These are organizations that exist primarily to serve the public
at large rather than primarily the members of the organization. They may do
so in a variety of ways, however—providing health and education services,
sponsoring cultural or religious activities, advocating for certain causes,
aiding the poor, financing other nonprofits, and many more. Altogether, over
1.6 million such organizations exist at the present time, and they comprise
by far the largest portion of the sector in financial terms, accounting for an
enormous $1.7 trillion in revenue, or 88 percent of the sector's total.[8]

TREATMENT IN TAX LAW

This distinction between primarily member-serving and primarily public-
serving nonprofit organizations is far from perfect, of course. Even the
member-serving organizations produce some public benefits, and the
public-serving organizations often deliver benefits to their members. Yet the
distinction is significant enough to find formal reflection in the law.

In particular, public-serving organizations are the only ones entitled to tax-
exempt status under Section 501(c)(3) of the federal tax law. What makes
this so important is that this gives such organizations a tax advantage not
available to other nonprofit organizations. In particular, in addition to

being exempt from most taxes themselves, like all nonprofit organizations, 501(c)(3) organizations are also eligible to receive tax-deductible gifts from individuals and corporations. This gives the individuals and corporations a financial incentive to make contributions to these 501(c)(3) organizations because they can deduct the gifts from their income before calculating the taxes they owe. The chief justification for this is that the organizations are considered to be serving purposes that government might otherwise have to support through tax revenues if contributions were not available to them.[9]

Most public-benefit nonprofit organizations are tax-exempt under Section 501(c)(3) of the federal tax law, which is reserved for organizations operating "exclusively for religious, charitable, scientific, literary, or educational purposes."

To be eligible for this status, organizations must operate "exclusively for religious, charitable, scientific, literary, or educational purposes."[10] The meaning of these terms is rooted in English common law, however, and is quite broad, essentially embracing organizations that promote the general welfare in any of a wide variety of ways.[11] Included, therefore, are not only agencies providing aid to the poor, but also most of the educational, cultural, social service, advocacy, self-help, health, environmental, civil rights, child welfare, and related organizations that most people have in mind when they think about the nonprofit sector. The one major exception is public-serving organizations heavily engaged in "lobbying," that is, promoting particular pieces of legislation or regulation. Because of limitations on the extent of lobbying permitted for 501(c)(3) organizations, organizations wanting to engage more actively in lobbying can register as tax-exempt under section 501(c)(4) of the Internal Revenue Code, which allows them to engage without limit in such legislative lobbying activities but, in return, denies them access to tax-deductible charitable contributions.[12]

FOCUS ON PUBLIC-SERVING ORGANIZATIONS

Because of their essentially public character, the public-serving nonprofit organizations are the ones that most observers have in mind when they speak about the "nonprofit sector" in the United States. These are therefore the organizations that will be the principal focus of the balance of this primer.

Anatomy of the Public-Serving Nonprofit Sector

OVERVIEW

As already noted, the *public-serving* component of the nonprofit sector is by far the largest part, but it is itself quite diverse. Broadly speaking, it consists of four very different *types* of organizations, as shown in Figure 3.2.

- The first, and by far largest, group of public-serving nonprofit organizations are those that deliver the services and perform the expressive functions for which the sector is best known. We will refer to them as *service and expressive organizations*. They provide health care, education, counseling, day care, adoption assistance, cultural performances, and dozens of other services or give expression to various causes, such as civil rights, environmental protection, or the right to life.

- The second are the 501(c)(4) *social welfare/social action agencies* noted above, which include a variety of service clubs as well as a number of lobbying organizations.

- Third, reflecting the considerable specialization of the U.S. nonprofit sector, the public-serving portion of this sector includes a group of organizations that specialize in generating and distributing private charitable support to the other portions of the sector. We will refer to them as *funding intermediaries*; they include a variety of types of organizations, including foundations as well as various federated fundraising entities such as the United Way or the American Cancer Society.

- Finally, the public-serving component of the nonprofit sector includes *religious congregations*, that is, organizations that principally engage in religious worship (for example, churches, synagogues, mosques). In some accounts, these organizations are grouped with the member-serving part of the sector because they principally serve the members of the congregations, but since American law grants them tax exemption under section 501(c)(3) of the Internal Revenue Code, we treat them along with the other 501(c)(3) organizations as public-serving organizations, broadly conceived. As we will see, however, these organizations enjoy a special status even within the 501(c)(3) group of organizations.

Let us examine each of these broad types of public-serving nonprofit organizations in a bit more detail, focusing particularly on the service and expressive organizations.

SERVICE AND EXPRESSIVE ORGANIZATIONS

Numbers of Organizations. By far the largest component of the public-serving nonprofit sector in the United States, both in terms of numbers of organizations and in terms of revenues, is the service and expressive organizations. Solid data on the scope of this nonprofit service and expressive subsector, or of its constituent parts, are difficult to piece together, however, and sensitive to differences in record-keeping. For example, some organizations treat their branches as separate organizations and others as integral parts of a single parent organization. In addition, many organizations carry out a multitude of activities and cannot easily be classified in one category. Based on the available data, however, it appears that there were approximately nearly 1 million such organizations registered with the Internal Revenue Service as of 2009—though, as noted earlier, most of these are quite small, and many may be inactive.[13] Detailed financial and other information is available only on those with at least one paid employee or that file the required Form 990 with the Internal Revenue Service. As of 2007, there were just over 250,000 such organizations.[14]

As shown in Figure 3.4, these organizations are not distributed evenly among the various service fields. Rather:

FIGURE 3.4: U.S. Nonprofit Service and Expressive Organizations' Shares of Total Organizations and Revenues, by Field, 2007

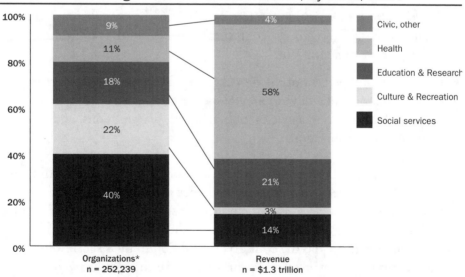

*Organizations reporting to the IRS
Source: See Chapter 3, endnotes 2,3,4.

- The *social service agencies* are the most numerous; 40 percent of all reporting nonprofit service and expressive organizations fall into this category. Included here are child day care centers, individual and family counseling agencies, soup kitchens, shelters, low-income housing agencies, and other human service agencies.

- The next-largest group of nonprofit service and expressive organizations are *culture and recreation* providers, which includes symphonies, museums, art galleries, theaters, zoos, botanical gardens, sports clubs, and the like. Together, these cultural and recreational organizations represent 22 percent of the reporting nonprofit organizations.

- The third-largest group of nonprofit service and expressive organizations are the *educational and research institutions*, including nonprofit elementary and secondary schools as well as nonprofit universities and colleges, libraries, and research institutes. Roughly 46,000 such nonprofit educational and research institutions reported to the IRS in 2007, and they comprise 18 percent of the sector's institutions.

501(c)(3) organizations are both exempt from federal income taxation themselves and eligible to receive tax-deductible gifts from individuals and corporations.

- *Health organizations*, including hospitals, nursing homes, clinics, and medical research laboratories, comprise 11 percent of the nonprofit service and expressive organizations.

- Finally, about 9 percent of the organizations fall into a *civic and other* category that includes environmental organizations, civic clubs, civil rights and social action agencies, public benefit organizations, and international organizations.

Revenues: A Major Economic Force. Because of the growth of government spending in recent decades and the prominence given to government policies, it is widely believed that the nonprofit service and expressive set of organizations may have shrunk into insignificance. Yet nothing could be further from the truth. To the contrary, in addition to their social value, nonprofit service and expressive organizations have entered the twenty-first century as a major economic force. In particular, these organizations had revenues in 2007 of approximately $1.323 trillion, or the equivalent of nearly 10 percent of the U.S. gross national product. In many local areas, in fact, the expenditures of the nonprofit sector easily outdistance those of local government. For example, a recent study of the nonprofit sector in Baltimore, Maryland, revealed that nonprofit expenditures in this metropolitan area exceeded the total expenditures of the city government and the five surrounding county governments.[15]

The distribution of revenues differs widely from the distribution of organizations, however. As shown in Figure 3.4, there are several notable differences:

- *Health dominance.* The health subsector, composed in part of huge hospital complexes, accounts for the lion's share of the sector's total revenues even though it comprises a relatively small proportion of the organizations. Specifically, with 11 percent of the organizations the health subsector accounts for 58 percent of all nonprofit service and expressive organization revenues.

- *Significant education presence.* The education subsector, containing major universities as well as colleges and preparatory schools, accounts for another 21 percent of the revenues. Health and education organizations alone thus account for nearly 80 percent of the sector's revenues.

- *Modest social service scale.* Social services, the field with the largest number of reporting organizations (100,255, or 40 percent of the total), accounts for a much smaller 14 percent of the revenues. Still, at $185 billion, this remains a sizable industry.

- *Numerous, but generally small, arts and culture organizations.* Arts and recreation organizations account for nearly one out of every four nonprofit service and expressive organizations yet account for only 4 percent of nonprofit service and expressive organization revenue.

- *Balance of the sector.* Finally, the remaining 9 percent of the organizations, including civic, environmental, and community service agencies, account for 4 percent of the revenue.

Quite clearly, this is a sector with a great deal of diversity in the size of its component organizations and subfields.

Sources of Revenue: Overview. Where do these public-serving nonprofit service and expressive organizations get their $1.3 trillion in revenue? Unfortunately, there is a great deal of confusion about this, both among opinion leaders and the general public. One widespread belief has been that large charitable foundations provide most of the income of America's nonprofit service and expressive organizations. Another is that charitable contributions as a whole, including individual and corporate gifts in addition to foundation grants, account for the bulk of this income.

In fact, however, charitable contributions reaching nonprofit service and expressive organizations totaled about $135.1 billion as of 2007—a substantial figure indeed, but well below the $1.3 trillion in nonprofit service and expressive organization income.[16] And as we will see more fully below, foundations comprise a very small portion even of these charitable contributions, let alone of the entire revenue of the nation's nonprofit service and expressive organizations. Clearly, as important as private charitable support may be to the independence of the nonprofit sector, it hardly comprises the major source of income.

Where, then, does the rest of nonprofit revenue come from? The answer to this question may be found in Figure 3.5. This figure groups the many different sources of nonprofit income—charitable donations, both cash and in-kind; bequests; membership fees; private payments for services; interest and dividends on investments; government grants; government contracts; and government reimbursement payments—into three broad categories: private giving, fees and charges, and government support.

Private giving, or philanthropy, includes charitable donations made by living individuals, bequests, foundations, corporations, and federated giving campaigns such as United Way.

Fees and charges include private payments for services (such as college tuition or admission fees at museums), membership dues, and earnings from investments (for example, interest earnings or dividends).[17]

Government support takes the form of grants, reimbursements for services for eligible clients (for example, Medicare or Medicaid payments to hospitals or nursing homes), fee-for-service contracts between government and nonprofit providers, and government grants.

Key features of the nonprofit revenue structure include the following, as Figure 3.5 shows:[18]

- *Fees dominate the revenue picture overall.* The major source of support of America's nonprofit public-benefit service and expressive organizations are fees, service charges, and other commercial income. As noted above, this source includes tuition payments at nonprofit schools, charges for hospital care not covered by government health insurance, other direct payments for nonprofit services, and income from investments and sales of products. This source alone accounts for over half (52 percent) of all nonprofit service and expressive organization revenues.

FIGURE 3.5: Sources of Nonprofit Service and Expressive
Organization Revenue, 2007

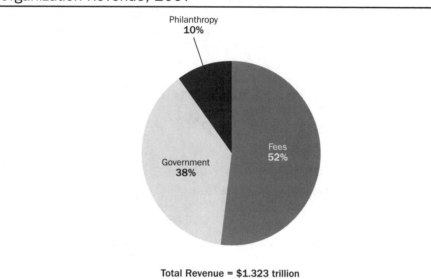

Philanthropy
10%

Fees
52%

Government
38%

Total Revenue = $1.323 trillion

Source: See Chapter 3, endnote 18.

- *Substantial government support.* The second-largest source of income of
  America's nonprofit public-benefit service and expressive organizations
  as of 2007 is government. Government grants, contracts, and
  reimbursements account for 38 percent of nonprofit service and expressive
  organization income. This reflects a widespread pattern of partnership
  between government and the nonprofit sector in carrying out public
  purposes, from the delivery of health care to the provision of education.[19]

- *Private giving.* Far from being the leading source of nonprofit revenue,
  private giving turns out to be the smallest in relative terms. As noted
  above, private charitable contributions come from four different sources:
  foundations, bequests, corporations, and living individuals. As Figure 3.6
  shows, living individuals account for the bulk (75 percent) of the gifts,
  followed by foundations (nearly 13 percent), bequests (about 7 percent),
  and corporations (about 5 percent).[20] Not all of the charitable giving in a
  given year finds its way into the annual revenue of operating service and
  expressive nonprofit organizations, however. Rather, some portion flows to
  foundations and federated giving campaigns for distribution to nonprofits,
  occasionally with a delay. The charitable giving figures thus contain some
  double-counting as the same dollars can be recorded as gifts by individuals

FIGURE 3.6: Sources of Private Giving, 2008

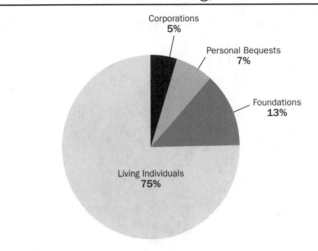

Source: See Chapter 3, endnote 20.

to foundations or federated funding organizations like United Way, and then as gifts by these foundations or federated funding organizations to recipient nonprofit organizations. When this double-counting is eliminated, we are left with $135.1 billion in private contributions received by nonprofit service and expressive organizations in 2007, as noted earlier, out of the $326.1 billion in charitable gifts recorded by *Giving USA* for 2007. Most important for our purposes here, this charitable giving represented only 10 percent of the total income that nonprofit service and expressive organizations received, leaving the sector's organizations to find the remaining 90 percent of their revenue from other sources.

Variations in Sources of Revenue by Field. This overall pattern of nonprofit service and expressive organization finance does not hold in all fields, however, though certain commonalities are evident. In particular, as shown in Figure 3.7:

- *Fee dominance in most major fields.* Not only are fees, charges, and other commercial income the major source of support for America's nonprofit service and expressive organizations overall, but also this is the major source of support for nonprofits in three of the five broad fields in which these organizations operate, providing 72 percent of the revenue in the field of education, 53 percent in arts and recreation, and 45 percent in social services. But fees also provide a sizable share of income for nonprofit health organizations as well. Clearly, fee income has become ubiquitous in this core component of the nation's nonprofit sector.

- *Government funding especially prominent in health care and social services.* Government support edges out fee income as the major source of nonprofit support in the health field and ranks second in two of the four other fields (social services and education). Government would rank number one as well in the social services field, moreover, were it not for the fact that we include housing and community development organizations in the social services field, and these organizations receive considerable fee income from the housing units they often own and manage.

- *Private philanthropy dominance among civic and other organizations.* Private philanthropy is the major source of revenue in only one field of nonprofit activity of the five we have identified, the catch-all "other" category of organizations, embracing civic, environmental, and international organizations. Over half (54 percent) of the revenues of these organizations came from philanthropy in 2007. Philanthropy also provided a sizable 37 percent of the support to nonprofit arts and recreation organizations, making it the second-largest source of support for these organizations.

In short, the funding structure of the nonprofit public-serving service and expressive sector differs substantially from what is often assumed. Fees and

FIGURE 3.7: Sources of Service and Expressive Nonprofit Organization Revenue, by Activity Field, 2007

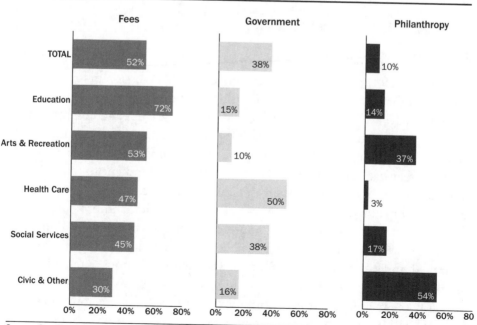

government support have displaced philanthropy as the chief sources of nonprofit support, though philanthropy continues to play an especially important role in advocacy, civic engagement, and culture and recreation.

Contributions of Time. In addition to the cash income they receive, nonprofit service organizations also have access to the contributed time of numerous volunteers. As noted above, recent estimates indicate that about 62 million Americans volunteered an average of 132 hours per year (2.5 hours per week) to various charitable and other organizations in 2007, and public-serving nonprofit service organizations are the beneficiaries of about 57 percent of this time.[21] Conservatively estimated, these organizations would have had to spend about $54 billion to hire employees to carry out this work.[22] Therefore, it is possible to consider this volunteer time as an additional $54 billion of philanthropic support to the service and expressive nonprofit organizations, boosting the philanthropic source of their support from 10 to 13 percent.

Private giving from all sources accounts for only about 10 percent of overall nonprofit service and expressive organization revenue. The balance of this revenue comes from fees and government support.

SOCIAL WELFARE AND "ACTION" ORGANIZATIONS

A second class of public-serving nonprofit organizations falls under Section 501(c)(4) of the Internal Revenue Code. This section grants tax exemption for a broad array of organizations that promote community benefit or advance "social welfare," including civic leagues and community improvement organizations of varied sorts. Recent examples of organizations granted exemption under this section of the Internal Revenue Code include organizations that encouraged industrial development to relieve unemployment in an economically depressed area, helped secure accident insurance for students and employees in a school district, and provided bus transportation between a community and a major employment hub when regular bus service was not available.[23] Like "charitable" organizations exempted under Section 501(c)(3), the "welfare organizations" granted exemption under Section 501(c)(4) must serve a broad public and not primarily the members of the organization. They are therefore appropriately included within the public-serving component of the nonprofit sector.

Although the "social welfare" focus required of 501(c)(4)s makes them quite similar in purpose to the 501(c)(3) service and expressive organizations discussed above, one crucial feature separates the two: unlike 501(c)(3) organizations, which are restricted to devoting only an "insubstantial part" of their activities to lobbying (that is, attempting to influence legislation), 501(c)(4)s have no limits on their lobbying activity.[24] Many of the organizations seeking exemption as 501(c)(4) organizations in recent years have therefore been organizations that wish to engage substantially in legislative lobbying. Indeed, many 501(c)(3) organizations form 501(c)(4) "political action" affiliates to handle their lobbying activities or join coalitions that have 501(c)(4) status.

The privilege of engaging in lobbying without limit does not come without a cost for 501(c)(4) organizations, however. Rather, unlike 501(c)(3) organizations, 501(c)(4)s do not have access to tax-deductible contributions from individuals or corporations. Donors making contributions to these organizations must therefore pay taxes on the income supporting these contributions, thus limiting the financial incentive to give to 501(c)(4)s.

Altogether, 110,538 organizations were registered on the IRS Exempt Organization Master File as "civic leagues or social welfare organizations" as of 2009. Of these, just under 20,000 were of sufficient scale to file the required Form 990 with the IRS. Collectively, these reporting 501(c)(4)s had revenues of $84.6 billion as of 2007, as shown in Figure 3.2.

Unlike 501(c)(3) organizations, 501(c)(4)s do not have access to tax-deductible contributions from individuals or corporations.

FUNDING INTERMEDIARIES

Among the public-serving nonprofit organizations in the United States, probably the least well understood is a third category, which we refer to as *funding intermediaries*. These are organizations whose sole, or principal, function is to channel financial support, especially private charitable support, to other nonprofit organizations. The existence of these funding intermediaries reflects the highly specialized and developed character of the U.S. nonprofit sector, which has led to the emergence of organizations that are dedicated exclusively to fundraising and fund distribution. But it also reflects the importance of private charitable giving in the United States and the scale of the "industry" that has emerged to generate and channel it. Although, as we have seen, private charitable giving is by no means the only, or even the largest, source of support for American nonprofit service organizations, it is nevertheless quite important because of the role it plays in helping to ensure the sector's independence and autonomous character.

The role of the funding intermediaries is to help generate this private funding, to manage it once it is accumulated, and to make it available for use by the other organizations in the sector. Broadly speaking, as shown in Figure 3.8, three distinct types of such funding intermediaries exist: foundations, support organizations, and professional fundraisers. Let us look briefly at each.

Foundations. Private foundations (for example, the Ford Foundation, the Rockefeller Foundation, the W.K. Kellogg Foundation) are among the most visible components of the nonprofit sector—so much so that there is

FIGURE 3.8: Nonprofit Funding Intermediaries

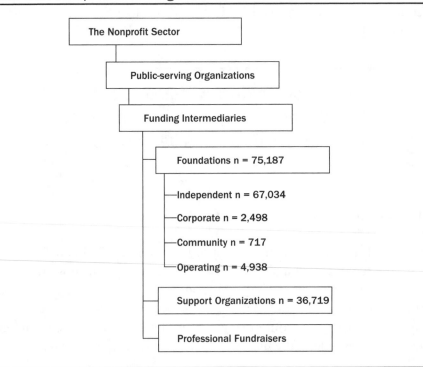

Source: See Chapter 3, endnotes 26 and 32.

a tendency to overstate their role and confuse them with the public-serving nonprofit sector as a whole. This latter problem is particularly acute among overseas observers because the term "foundation" is used quite differently in many other countries. In particular, in Europe the term "foundation" is used to refer to any nonprofit organization with an endowment, whereas in the United States the term is typically reserved for organizations with the more specialized function of accumulating assets for the purpose of making grants to other nonprofit organizations, typically out of the earnings from the assets, although foundations increasingly use their assets in other "program-related" ways as well.[25]

Altogether, as noted in Table 3.2, there were over 75,000 foundations in the United States as of 2007, with total assets of $682 billion. Collectively, these foundations delivered $44 billion in so-called "qualifying distributions" to various charitable nonprofit organizations in that year. Included here, however, are four somewhat different types of foundations:

Independent Grantmaking Foundations. The economically most sizable type of foundation by far is the so-called independent grantmaking foundation. These are nonprofit organizations set up to administer an endowment typically left for charitable purposes by a single individual. Under the Tax Reform Act of 1969, these organizations are required to pay out, in grants and other "qualifying distributions," a minimum of 5 percent of their assets each year.[26] Of the more than 75,000 foundations in existence as of 2007, over 67,000, or nearly 90 percent, were independent grantmaking foundations, as shown in Table 3.2. These independent foundations controlled 83 percent of all foundation assets and accounted for 73 percent of all foundation grants.

Private foundations are among the most visible components of the nonprofit sector—so much so that there is a tendency to overstate their role and confuse them with the public-serving nonprofit sector as a whole.

TABLE 3.2 America's Grantmaking Foundations, 2007

Type	Entities		Assets		Grants	
	Number	%	Billion $	%	Billion $	%
Independent	67,034	89%	$564.2	82.7%	$32.2	72.7%
Corporate	2,498	3%	21.9	3.2%	4.4	9.9%
Community	717	1%	56.7	8.3%	4.3	9.7%
Operating	4,938	7%	39.4	5.8%	3.4	7.7%
Total	75,187	100%	682.2	100.0%	44.3	100.0%

Source: Foundation Center, *Foundation Yearbook*, 2009.

Corporate Foundations. Somewhat different from the independent foundations are the corporate or company-sponsored foundations. Unlike the independent foundations, which receive their endowments from wealthy individuals, corporate foundations receive their funds from business corporations that want to avoid the fluctuations that come from financing corporate charitable activities from current income alone. By creating corporate foundations, corporations are able to maintain more professional staffs and stable giving programs because the foundations can receive excess funds during years of corporate prosperity to build up endowments for use when corporate profits are lower. Altogether, there were nearly 2,500 corporate foundations in 2007, and they controlled 3.2 percent of all foundation assets but accounted for 10 percent of all foundation grants. This excludes, of course, the amounts that corporations give to charitable purposes directly, rather than through separate foundations.

Community Foundations. A third form of foundation is the community foundation. Where both independent and corporate foundations receive their funds from a single source, community foundations receive them from a number of sources in a given community. They are thus "public charities" in formal legal terms, but operate like foundations. The basic concept of a community foundation is that wealthy individuals who might otherwise leave a bequest to a particular organization or cause that may cease to exist or be relevant after their death, or create a separate foundation on a scale that is too small to support a regular staff, can choose instead to leave bequests or establish "donor-advised funds" within a broader community foundation that manages a number of such funds. This arrangement guarantees that the resources will be used for the purposes that the donors wish but not be tied to organizations or purposes that cease to be relevant or operational over time. Altogether, 717 community foundations were in existence as of 2007, and they accounted for over 8 percent of all foundation assets and nearly 10 percent of all foundation grants.

Operating Foundations. Finally, although most American foundations specialize in grantmaking, there were nearly 5,000 foundations as of 2007 that functioned both as grantmakers and as operators of actual charitable programs. This pattern, which is much more widespread in other countries, seems to be growing as well in the United States. As evidence of this, the number of such operating foundations in existence as of 2007, at 4,938, was more than twice the 2,323 that existed in 1996. These so-called operating foundations accounted for almost 6 percent of foundation assets and nearly 8 percent of all foundation "grants," though the grants in this case may consist of qualifying distributions in support of charitable activities carried out by the operating foundations themselves.

The Relative Position of Foundations. Like many other parts of the nonprofit sector, foundations have grown massively in recent years, both in numbers and in economic scale. Thus, as shown in Table 3.3, the number of foundations increased by nearly 250 percent between 1975 and 2007, from just under 22,000 institutions to over 75,000. During this period also, the scale of both foundation assets and grants swelled by 600 percent, after adjusting for inflation.

TABLE 3.3: Growth in U.S. Grantmaking Foundations, 1975–2007

Variable	1975	2007	% change
Entities	21,887	75,137	243%
Assets (billion $)*	$98.3	$682.2	594%
Grants (billion $)*	$6.3	$44.3	603%

*In constant 2007 U.S. dollars.
Source: Foundation Center, *Foundation Yearbook*, 2008 and 2009

Because of the considerable scale and recent growth of the American foundation universe, there is often a tendency to exaggerate the role that foundations can play. It is therefore important to bear a number of crucial facts in mind in assessing their position in the American nonprofit sector.

- In the first place, although the number of American foundations is quite large, most foundations are quite small. In fact, as shown in Figure 3.9, as of 2006 the top 0.4 percent of all foundations—270 institutions in all—controlled 50 percent of all foundation assets and the top 8.5 percent accounted for 87 percent of the assets. By contrast, the bottom 61.5 percent of all foundations accounted for only 2 percent of all foundation assets. (For a list of the 10 largest foundations in terms of assets, see Table 3.4).

FIGURE 3.9: Distribution of Foundations and Foundation Assets, by Size Class, 2006

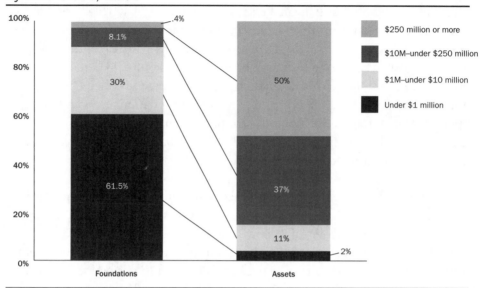

Source: Foundation Center, *Foundation Yearbook,* 2008, p. 13.

TABLE 3.4: Ten Largest U.S. Foundations by Size of Assets, 2007 (billion $)

Foundation	Assets (billions)
Bill and Melinda Gates Foundation	$38.9
Ford Foundation	$13.8
J. Paul Getty Trust	$11.2
Robert Wood Johnson Foundation	$10.7
William and Flora Hewlett Foundation	$9.3
W.K. Kellogg Foundation	$8.1
Lilly Endowment	$7.7
John D. and Catherine T. MacArthur Foundation	$7.1
David and Lucile Packard Foundation	$6.6
Andrew W. Mellon Foundation	$6.5

Source: Foundation Center, *Foundation Yearbook,* 2009.

- Similarly, although the overall scale of foundation assets seems quite large, it pales in comparison to the assets of other institutions in American society. Thus, as Figure 3.10 shows, compared to the $682 million in foundation assets as of 2007, U.S. money market funds had assets of $3.03 billion (five times as much), U.S. life insurance companies had assets of $4.95 billion (eight times as much), U.S. pension funds had assets of $6.39 billion (eleven times as much), and U.S. mutual funds, commercial banks, and nonfinancial corporations each had assets well above eleven times more than foundations.[27] Clearly, the assets of America's charitable foundations hardly make these institutions dominant players in America's capital markets.

- Finally, private foundation grants, while important in helping to preserve the independence of America's nonprofit organizations, hardly represent the dominant share even of the income of nonprofit service and expressive organizations. As shown in Figure 3.6 above, foundations (including corporate foundations) accounted for only about 13 percent of the $314.1 billion in private philanthropic contributions that Americans made in 2007. Even when we focus exclusively on the giving that flows to nonprofit service and expressive organizations of the sort that foundations support and exclude giving to religious congregations, the foundation share of private giving is still only about 20 percent. And since private charitable contributions represent only about 10 percent of the *total income* of these nonprofit organizations, as noted above, this means that foundations

FIGURE 3.10: Financial Assets, Foundations versus Other Financial Institutions, 2007 ($ billions)

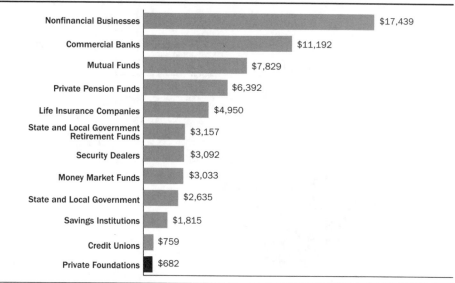

Nonfinancial Businesses	$17,439
Commercial Banks	$11,192
Mutual Funds	$7,829
Private Pension Funds	$6,392
Life Insurance Companies	$4,950
State and Local Government Retirement Funds	$3,157
Security Dealers	$3,092
Money Market Funds	$3,033
State and Local Government	$2,635
Savings Institutions	$1,815
Credit Unions	$759
Private Foundations	$682

Source: Board of Governors of the Federal Reserve System, "Federal Reserve Statistical Release, 2.1, Flow of Funds Accounts of the U.S." (12 March 2009), www.federalreserve.gov/releases/Z1/20090312.

provide just slightly over 2 percent of nonprofit service-organization total revenue, as shown in Figure 3.11.[28]

Foundations as "Philanthropic Banks." One very interesting recent development that holds significant promise for expanding the impact that foundations can have is the growing use by at least some foundations of so-called program-related investments (PRIs) and other non-grant forms of assistance. PRIs were authorized by the 1969 Tax Reform Act. They allow foundations to count toward their 5 percent "payout" requirement the costs of loans, loan guarantees, and other financial instruments that allow foundations to recoup all or a portion of their "investments," to support projects that achieve some degree of financial return, and to leverage the resources of private investors to promote social objectives. To qualify as a PRI, a non-grant form of assistance must meet three criteria: 1) the primary purpose must be to serve the charitable mission of the foundation; 2) financial gain cannot be a significant objective; and 3) the investment cannot promote a political party or candidate.[29]

The use of PRIs developed quite slowly through much of the period since enactment of the 1969 legislation. One study reported only 40 foundations involved in any type of "mission investing" as of 1995, rising to about 80 as of 2005.[30] But interest in the use of non-grant forms of assistance has ballooned in the early years of the twenty-first century and seems destined to expand further, not simply through PRIs, which are tied to a foundation's grant budget, but also through more aggressive use of foundation

FIGURE 3.11: Foundation Share of U.S. Nonprofit Service and Expressive Organization Revenue, 2007

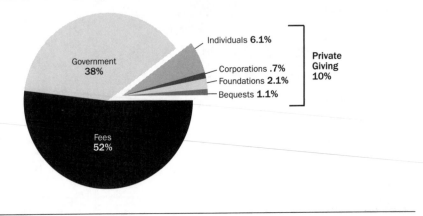

Source: See Chapter 3, endnote 29.

investments, which are increasingly being deployed to promote charitable missions and to leverage the resources of private investors. This surge of interest has been fueled by the success of the international microfinance field; the passage in the 1970s and 1980s of the low-income housing tax credit and the Community Reinvestment Act, which stimulated the flow of private investment capital into neighborhood renewal and low-income housing construction; the emergence of a number of intermediary organizations helping to channel new forms of foundation assistance into a variety of social ventures; and the general stress on "sustainability" of social-purpose organizations and on "social ventures" as the vehicles most likely to achieve it. In the process, a new field of "mission investing" has surfaced and a "new frontier of philanthropy" established, and a growing number of foundations have begun to function as veritable philanthropic "banks," with a variety of "windows" offering a broad menu of financial vehicles in addition to grants to help organizations at different stages of their development.[31]

One interesting recent development is the growing use by some foundations of program-related investments and other non-grant forms of assistance.

Summary. In short, the United States has an extraordinary number of private, charitable foundations. These foundations control significant assets and make important contributions to the American nonprofit sector. Nevertheless, it would be wrong to exaggerate the role that these organizations play. They are by no means the dominant source of charitable donations and represent an even smaller share of the overall income of American nonprofits. Their main function, therefore, may be to serve as creative catalysts for social problem-solving and sources of innovation helping to shape government policies. In recent years, however, a number of foundations have expanded their use of new instruments of assistance that can extend their reach and leverage additional resources for social problem solving.

Support Organizations. Beyond the foundations, a second broad group of "funding intermediaries" in the American nonprofit sector are so-called "support organizations." These are organizations that collect private donations on behalf of a number of service and expressive organizations or otherwise accumulate assets for distribution to other nonprofit organizations.

Internal Revenue Service data reveal 36,719 such support organizations with total revenues of $90.4 billion as of 2007.[32] Many of these are established as the fundraising arms of operating nonprofit organizations or even of public institutions, such as state universities. Others are *federated funders*. Unlike foundations, these federated funding organizations generate their support from a sizable number of individuals. They thus resemble community foundations except that their support base is usually quite a bit broader than this. Examples here would be the United Jewish Appeal, the American Cancer Society, the American Heart Association, federated arts appeals, and the like.

Perhaps the best known of these federated funding organizations is United Way. United Way is a network of some 1,900 local "community chests" that raise funds from individuals and corporations on behalf of a number of local social service agencies. What is distinctive about the United Way system, however, is its use of a particular mode of fundraising, namely "workplace solicitation." This essentially involves a direct charitable appeal to workers in their workplace coupled with a system allowing employers to deduct the pledged contributions made by their employees automatically from the employees' paychecks each pay period. In order to ensure employer support, United Way has typically involved the corporate community actively in the organization of each year's United Way "campaign" and has historically restricted the distribution of the proceeds of the campaign to a set of approved United Way "member agencies." This latter feature has come under increasing attack in recent years, however, with the result that many local United Ways have established "donor option" plans, which permit donors to designate which agencies will receive their contributions.

Because of its obvious efficiencies, United Way's workplace campaigns have been quite effective, so much so that many other federated fundraising organizations have sought to break the monopoly that United Way has long had on the workplace as a solicitation site.[33] In 2007–2008, for example, local United Ways throughout the United States collected a total of $4.19 billion in contributions.[34] While this is quite significant, it represented just over 3 percent of all private charitable donations reaching American nonprofit service and expressive organizations, and 0.3 percent of all nonprofit service and expressive organization revenue. In the human service field in which it focuses, however, United Way provides closer to 16 percent of all the charitable support and about 7 percent of total revenue.

While United Way is the best known of the federated funding organizations, it is by no means the only one. Also prominent are the numerous united health appeal organizations, such as the American Cancer Society, the American Heart Association, the American Diabetes Association, and others. These organizations sponsor public appeals through mail, by telephone, or via house-to-house solicitations to generate funds for use in health research and related purposes. The American Cancer Society, the largest of these federated fundraising organizations, for example, raised $898 million in 2009 through a combination of direct public appeals, special events, and bequests, which it then used to support medical research, public health education campaigns, medical education, and patient support.[35]

A donor-advised fund allows a donor to create a charitable fund in a sponsoring organization and then direct distributions from this fund over time to support the donor's charitable purposes.

Thanks in part to the rise of internet-based fundraising, recent years have witnessed an expansion of the role of federated fundraising, even as individual nonprofit organizations have increased their direct appeals as well. Federated fundraising minimizes costs, especially for direct mail and related types of campaigning, but it also creates serious challenges in figuring out how to distribute the proceeds of federated campaigns and how to create donor identification with the causes and agencies being supported.

Another rapidly growing form of federated fundraising takes the form of commercially originated *donor-advised funds*. A donor-advised fund is a charitable vehicle that allows a donor to create a charitable fund in a sponsoring organization and then direct distributions from this fund over time to support the donor's charitable purposes. The donor secures the tax deduction for his or her contribution at the time of the creation of the fund, but the payout can stretch over time.

Donor-advised funds have long been a favored vehicle for community foundations, allowing these institutions to build up endowments consisting of the bequests or lifetime gifts of community residents that the foundation, or the foundation and the donor's family, can then oversee upon the death of the donor. The new development is the appearance of donor-advised funds created by some of the nation's leading investment firms, such as Vanguard, Fidelity, and Schwab. The appeal to donors is that the same entity managing their regular investment accounts can handle the management of their charitable resources. Commercially originated donor-advised funds have therefore surged in popularity. Thirty-eight such funds were thus in existence as of 2007, with combined assets of $11 billion.[36] The top three—Fidelity, Schwab, and Vanguard—controlled approximately $8.8 billion in assets as of 2008 and made close to $2 billion in charitable donations.[37] Although less than two decades old, these gift funds have already surpassed the nation's community foundations in the number of donor-advised fund accounts they manage.[38]

Religious congregations are the only nonprofit organizations automatically entitled to tax exemption.

Professional Fundraisers. A final group of financial intermediaries of great importance to the nonprofit sector are professional fundraisers, the individuals and firms professionally involved in raising private contributions on behalf of private, nonprofit organizations. Larger nonprofit organizations typically employ one or more professional fundraisers on their regular staffs, and the typical large university or cultural institution may have a "development office" that employs fifty or more fundraisers. These professional fundraisers have their own professional association, the Association of Fundraising Professionals (AFP), as well as extensive networks of workshops and training courses. As of 2010, AFP boasted 30,000 members in 213 chapters throughout the world.[39] In addition, although they are not covered directly in this primer, it is useful to note that a significant number of for-profit fundraising firms exist. For example, the Giving Institute, formerly the American Association of Fundraising Counsel, Inc., represents 36 of these for-profit consulting firms. Such firms work on retainers from nonprofit organizations to manage fundraising campaigns. Somewhat ironically, it is the for-profit firms in what is now the Giving Institute that initiated *Giving USA*, the authoritative sourcebook on charitable giving to nonprofit organizations in the United States.

RELIGIOUS CONGREGATIONS

Yet a fourth class of public-benefit nonprofit organizations are religious congregations, though there is some debate about whether they should be treated as public-benefit or member-benefit organizations since 70 to 80 percent of their revenues are used to provide services to their congregants.[40] Congregations are places of religious worship, as distinguished from religiously affiliated service organizations, such as Christian schools, social service agencies like Catholic Charities, or religiously affiliated hospitals or nursing homes, which are included among the service and expressive organizations discussed earlier in this chapter.

Religious congregations are the only nonprofit organizations automatically entitled to tax exemption under Section 501(c)(3) of the tax code, and thus to the receipt of tax-deductible donations without even having to file an application for formal recognition from the Internal Revenue Service. They are also exempt from the reporting requirements that the law places on all other types of 501(c)(3) organizations.

Such treatment is a legacy of the English legal tradition, especially the Elizabethan Statute of Charitable Uses, which considered religious organizations to be "public charities." But it also reflects the strong separation of church and state built into the American constitution. Because the power to tax is the power to destroy, it has long been felt that to require religious congregations to secure approval from government to be incorporated or exempted from taxation would be to give government too much potential control over them. A self-declared religious congregation is therefore automatically treated as a 501(c)(3) organization exempt from taxes and eligible to receive tax-deductible gifts.

What constitutes a religious congregation or church for this purpose is open to dispute, however. Federal authorities have historically been loath to define the term very precisely in view of the First Amendment's prohibitions on any laws regarding the establishment of religion or the free exercise thereof.[41] But the emergence of various self-styled religious organizations that turn out to be fronts for nonexempt activities has led the courts and the Internal Revenue Service to be somewhat more precise. Thus, churches and religious organizations are expected, among other things, to have some recognized creed or form of worship, to be sacerdotal in character, to have regular religious services, and to operate, like other 501(c)(3) organizations, for other than private gain.[42]

Because religious congregations are not required to register or provide information on their operations to any government agency, it is difficult to gauge their numbers or scale of operations. Approximately 113,000 religious congregations are thought to be registered with the IRS even though they are not required to do so. However, only 17,521 submitted Form 990 filings with the Internal Revenue Service as of 2007. Based on data assembled by the National Council of the Churches of Christ, the Association of Religion Data Archives (ARDA), and the National Congregation Study, we estimate the total number of congregations in the United States at approximately 429,000. Based on the National Congregations Study and data on charitable giving to religious congregations assembled by *Giving USA*, we estimate congregation revenues to be approximately $119.2 billion as of 2007. Most (85 percent) of this revenue comes from private giving, but congregations receive the remaining 15 percent of revenue from fees and other types of charges, such as rentals of their facilities.[43]

Comparison to Other Countries

The American nonprofit sector is thus an enormous economic and social force. But how does it compare to its counterparts in other parts of the world?

For many Americans, the answer to this question is obvious. Since at least the time of Alexis de Tocqueville's 1835 chronicle of *Democracy in America*, which called dramatic attention to America's singular attachment to private associations in contrast to European arrangements for handling important public matters, American folklore has held firmly to the belief that nonprofit associations are somehow a uniquely American phenomenon, or at least that the American nonprofit sector is the largest and most robust in the world.

In fact, however, recent research has exploded this comforting American myth. While the U.S. nonprofit sector is quite large, it is certainly not the only one in the world. Nor is it even the largest. Work by statistical officials in India, for example, has identified over 3 million registered nonprofit organizations in that country compared to the 1.9 million recorded in the United States. When measured as a share of the country's economically active population, moreover, the U.S. nonprofit sector falls below that in many other countries, such as the Netherlands, Belgium, Canada, and Israel, as shown in Figure 3.12.[44]

Clearly, while America may have a particularly highly developed nonprofit sector, similar organizations are very much present in other parts of the world as well. Indeed, a veritable "global associational revolution" appears to be under way around the world, a significant upsurge of organized, private, voluntary activity in virtually every corner of the globe.[45] People in other countries have thus found themselves drawn to nonprofit organizations at least as avidly as Americans, which makes it all the more important to understand the evolving shape and role of such organizations in the American context.

FIGURE 3.12: Nonprofit Sector Workforce as a Percent of Economically Active Populations, U.S. versus 42 Countries

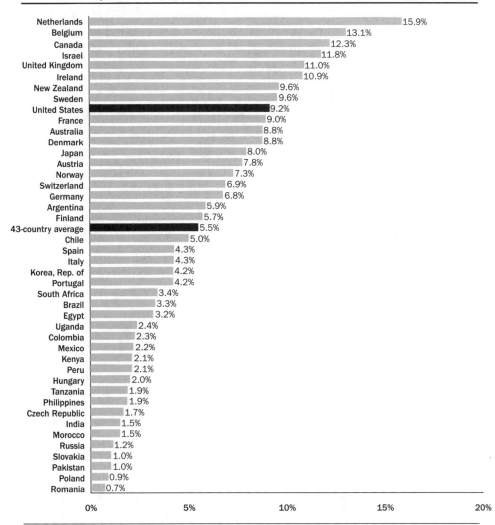

Source: Lester M. Salamon, S. Wojciech Sokolowski, and Associates. *Global Civil Society: Dimensions of the Nonprofit Sector, Volume III* (Kumarian Press, 2011).

Summary

Four principal conclusions flow from this overview of the American nonprofit sector:

1. *The nonprofit sector is quite diverse.* It includes both primarily member-serving and primarily public-serving organizations. Even among the public-serving organizations of greatest concern to us here, a great deal of specialization has taken place. Some organizations are essentially funding intermediaries, others are places of sacramental religious worship, and others perform the wide range of service and expressive functions for which the sector is best known.

2. *The U.S. nonprofit sector is much larger than is commonly believed.* Even the service and expressive component of the sector's public-benefit organizations had expenditures in 2007 on a scale equal to 9 percent of the entire U.S. gross national product.

3. *Private giving comprises a much smaller share of the income of the U.S. nonprofit sector than is commonly recognized.* Important as private giving is to the vitality and independence of the nonprofit sector, it is hardly the largest source of nonprofit service and expressive organization revenue. Rather, most of the income of this sector comes from fees and service charges, with government a close second.

4. *While the American nonprofit sector is larger than its counterparts elsewhere in absolute terms, it is not the largest in the world in relative terms.* Nonprofit organizations have long been present in other countries as well, and their role and scope appear to be on the rise almost everywhere.

ENDNOTES

1. One recent estimate puts the number of informal grassroots organizations in the United States as of the early 1990s at 7.5 million, or about 30 per 1,000 inhabitants, though this is based on rather rough projections. By comparison, the number of organizations formally registered as tax-exempt entities under any of the 26 relevant provisions of the Internal Revenue Code was approximately 1.164 million as of 1995. See: David Horton Smith, "The Rest of the Nonprofit Sector: Grassroots Associations as the Dark Matter Ignored in Prevailing 'Flat Earth' Maps of the Sector," *Nonprofit and Voluntary Sector Quarterly*, 26:2 (June 1997): 118.

2. The estimate of 2.0 million identifiable nonprofit organizations noted here was derived by adding to the 1,526,882 organizations listed as registered tax-exempt organizations on the Internal Revenue Service's Exempt Organization Master File (EOMF) two categories of organizations known to be underrepresented in the IRS records: religious congregations and other charitable nonprofit organizations not recorded in IRS records but encountered in field research by various scholars.

    The IRS EOMF data were derived from IRS data files accessed at: www.irs.gov/taxstats/ charitablestats/article/0,,id=97186,00.html. Because religious congregations are not required to secure tax-exempt status or to file the information forms required of other charitable organizations, data on the scale of the religious congregation universe is highly imperfect. The estimate here is based on a number of sources. Data on the number of Christian denominational churches, including Protestant, Roman Catholic, and Orthodox faiths, was derived from Eileen W. Lindner, ed., *Yearbook of American and Canadian Churches 2010*, 78th Issue, prepared for the National Council of the Churches of Christ (Nashville: Abingdon Press, 2010). These data derive from surveys of denominational bodies and generally cover the year 2008, though data on some denominations cover earlier years. Data on Jewish synagogues, Muslim mosques, and Buddhist, Hindu, and other eastern religions (e.g., Bahai, Jain, Zoroastrian) were derived from the Association of Religion Data Archives (ARDA), accessed at: www.thearda.com/ mapsReports/reports/US_2000.asp. This source presents congregational and membership data only through 2000. Finally, an estimate of unaffiliated congregations was derived from the National Congregations Study, 2006-7, as reported in Mark Chaves, "Religious Congregations," in *The State of Nonprofit America*, 2nd ed., ed. Lester M. Salamon (Washington: Brookings Institution Press, 2012). Altogether, this yielded an estimate of 428,975 congregations, consistent with an estimate that the author derived from data in the U.S. Bureau of Economic Analysis, National Income and Product Accounts, Table 7.20, www.bea.gov/national/nipaweb/ but almost 100,000 higher than the 330,000 congregations that Hadaway and Marler estimated as of 2004. Although congregations are not required to register with the Internal Revenue Service, Boris (2006) reports that a review of the EOMF revealed an estimated 113,000 congregations registered in that file, suggesting that an additional 316,000 congregations need to be added to the IRS EOMF listing. See: C. Kirk Hadaway and Penny Long Marler, "How Many Americans Attend Worship Each Week? An Alternative Approach to Measurement," *Journal for the Scientific Study of Religion* 44:3 (2005): 307-22; Elizabeth T. Boris, "Nonprofit Organizations in a Democracy," in *Nonprofits and Government: Collaboration and Conflict*, ed. Elizabeth T. Boris and C. Eugene Steurle (Washington: Urban Institute Press, 2006), 29.

The existence of tax-exempt organizations other than churches not listed with the Internal Revenue Service was identified based on survey work conducted by the present author in cooperation with a team of colleagues in sixteen American cities of various sizes in the early 1980s. See: Lester M. Salamon, *Partners in Public Service: Government–Nonprofit Relations in the Modern Welfare State* (Baltimore: Johns Hopkins University Press, 1995), 59, n.1. This finding has since been verified by other researchers. See for example: Kirsten A. Grønbjerg, Helen Liu, and Thomas Pollak, "Incorporated but not IRS-Registered: Exploring the (Dark) Grey Fringes of the Nonprofit Universe," *Nonprofit and Voluntary Sector Quarterly* 39:3 (September 2009), 925-45. The number of such organizations was estimated by dividing their total income as reported in National Income and Product Account (NIPA) Table 7.20 by the average income of organizations with income of $25,000 or less that did file tax returns with the IRS. This yields a conservative estimate of 136,600 organizations. NIPA data were accessed at www.bea.gov/national/nipaweb.

3. Based on Internal Revenue Service data accessed through www.irs.gov/taxstats/charitablestats/ article/0,,id=97176,00.html#2.

4. Data on nonprofit revenues from Internal Revenue 990 and 990PF filings accessed through www.irs.gov/taxstats/charitablestats/article/0,,id=97176,00.html#2 and www.irs.gov/pub/irs-soi/07pf01ta.xls. The estimate of the revenues of nonprofit organizations not captured in IRS filings was derived from National Income and Product Account (NIPA) Table 7.20, accessed at www.bea.gov/national/nipaweb. The estimate of religious congregation revenue was developed by applying the share of total congregational revenue coming from charitable contributions, as shown by the National Congregations Study, to the estimate of total contributions to religious organizations provided by *Giving USA*. With congregational revenue from giving estimated to be 85 percent of total revenue as of 2007 and giving to religion estimated at $101.3 billion in 2007, this yielded an estimate of total religious income of $119 billion. For further detail on this estimate, see Chapter 11, n. 11. Data on gross national income of countries from the *Statistical Abstract of the United States,* accessed through www.census.gov/compendia/statab/cats/ international_statistics/economy.html.

5. Data on nonprofit employment from: Kennard T. Wing, Thomas H. Pollack, and Amy Blackwood, *The Nonprofit Almanac: 2008* (Washington, DC: The Urban Institute Press, 2008), 30, Table 2.2, 30 (cited hereafter as *Nonprofit Almanac 2008*). The estimate here was derived by

projecting the 2005 estimate provided in this source to 2007 by assuming that the growth rate of nonprofit employment between 2005 and 2007 would roughly equal the average for 2000–2005. Volunteer data are from the September Supplement to the Current Population Survey (2007) data available online at: www.census.gov/cps/. The full-time equivalent was calculated assuming 1,758 hours of full-time work per year, based on the *Economic Report of the President, 2009*. Value of volunteer time was calculated using a replacement cost approach and applying the average wage in the U.S. economy. Data on total U.S. workforce, average wage, and workers by industry secured from: *Quarterly Census of Employment and Wages,* retrieved from BLS web site: www.bls.gov/data/#employment.

6. As noted earlier, only organizations with $25,000 or more of income are required to complete a Form 990 reporting on their revenues, expenditures, and other financial parameters. Of the 322,554 501(c)(4) through 501(c)(9) organizations listed on the Exempt Organization Master File, only approximately 51,000, or about 16 percent, filed the 990 form in 2007.

7. The numbers of registered organizations by type were secured from the table "Entries in 2009 EOMF [Exempt Organization Master File], by legal status," available from the Internal Revenue Service web site at www.irs.gov/taxstats/charitablestats. For sources of estimates of the number of religious congregations, see note 2 above. Revenue figures are derived from IRS Statistics of Income Table 3: "Form 990 Returns of 501(c)(3)-(9) Organizations: Balance Sheet and Income Statement Items, by Code Section, Tax Year 2007," accessed on September 2, 2010 at www.irs.gov.taxsstats/charitablestats. Total revenues of all nonprofit organizations were computed from this table and from Table 1: "Domestic Private Foundations: Number and Selected Financial Data, by Type of Foundation and Size and End-of-Year Fair Market Value of Total Assets, Tax Year 2007," accessed through the IRS Statistics of Income web site. These data were augmented by data from NIPA Table 7.20 for religious organizations and other organizations not captured in IRS statistics. Except for religious congregations, revenues shown by type of organization cover only "reporting" organizations, i.e., those filing Form 990 or 990-PF.

8. Here, again, the revenue figure cited represents the revenue of the 281,474 public-serving nonprofit organizations that filed Form 990 or Form 990PF with the Internal Revenue Service plus estimates for nonreporting organizations. See note 4 above for further detail on relevant sources.

9. The justification for tax exemption in the case of religious organizations is naturally different from this, resting on the First Amendment's bar against any law that might prohibit the "free exercise" of religion. Taxation of churches has been judged to involve the kind of excessive entanglement of government with religion that the First Amendment has been interpreted to prohibit. Bruce Hopkins, *The Law of Tax-Exempt Organizations,* 6th ed. (New York: John Wiley and Sons, 1992), 202–3. Although nonprofit organizations are themselves exempt from federal and most state and local taxes, their employees pay sales and income taxes. For a useful analysis of the effects of nonprofit property tax exemption and efforts to secure so-called "payments in lieu of taxes," or PILOTS, from nonprofits, see: Evelyn Brody, ed., *Property-Tax Exemption for Charities: Mapping the Battlefield* (Washington, DC: The Urban Institute Press, 2002).

10. The formal language of the law is somewhat more complex than this. Section 501(c)(3) status is available for "Corporations, and any community chest, fund or foundation, organized and operated exclusively for religious, charitable, scientific, testing for public safety, literary, or educational purposes, or to foster national or international amateur sports competition (but only if no part of its activities involve the provision of athletic facilities or equipment), or for the prevention of cruelty to children or animals."

11. The English Statute of Charitable Uses of 1601, which is the basis of the legal definition of the term charitable, specifically included the following activities within the term charitable: "...relief of aged, impotent, and poor people;...maintenance of sick and maimed soldiers and mariners;

schools for learning, free schools, and scholars in universities; repair of bridges, ports, havens, causeways, churches, seabanks, and highways;...education and preferment of orphans;...relief, stock or maintenance of houses of correction;...marriages of poor maids; supportation, aid, and help of young tradesmen, handicraftsmen and persons decayed; relief or redemption of prisoners or captives; aid or ease of any poor inhabitants concerning payments of fifteens, setting out of soldiers and other taxes." For further detail, see: Hopkins (1992), 69–108.

12. For further detail on these provisions, see Hopkins (1992), 564–568, and Chapter 10 below.

13. This estimate was developed by subtracting from the 1,082,466 organizations registered as 501(c)(3) organizations on the Internal Revenue Service's Master File of Exempt Organizations as of 2009 the estimated 113,000 churches that choose to register with the Internal Revenue Service even though they are not required to, and the approximately 114,354 foundations and other funding intermediaries registered as 501(c)(3) organizations, and then adding the 136,600 additional organizations estimated from Bureau of Economic Analysis data to be missing from IRS listings. See note 4 above for references to these sources.

14. This estimate was developed by subtracting from the 313,121 501(c)(3) organizations that filed Form 990 returns with the IRS for the 2007 tax year the estimated 42,740 "supporting organizations" and the 17,483 religious organizations reported in the IRS Form 990 "Microdata File" for 2007, downloaded from www.irs.gov/taxstats/charitablestats/article/0,,id=97176,00.htm.

15. Lester M. Salamon, David Altschuler, and Jaana Myllyluoma, *More Than Just Charity: The Baltimore Area Nonprofit Sector in a Time of Change* (Baltimore: The Johns Hopkins Institute for Policy Studies, 1990), 9.

16. Based on data reported by the Internal Revenue Service from Form 990 returns. See note 18 for further detail on the formulation of these revenue estimates. This figure is well below the $326.1 billion in private giving reported for 2007 by *Giving USA*, the major source on private giving in the United States. The *Giving USA* total includes a great deal of double-counting, however. For example, it includes the giving made to private foundations as well as the grants that private foundations then make to nonprofit organizations. Similarly, it includes both the contributions to the numerous federated funders and support organizations created by various nonprofit organizations (e.g., hospitals, universities, social service providers) and the payments these entities subsequently make to the organizations they support. The $135.1 billion figure reported here includes the payments that service and expressive organizations receive from these "funding intermediaries" but not the contributions that these funding intermediaries first collect from the public. For further discussion of the revenues of funding intermediaries, see the subsequent section on them in this chapter.

17. As will become clear below, the term "fees and charges" as used here differs considerably from the term "program service revenue" used in IRS Form 990 and in much of the reporting on nonprofit revenue. The latter term includes a considerable amount of revenue that originates with government, not private purchasers. Included here is government contract revenue and government "voucher" payments through such huge government programs as Medicaid and Medicare. Because so much of the government support to nonprofit organizations takes the form of voucher payments and contracts, lumping this together with private purchases under a broad "program service revenue" concept obscures the important role that government plays in the financing of the modern nonprofit sector in the United States. On the growth of such "consumer side subsidies," see: Lester M. Salamon, *The Resilient Sector* (Washington, DC: The Brookings Institution Press, 2003), 17–19; and Lester M. Salamon, "The New Governance and the Tools of Public Action: An Introduction," in *The Tools of Government: A Guide to the New Governance*, ed. Lester M. Salamon (New York: Oxford University Press, 2002), 1–6.

18. The data reported here draw primarily on microdata files prepared by the Internal Revenue Service from Form 990 filings required of all nonprofit organizations with $25,000 or more of annual income. Foundations and other "funding intermediaries," as well as religious congregations, were removed from the data to avoid double-counting of contributions and to zero in on the service and expressive organizations of principal concern to us. The micro-data files were accessed through the IRS web site at www.irs.gov/taxstats/charitablestats/article/0,,id=97176,00.html.

    Because Form 990 merges government contract payments, government voucher payments such as Medicare and Medicaid, and direct purchases paid for by consumers together as "program service revenue," the data they generate obscure the true extent of government support flowing to nonprofit organizations. Since these government "purchases" are huge and the impact of government policy on the nonprofit sector is a matter of considerable importance, we felt it necessary to disentangle this "program service" category and provide a clearer picture of the totality of direct government support to nonprofit service and expressive organizations. To do so, we drew on four additional data sources: first, the Census Bureau's 2002 *Economic Census*; second, the Census Bureau's *Service Annual Survey* for 2006; third, the Bureau of Economic Analysis' (BEA) National Income and Product Accounts (www.bea.gov/national/Index.htm), especially Table 7.20; and finally, the Appendix to Chapter 4 of the 2008 *Nonprofit Almanac*, which represented an attempt by the authors of this publication to overcome this shortcoming of the 990 Form. More specifically, information about the revenue sources in the health service fields (ambulatory health services [North American Industrial Classification System, or NAICS, Code 621], hospitals [NAICS 622], and nursing homes [NAICS 623]) was obtained from the *Service Annual Survey* (SAS), which breaks down revenues of these employer firms by source, including Medicare, Medicaid, and other government payments (Table 8.10). It also breaks down the health service firms by tax exemption status (Tables 8.1, 8.2, and 8.3). Based on this information, we were able to differentiate the government portion of program service revenue for tax-exempt health service providers and provide a fuller estimate of revenue sources for this group of nonprofits.

    Information about revenue sources in social services (NAICS 624) was obtained from two sources: first, the aggregate amount was obtained from the 2006 *Service Annual Survey*; and second, the distribution among revenue sources was obtained from the 2002 *Economic Census* (Social Assistance, Table 3), which provides line-item detail on government payments for services, and government and private grants, among other revenue items.

    Likewise, we calculated the "philanthropy" share of organizations with revenue of $25,000 or less that filed 990 returns, applied that share to the revenue obtained from NIPA Table 7.20, and treated the remaining balance as "fees." It is unlikely that these types of organizations received any government funding of economically significant value.

19. For more detail on this government–nonprofit financial link, see Chapter 5 and Lester M. Salamon, *Partners in Public Service: Government-Nonprofit Relations in the Modern Welfare State* (Baltimore: Johns Hopkins University Press, 1995). For insight into the broader pattern of "third-party government" of which it is a part, see: Lester M. Salamon, ed. *The Tools of Government: A Guide to the New Governance* (New York: Oxford University Press, 2002). As indicated in note 18 above, existing data sources obscure the true extent of government funding of nonprofit activity by recording government voucher payments as "program service revenue," or market sales. The estimates reported here include such payments as part of government support to the nonprofit sector.

20. *Giving USA 2009* (Indianapolis: Giving USA Foundation, 2009), 3.

21. Estimates based on September 2010 Supplement to the U.S. Census Bureau, *Current Population Survey* data, available online at: www.census.gov/cps/.

22. The value of volunteering for service and expressive organizations was estimated by applying the 57 percent figure to the total value of volunteering ($95 billion) calculated as outlined in endnote 5 above.

23. Bruce R. Hopkins, *The Law of Tax-Exempt Organizations*, 9th ed. (New York: John Wiley and Sons, 2007), 391–2.

24. Under a 1976 law, "lobbying" is defined as "communicating a position on a particular piece of legislation to a legislative official, and/or calling on others to contact a legislative official in support or opposition to a particular piece of legislation." Nonprofit 501(c)(3) organizations are permitted to "advocate" for policies without limit, but they can devote to lobbying, i.e., attempting to influence particular pieces of legislation, only an "insubstantial part" of their revenues or expenditures. What constitutes an "insubstantial" part of an organization's activities has long been open to debate, however. To clarify this, in 1976 Congress gave nonprofits the choice of electing to come under an "expenditure test" that clarified and greatly simplified nonprofit lobbying. Under the expenditure test, nonprofits may spend up to 20 percent of their first $500,000 of exempt-purpose expenditures each year on lobbying. The percentage declines up to a ceiling of $1 million of spending on lobbying as income increases. Few organizations have elected to come under this expenditure test. By default, the rest of the nonprofits are governed by the "insubstantial part" test. For further details on the rules governing nonprofit involvement in the policy process, see Hopkins (2007), 637–71.

25. While foundations in their present form have existed since the turn of the century, they were given legal definition only in 1969, with the passage of the Tax Reform Act. This act differentiated foundations from other nonprofit institutions that have endowments and imposed extra restrictions on the foundations. The key defining feature of a foundation as opposed to other nonprofit institutions legally is that the foundations receive their support from a single individual or family. To be treated as other than a foundation and thus escape the special restrictions imposed on foundations, nonprofit organizations must therefore meet a "public support test," demonstrating that they receive their support from multiple sources. Entities that do so are referred to as "public charities." "Community foundations," which, as noted below, receive their support from multiple sources and therefore are legally "public charities" and not foundations, fall into a special category in the law. Some important differences exist in the definitions of foundations used by the Internal Revenue Service and the Foundation Center, which creates some confusion in the estimates of the size of the foundation universe. The IRS essentially defines a foundation as any nonprofit 501(c)(3) organization that fails to meet the "public support test." This means that libraries, museums, homes for the aged, and other nonprofits could be counted as foundations if they were endowed by an individual or single family or were initially established as "public charities" but then lost that status by being unable to prove that they have sustained support from a broad public. The Foundation Center, by contrast, defines a foundation more narrowly as a "nonprofit, nongovernmental organization with a principal endowment of its own that maintains or aids charitable, educational, religious, or other activities serving the public good, primarily by making grants to other nonprofit organizations." As we shall see below, however, some foundations operate programs directly in addition to making grants. Generally speaking, we use the Foundation Center definition and data here. Compared to the 75,187 foundations identified by the Foundation Center as existing as of 2007, the Internal Revenue Service identified 82,709 foundations as of the 2007 tax year, of which 70,807 were identified as "grant-making." The IRS listing includes only organizations that file Form 990-PF, which means it excludes community foundations since these do not meet the legal definition of a foundation. See: IRS, Statistics of Income, Table 1: "Domestic Private Foundations: Number and Selected Financial Data, By Type of Foundations, Tax Year 2007" (August 2010), available at www.irs.gov/taxstats/charitablestats/article/0,,id=96996,00.html. Foundation Center data from: Foundation Center, *Foundation Yearbook,* 2009.

26. "Qualifying distributions" include grants, so-called program-related investments, and administrative expenses. The payout requirement is set at 5 percent of the average market value of the foundation's investments in the prior year, with various provisions for carry-overs and supplementation in subsequent years if the figures do not match in a particular year. Program-

related investments are loans, loan guarantees, and other types of financial transactions that can count toward a foundation's "payout" requirement even though they do not take the form of grants.

27. Source: Board of Governors of the Federal Reserve System, Federal Reserve Statistical Release Z.1, Flow of Funds Accounts of the U.S. (Washington, DC, 2009). Accessed at: www.federalreserve. gov/releases/Z1/20090312.

28. Based on data in *Giving USA* 2009, 3–4. Assumes that most giving to religion is from individuals and that limited foundation giving flows to religious congregations.

29. Christie Baxter, *Program-Related Investments: A Technical Manual for Foundations* (New York: John Wiley and Sons, 1997), 7.

30. Sarah Cooch and Mark Kramer, *Compounding Impact: Missing Investing by U.S. Foundations* (Boston: FSG Social Impact Advisors, April 2007), 14.

31. For further information on these developments, see: Steven Godeke and Doug Bauer, *Philanthropy's New Passing Gear: Mission-Related Investing—A Policy and Implementation Guide for Foundation Trustees* (New York: Rockefeller Philanthropy Advisors, 2008); and Lester M. Salamon, ed. *New Frontiers of Philanthropy: A Guide to the New Tools and New Actors that are Reshaping Global Philanthropy and Social Investing* (San Francisco: Jossey-Bass Publishers, 2012).

32. Based on microdata files accessed at: www.irs.gov/taxstats/charitablestats/article/0,,id=97176,00. html.

33. During the Carter Administration, several alternative funds, such as the Black United Fund and the United Health Appeal, secured permission to solicit contributions in the federal workplace. This was later revoked by the Reagan Administration, provoking a legal battle that has ended with a broadening of the access to the federal workplace and a greater willingness of the United Way to accept the donor option approach. For this and other features of United Way, see: Eleanor Brilliant, *The United Way: Dilemmas of Organized Charity* (New York: Columbia University Press, 1991).

34. *Giving USA 2009*, 155.

35. www.cancer.org/acs/groups/content/@ocoo-ocmdo/documents/document/acsq-019007.pdf.

36. Andrew W. Hastings, "Donor Advised Fund Market: An analysis of the overall market and trends by National Philanthropic Trust" (National Philanthropic Trust, November 2008), 2.

37. *Giving USA 2009*, 153; Fidelity Charitable Gift Fund, *Annual Report, 2008* (Cincinnati: Fidelity Charitable Gift Fund, 2008), 5.

38. According to one analysis, the nation's corporate-originated donor-advised funds managed close to 72,000 donor-advised funds as of 2007 compared to approximately 26,000 by the nation's more than 700 community foundations. Hastings, "Donor-Advised Fund Market" (2008).

39. Accessed through: www.afpnet.org/.

40. See, for example, Mark Chaves, "Religious Congregations," in *The State of Nonprofit America*, 2nd ed., ed. Lester M. Salamon (Washington, DC: Brookings Institution Press, 2012).

41. The First Amendment to the U.S. Constitution declares that "Congress shall make no law respecting an establishment of religion, or prohibiting the free exercise thereof."

42. Organizations that are church-related but that would be eligible for tax-exempt 501(c)(3) status for other than religious reasons (e.g., church-affiliated educational organizations, hospitals, orphanages, old-age homes) are not treated as churches and are required to register and abide by IRS reporting requirements. Reflecting this, we do not treat them here as religious congregations, but rather as service organizations. On the legal treatment of churches and church-related charitable organizations, see: Hopkins (1992), 775–77.

43. For the derivation of the estimates of the number and revenues of congregations, see notes 2 and 4 above.

44. Lester M. Salamon, S. Wojciech Sokolowski, and Associates, *Global Civil Society: Dimensions of the Nonprofit Sector, Volume III.* (Sterling, VA: Kumarian Press, 2011).

45. Lester M. Salamon, "The Rise of the Nonprofit Sector," *Foreign Affairs* 73:4 (July/August 1994), 109–122.

The Nonprofit Sector in Context: The Government and Business Presence

Important as the nonprofit sector is to American society and the American social welfare system, it hardly operates in a vacuum. Nor does it have a monopoly on providing for public needs. To the contrary, one of the signal developments of the past half-century of American life has been the expansion of governmental social welfare activity, so much so that some observers have feared that government may have displaced the nonprofit sector altogether.

As we have seen, this fear has been largely unwarranted. The presumed conflict between an activist government and a vibrant nonprofit sector has not really materialized in the American setting (nor, as it turns out, in most of the so-called "welfare states" of Europe).[1] Although tensions clearly exist, a widespread partnership has developed between the two sectors, and with for-profit businesses as well, creating a "mixed economy" of welfare in which public and private, nonprofit and for-profit, action are mixed in often complex and confusing ways.[2] Thus:

- Nonprofit organizations help to identify problems and mobilize pressure on government to respond.

- Government establishes programs and raises resources and then turns to both nonprofit and for-profit organizations to deliver the services.

- Private households purchase welfare services on their own from both nonprofit and for-profit providers.

- For-profit businesses form alliances with nonprofit organizations and local governments to improve schools, upgrade neighborhoods, and promote the arts.

The purpose of this chapter is to outline the basic scope and structure of governmental involvement in this "mixed economy," focusing particularly on the social welfare sphere; and to assess how valid the claim is that government has surpassed the nonprofit sector in the provision of social welfare services. In addition, the chapter outlines the role that private for-profit businesses have come to play in many of the traditional fields of nonprofit activity.

The presumed conflict between an activist government and a vibrant nonprofit sector has not really materialized. Although tensions exist, a widespread partnership has developed.

To do so, the discussion falls into three major sections. The first provides an overview of government social welfare spending in the United States, the distribution of this spending between the national government and state and local governments, and the relationship between the levels of such spending in the United States and those in other countries. Against this backdrop, we then zero in on those areas where nonprofit organizations are involved and compare the level of government involvement in these areas with the levels of nonprofit activity in the same fields. Finally, we examine the role that for-profit providers are now playing in these same fields.

What emerges from this analysis are five basic conclusions:

- First, government social welfare spending is quite extensive in the United States.

- Second, despite the expansion of national government activity, state and local governments still play a significant role in many fields.

- Third, government social welfare spending in the United States, however significant, is still well below comparable levels in most other advanced industrial societies.

- Fourth, far from being overshadowed by government, the nonprofit sector in the United States is almost as large as government in the fields where both are actively involved.

- Fifth, for-profit businesses have moved extensively into many fields that nonprofits once dominated.

The remainder of this chapter examines the bases for these conclusions.

The Government Role: Basic Parameters

OVERVIEW

In 2009, the latest year for which data are available, federal, state, and local governments in the United States spent a total of $3.1 trillion on "social welfare services." Included here are old-age pensions, unemployment insurance, veterans' benefits, education, health care, welfare aid for the poor, nutrition assistance, day care, social services, housing, and related services. This represented approximately 16 percent of the total U.S. gross domestic product and three-fifths (61 percent) of all government spending—federal, state, and local.[3] As noted in Figure 4.1:

FIGURE 4.1: Government Spending on Social Welfare and Education, 2009

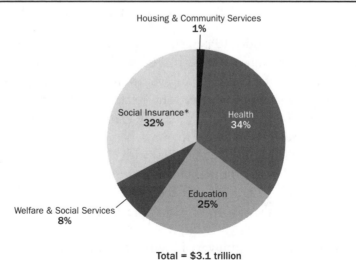

Total = $3.1 trillion

*Social insurance includes disability, retirement, and unemployment; excludes government employee retirement plans.
Source: U.S. Bureau of Economic Analysis, National Income and Product Accounts, Table 3.16, 2009.

- The largest portion (34 percent) of this social welfare spending went for health benefits, up from 28 percent fifteen years earlier. This included payments for Medicare, the federal health program providing health insurance for the elderly; Medicaid, a joint federal-state program providing reimbursement to hospitals and nursing homes for health services to the poor; and veterans' health care.

- The second-largest portion of social welfare spending (32 percent) went for social insurance. Included here is the federal social security program, which provides pension benefits to retired workers; unemployment insurance, which provides cash payments to unemployed persons in covered occupations for a limited period following loss of a job; disability payments to persons injured while working; and pension payments to injured war veterans. These benefits are typically conditioned only on past work or military experience and are not income-related. Not included, however, are government employee retirement payments.

In 2009, the latest year for which data are available, federal, state, and local governments in the United States spent a total of $3.1 trillion on "social welfare services."

- About one-fourth (25 percent) of government social welfare spending goes for education, of which the lion's share is for elementary and secondary education and a much smaller share for higher education.

- This leaves just under 10 percent to be split among all the rest of the activities, including the needs-based "welfare" program, housing aid, and an assortment of child nutrition, vocational rehabilitation, institutional care, income support, food aid, and related social services. Included here is the Temporary Assistance to Needy Families (previously Aid to Families with Dependent Children) Program, the basic cash assistance program for low-income female-headed families with children; the Special Nutrition Assistance Program (formerly known as the Food Stamp Program), which provides food assistance to the needy; public housing; and a variety of employment assistance and social service programs.

Quite clearly, the basic, universal, non-needs-tested assistance programs for the elderly and for education dominate the government role in the social welfare field. This means that the overwhelming majority of government social welfare spending actually flows to the broad middle class. By contrast, the assistance targeted particularly on the poor is far more limited.

FEDERAL VERSUS STATE AND LOCAL ROLES

Much of the impetus for the growth of government social welfare spending over the past four or five decades has come at the national level, giving rise to the common assumption that state and local involvement, once dominant, has now effectively disappeared. In fact, however, state and local governments retain a substantial role in the social welfare field, both in financing government social welfare services and, even more so, in actually delivering or managing the delivery of these services. In particular:

• Of the $3.1 trillion in government social welfare spending in 2009, 63 percent came from the federal government. The remaining 37 percent came from state and local governments.[4]

• As shown in Figure 4.2, federal spending dominates in two major areas: pensions (Social Security and veterans' payments) and housing.

• State and local governments have the decidedly dominant role in education, especially elementary and secondary education. Overall, 87 percent of public education spending originates at the state and local level.

FIGURE 4.2: Federal versus State and Local Government Social Welfare and Education Spending, by Field, 2009

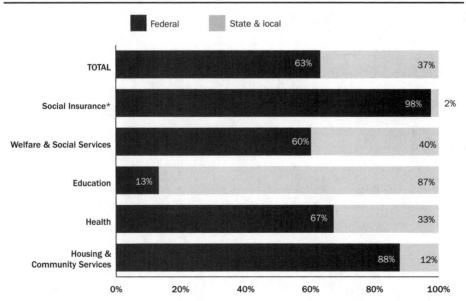

*Social insurance includes disability, retirement, and unemployment; excludes government employee retirement plans.
Source: U.S. Bureau of Economic Analysis, National Income and Product Accounts, Table 3.16, 2009.

- In addition, state and local governments account for 40 percent of the support for a broad range of other social welfare service activities, including day care, child placement and adoption services, foster care, and welfare assistance.

- Even in the huge health care field, which has come to embrace a considerable portion of social services, the states provide a third of the funding. This reflects state and local financing of much of public health and the "matching" requirements built into the federal Medicaid program.

- Beyond their financing role, moreover, state and local governments frequently play a major role in the implementation of even the federally financed activity. Thus, the federal Medicaid and Temporary Assistance to Needy Families (welfare) programs are essentially administered by state and local governments. State and local governments also operate the federal Social Service Block Grant and Community Development Block Grant programs as well as most other federally financed social service activities.

In short, the expansion of federal social welfare activity has by no means displaced the state and local governments, and this was true well before the "devolution" innovations of the mid-1990s that will be highlighted in Chapter 5 below. To the contrary, federal aid has helped to expand the role of state and local governments, and these governments retain a vital role in both the financing and delivery of social welfare services.

COMPARISON TO OTHER COUNTRIES

While the government role in social welfare provision is quite extensive in the United States, it still lags behind that in most other developed countries of the world. Compared to the 16 percent of gross domestic product (GDP) that government social spending represents in the United States, most of the developed nations of Europe devote 25 percent or more of their GDP to government-funded social welfare activities (see Figure 4.3).[5] This reflects the different conceptions about public versus individual responsibility for social welfare between the United States and Europe. What is treated as a public responsibility in Europe is often considered a private responsibility, to be financed out of private earnings, in the United States.

Nor is it the case that America's generally higher rate of charitable giving makes up for its relatively lower level of government social welfare spending, as is often claimed. While the United States does have a significantly higher rate of private charitable giving as a share of GDP than most other developed countries, as Figure 4.4 shows, the difference amounts to only 0.7 to 1.8 percent of GDP, hardly enough to offset the 5.4 to 13.3 percent of GDP by which the United States lags behind other developed countries in overall government social welfare spending, and thus hardly enough to earn the United States the reputation of being more "generous" than these other countries to those in need, as is sometimes claimed.[6]

Government Versus the Nonprofit Sector

At first glance, the $3.1 trillion in government social welfare spending appears to overshadow by a substantial margin the $1.3 trillion in nonprofit service and expressive organization expenditures identified in Chapter 3 above, not to mention the $135 billion in private charitable support flowing to these organizations. This is true even after taking account of the fact that the government spending data reported so far are for 2009 and the nonprofit revenue data from 2007.

FIGURE 4.3: Government Social Welfare Spending as a Percent of GDP, U.S. versus Selected OECD Countries and OECD Average, 2005

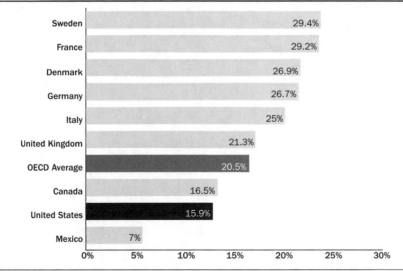

Source: See Chapter 4, endnote 5.

For-profit businesses are increasingly active in many of the fields where nonprofit organizations operate.

For purposes of comparing the scale of government activity to the scale of nonprofit activity, however, it is not appropriate to include all of what is here referred to as "social welfare expenditures." The nonprofit sector is not involved in certain types of social welfare services, such as the provision of retirement or unemployment benefits. Moreover, its involvement in the provision of elementary and secondary education is also minimal, as most educational services at this level are provided by local governments. When these categories are excluded and we examine government spending for 2007, the latest year for which we have nonprofit revenue data, we are left with $1.9 trillion of government social welfare spending. What this means is that for every four dollars of government spending in these fields, nonprofit organizations spend three dollars, or 75 percent as much.[7]

Of this $1.9 trillion of government spending, moreover, $1.17 trillion represents federal spending and $0.732 trillion represents state and local government spending. What this means is that nonprofit expenditures in these fields were nearly twice as large as all state and local government

FIGURE 4.4: Private Philanthropy as a Percent of GDP, U.S. versus Selected Developed Countries

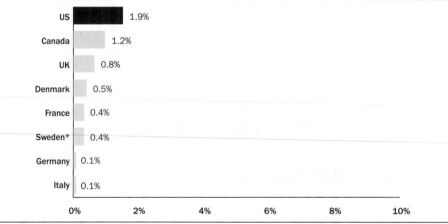

*Giving to religion not included.
Source: See Chapter 4, endnote 6.

spending and 20 percent higher than federal government spending (see Figure 4.5).

To be sure, a significant share of the revenue that supports nonprofit expenditures comes from government support, but the key point is that the growth of government in these fields has hardly displaced the role of nonprofit organizations. To the contrary, the nonprofit role has grown apace.

The For-Profit Role

In addition to government and nonprofit organizations, for-profit businesses are also increasingly active in many of the fields where nonprofit organizations operate. This reflects in part the presence of governmental funding to underwrite the costs of human services for the poor, and in part the growing demand for such services among middle-class clients who can pay market prices. Thus, as shown in Figure 4.6, for-profit firms as of 2007 accounted for:

• 70 percent of all private nursing home employment;

• 69 percent of all private home health care employment;

• 63 percent of all child day care employment;

FIGURE 4.5: Social Welfare Spending in Fields of Nonprofit Activity*: Government versus Private Nonprofit Service Organization Spending, 2007

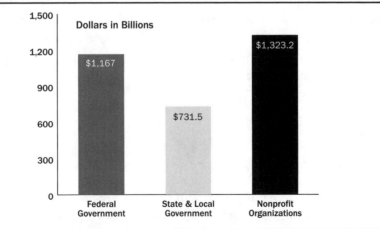

*Excludes retirement, unemployment, and primary and secondary education.
Source: U.S. Bureau of Economic Analysis, National Income and Product Accounts, Table 3.16, 2007; *See also* Chapter 3, endnote 4.

FIGURE 4.6: For-Profit Share of Private Employment in Selected Service Fields, 2007

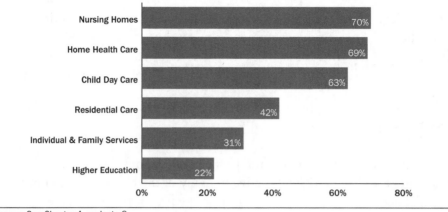

Source: See Chapter 4, endnote 8.

- 42 percent of all employment in private residential care facilities;

- 31 percent of all employment in individual and family service agencies; and

- 22 percent of all private higher-education employment.[8]

As will become clear in subsequent chapters, the for-profit share has been long-standing in some fields, such as nursing home care. In other fields, however, such as child day care, home health care, residential care, individual and family services, and specialty hospitals, recent years have seen a significant expansion of for-profit involvement, posing a considerable challenge to nonprofit providers. One reason for this expansion seems to be the superior access to capital available to for-profit firms thanks to their ability to raise capital by selling stock, a route that does not exist for nonprofits since they cannot be "owned" and are barred from distributing dividends to a set of shareholders.

Summary

Five main conclusions thus flow from the analysis in this chapter:

1. Government is a major presence in many of the fields in which nonprofit organizations are active, including health, education, and social welfare. In fact, over half of all government spending in the United States goes for these general purposes.

2. Although the growth of federal government spending has been critical in creating this government presence, state and local governments have played an important part as well and retain a significant presence. In fact, nearly 40 percent of all government social welfare spending originates at the state and local government level, and state and local governments help to implement many of the federally financed programs as well.

3. Although sizable, the level of government social welfare spending in the United States, when measured as a share of gross national product, lags significantly behind that in most other advanced industrial societies. In part, this reflects the greater reliance Americans place on private charity and the nonprofit sector. But in even greater part it reflects the greater reliance Americans place on private purchase of social welfare services.

4. Reflecting the importance of private purchase of social welfare services, for-profit firms have established a significant presence in the fields where nonprofits are active, equaling or exceeding the nonprofit presence in many of these fields.

5. Finally, despite the significant presence of both government and the for-profit sector, the nonprofit sector has maintained a very significant role. In fact, the level of nonprofit expenditures on social welfare services in the fields in which nonprofits and government are both extensively involved outdistances that of all state and local governments and is on a par with that of the federal government. Far from withering away with the growth of government, the nonprofit sector seems to have blossomed as well, though it now faces increasing competition from for-profit firms.

In short, a complex "mixed economy" of welfare exists in the United States, with nonprofit, for-profit, and governmental institutions all deeply involved, sometimes on their own, but increasingly in collaboration with each other. This reality flies in the face of some of our political rhetoric, which tends to portray these sectors as inherently in conflict. But it seems to be the reality that actually exists. As we will see in the next chapter, moreover, it is also a reality that has developed over a considerable period of time.

ENDNOTES

1. See, for example: Lester M. Salamon, S. Wojciech Sokolowski, and Associates, *Global Civil Society, Vol. III* (Sterling, VA: Kumarian Press, forthcoming); Ugo Ascoli and Costanzo Ranci, eds., *Dilemmas of the Welfare Mix: The New Structure of Welfare in an Era of Privatization* (London: Kluwer Academic/Plenum Publishers, 2002); Lester M. Salamon, "Putting Civil Society on the Economic Map of the World," *Annals of Public and Cooperative Economics* 81:2 (Summer 2010), 167–210.

2. For a statement of the theoretical rationale for this arrangement, see: Lester M. Salamon, "Of Market Failure, Voluntary Failure, and Third-Party Government: Toward a Theory of Government–Nonprofit Relations in the Modern Welfare State," *Journal of Voluntary Action Research* 16:1–2 (January–June 1987), 29–49; and Lester M. Salamon, *Partners in Public Service: Government-Nonprofit Relations in the Modern Welfare State* (Baltimore: Johns Hopkins University Press, 1995), 33–52.

3. Social insurance includes disability, social security, and unemployment insurance but not government employee retirement. U.S. Bureau of Economic Analysis, National Income and Product Accounts, Table 3.16, "Government Current Expenditures by Function, 1959–2009," revised as of September 20, 2010. Accessed at: www.bea.gov/national/nipaweb/SelectTable. asp?Selected=N. U.S. Gross Domestic Product from *Statistical Abstract of the United States 2010*, accessed at www.census.gov/statab/www/.

4. For the source of data in this paragraph, see endnote 3 above.

5. Social spending includes old-age pensions, survivors' benefits, incapacity-related benefits, health care, family benefits, labor market programs, unemployment benefits, housing benefits, and other social policy areas. See: Organization for Economic Cooperation and Development, "Social and Welfare Statistics," stats.oecd.org/WBOS/index.aspx.

6. Private giving data from: Salamon, Sokolowski, and Associates, *Global Civil Society* (forthcoming). Although it is difficult to draw firm conclusions about the consequences of these divergent spending patterns, some crucial social indicators suggest that at least some Americans pay a price for the country's generally lower rates of social welfare spending. Thus, of the countries listed in Figure 4.3, the U.S. has the highest rate of infant mortality, perhaps the best summary indicator of social well-being, and the lowest life expectancy rate. *Statistical Abstract of the United States* Table 1303. Births, Deaths, and Life Expectancy by Country or Area: 2009 and 2010. Accessed at: www. census.gov/compendia/statab/cats/international_statistics.html.

7. Data in this paragraph and the following one from U.S. Bureau of Economic Analysis, Table 3.16, 2007. Accessed at: www.bea.gov/national/nipaweb/SelectTable.asp.

8. For all but higher education, the data presented here are based on: U.S. Census Bureau, *Economic Census*, 2007, various tables. Higher education data are based on: U.S. Bureau of Labor Statistics, *Quarterly Census of Employment and Wages*, 2005. Data on nonprofit employment were extracted from this source by the Johns Hopkins Center for Civil Society Studies.

5

How Did We Get Here? Historical Developments and Recent Trends

That the nonprofit sector retains a significant role in the American social welfare system is due in no small measure to how that system has evolved. This evolution has also been responsible, in more recent years, for a variety of strains that nonprofit organizations have experienced. To understand the current position of the nonprofit sector in America's "mixed economy," therefore, it is necessary to understand how that "mixed economy" has developed and what it has undergone in recent years.

To do so, this chapter is divided into five major sections examining, respectively, the early origins of government-nonprofit relationships in the United States; the New Deal era of the 1930s; the Great Society era of the 1960s; the decade of retrenchment in the 1980s; and the important developments since 1990. In each, we first examine some of the signal developments of particular relevance to the nonprofit sector and then outline the implications these developments have had for nonprofit organizations and the structure and scale of our resulting nonprofit sector.

What emerges most clearly from this discussion is the realization that our understanding of the historical evolution of government and nonprofit roles in the American version of the modern welfare state has been seriously distorted by the ideological prism through which that history is now viewed.

To understand contemporary realities, therefore, it is necessary to re-examine this historical record and rescue the facts from the myths that now surround them. The purpose of this chapter is to undertake such a re-examination.

Early Origins

According to contemporary conventional wisdom, government involvement in social welfare activities is a relatively recent development in the United States, dating to the New Deal of the 1930s or the Great Society of the 1960s. Prior to this, it is believed, social welfare functions were largely the responsibility of private philanthropy and private nonprofit groups, with little government involvement. Furthermore, according to this conventional wisdom, the growth of government involvement is thought to have displaced philanthropy and the nonprofit sector, putting government bureaucrats into places formerly occupied by selfless volunteers. As Ronald Reagan classically put it early in his presidency, "We have let government take away the things we once considered were really ours to do voluntarily."[1]

Compelling though this interpretation of the history of government and nonprofit roles may be, however, it hardly squares with the available evidence. Indeed, neither the early period of splendid isolation nor the later period of supposed governmental usurpation does justice to the known facts.

As far as the early period is concerned, contrary to contemporary belief, government involvement in social welfare and education functions is not a recent development in the United States. State and local governments were playing significant roles in supporting education, health, and welfare well before the United States became a nation and extended these functions during the nineteenth and early twentieth centuries.[2] What is more, state and local authorities were not the only levels of government involved. Well before the New Deal extended the federal role, the federal government was deeply engaged in the provision of social welfare assistance. Indeed, by the latter nineteenth century, federal income assistance in the form of pensions to war veterans and their families was consuming 40 percent of the federal budget. And the first social service program of the federal government was enacted not in the 1970s, but in 1874.[3]

Most important for our purposes here, this government involvement was not perceived as a substitute for nonprofit activity. Rather, well before the American Revolution, colonial governments had established a tradition of assistance to private nonprofit institutions, and this tradition persisted well into the nineteenth and early twentieth centuries.[4] Indeed, America's first nonprofit organization, Harvard College, was also the first recorded beneficiary of this tradition. Soon after its founding in 1636, the colonial government of Massachusetts enacted a special tax, "the colledge corn," to support this institution. The commonwealth government also paid part of the salary of Harvard's president until 1781 and elected the college's Board of Overseers until after the Civil War. The state of Connecticut had an equally intimate relationship with Yale, and the state's governor, lieutenant governor, and six state senators sat on the Yale Corporation board from the founding of the school until the late 1800s. The prevailing sentiment was that education served a public purpose and therefore deserved public-sector support regardless of whether it was provided in publicly or privately controlled institutions.[5]

Well before the American Revolution, colonial governments established a tradition of government assistance to nonprofit institutions, and this tradition persisted well into the nineteenth and early twentieth centuries.

Nor was this pattern restricted to the field of education. A survey of seventeen major private hospitals in 1889, for example, revealed that 12 to 13 percent of their income came from government, while a special 1904 Census Bureau survey of benevolent institutions found that the government share of private hospital income exceeded 20 percent in a number of states. So widespread was the allocation of public funds for the support of private voluntary hospitals, in fact, that an American Hospital Association report referred to it in 1909 as "the distinctively American practice."[6]

As the social and economic problems associated with urbanization and industrialization escalated in the late nineteenth century, moreover, collaborative ties between governments and nonprofits grew apace. In New York City, for example, government payments to benevolent institutions for the care of prisoners and the poor grew from 2 percent of total city expenditures on the poor in 1850 to 57 percent by 1898. In the District of Columbia, about half of the public funds allocated for aid to the poor went to private charities as of 1892, and private charitable organizations received two-thirds of the funds the district granted between 1880 and 1892 for construction of facilities to care for the poor. Indeed, the early federal social service program mentioned above took the form of a grant-in-aid to a private nonprofit organization, and a religiously affiliated one at that, the Little Sisters of the Poor in the District of Columbia.[7]

These were not geographically isolated instances, moreover. To the contrary, a 1901 survey of government subsidization of private charities found that "except possibly two territories and four western states, there is probably not a state in the union where some aid [to private charities] is not given either by the state or by counties and cities." In many places, furthermore, this public support was extensive enough to surpass private charity as the principal source of income for nonprofit organizations. This was the case in New York State, for example, as of the late 1880s and of the District of Columbia by the end of the nineteenth century.[8]

In short, the presumed golden age of splendid isolation between government and the nonprofit sector in America is a convenient myth. Rather, as one close student of the history of America's nonprofit sector has written, "Collaboration, not separation or antagonism, between government and the Third Sector...has been the predominant characteristic.... Through most of American history government has been an active partner and financier of the Third Sector to a much greater extent than is commonly recognized."[9]

The New Deal System[10]

While the seeds of the current cooperative pattern of government-nonprofit relations were firmly planted early in American history, political and legal obstacles prevented their full flowering until the Great Depression of the 1930s, and even then only partially. Instead, powerful political forces fastened onto the nation's consciousness a comforting myth of privatism that allowed Americans to believe that the task of responding to the enormous poverty and distress created by the massive urbanization and industrialization of the late nineteenth and early twentieth centuries could be left largely to local governments and private, charitable groups. As a result, attempts to extend basic retirement, unemployment, and health care protections of the sort being adopted in other industrialized societies to working families in the United States were resisted.

The Great Depression of the 1930s made clear, however, that such a private and localized system of aid, however well intentioned, was not capable of providing on its own the protections that an urban-industrial society required. In response to the widespread distress of the Depression era, President Franklin D. Roosevelt was therefore able to push through a system of federal protections.

The United States emerged from the Second World War with a social welfare system that, despite the New Deal innovations, remained characterized by ... patchy coverage, limited funding, and state and local dominance.

At the heart of the resulting New Deal system of social welfare aid were three principal programs:

- **Old-age pensions** (the Social Security Program), financed largely by worker contributions to a Social Security Trust Fund;

- **Unemployment insurance**, providing temporary income coverage for persons who lose their jobs, financed partly by worker contributions and partly by employer contributions; and

- **Needs-tested cash assistance** (Old Age Assistance, Aid to Dependent Children, Aid to the Blind) for specific categories of people considered unable to work and thus ineligible for help from the regular, work-conditioned insurance programs (for example, widows with young children).

These innovations represented major steps toward providing individuals some protection against the impersonal threats of an increasingly urban-industrial society. At the same time, however, because of the political opposition they faced, they were far from complete. Thus, neither Social Security nor Unemployment Insurance provided universal coverage. Eligibility was work-conditioned and even then extended only to certain types of workplaces (for example, small businesses and farms were excluded). Cash assistance was available for those not covered by the social insurance programs, but it, too, was limited to narrow categories of people (widows with children, the aged, the blind), and, though part of the cost was covered by the national government, responsibility for determining benefit levels and eligibility and for administering the programs was vested in state governments, which were often quite restrictive.

As a consequence, the United States emerged from the Second World War with a social welfare system that, despite the New Deal innovations, retained many features of the pre–New Deal era. In particular, well into the 1960s the system remained characterized by:

- **Patchy coverage.** Key segments of the population remained uncovered or inadequately protected. For example, expansion of Social Security coverage turned out to be much slower than hoped, so that farm workers, employees of small businesses, and others remained outside its protections. In addition, no assistance was available for health care costs. And cash "welfare" assistance under the Aid to Dependent Children Program, controlled by local officials, was unavailable to intact families and held down so as not to interfere with wage rates on low-pay agricultural and household jobs.

- **Limited funding.** Reflecting these limitations, spending on social welfare protections remained quite limited. As of 1950, for example, less than 9 percent of the U.S. gross national product was devoted to government

FIGURE 5.1: Historical Trends in Government Social Welfare and Education Spending, Total versus Federal and State, 1959–2009 (Constant 2009 Dollars*)

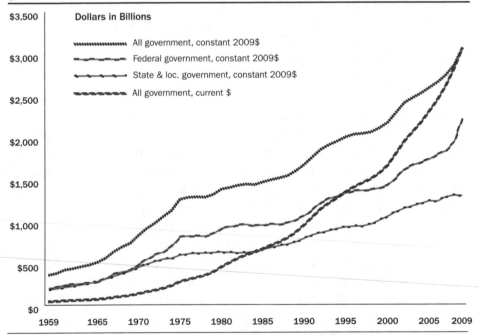

*Adjusted for inflation using deflator for personal consumption expenditures, NIPA Table 1.14.
Source: Bureau of Economic Analysis, National Income and Product Accounts (NIPA), Table 3.16: Government Current Expenditures by Function, 1959–2009.

social welfare spending.[11] Although some growth was evident in the 1950s, it remained quite limited in current dollar terms well into the early 1960s, as Figure 5.1 shows. Especially lacking was spending on health or social services.

- **State and local government dominance.** Despite the federal entrance in the 1930s, state and local governments continued to dominate the field. Not until 1970 did federal spending on social welfare and education outdistance state and local spending, as Figure 5.1 also shows.[12]

- **Education salience.** The major reason for the state and local prominence was that education continued to dominate the field, and education has traditionally been a state and local government function in the United States. Up through the mid-1950s, education constituted the largest component of social welfare spending, accounting for 40 percent of the total. As Figure 5.2 shows, it then ran neck-and-neck with social insurance (social security and unemployment insurance) during the 1960s and early 1970s before social insurance, and later health, pulled ahead.

FIGURE 5.2: Historical Trends in Government Social Welfare and Education Spending, by Field, 1959–2009 (Constant 2009 Dollars*)

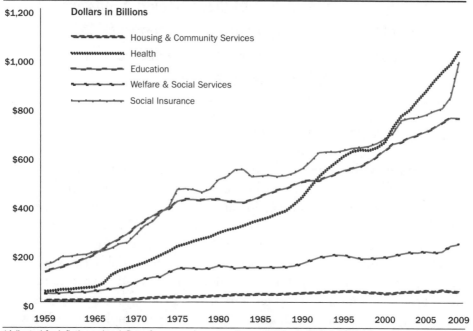

*Adjusted for inflation using deflator for personal consumption expenditures, NIPA Table 1.14.
Source: Bureau of Economic Analysis, National Income and Product Accounts (NIPA), Table 3.16: Government Current Expenditures by Function, 1959–2009.

While the New Deal reforms did not directly bolster the prevailing partnerships between government and the nonprofit sector, they clearly established a federal presence in the social welfare arena and thereby broadened the foundation on which such partnerships could build. It did not take long, moreover, for Congress to begin such building. A first step occurred soon after the end of World War II, when Congress was persuaded by the American Hospital Association to respond to the toll that the war had taken on U.S. hospitals by establishing a new program to finance the construction and renovation of hospitals throughout the country. The resulting Hill-Burton program, enacted in 1946, ultimately helped to finance the construction or rehabilitation of 9,200 hospitals, many of them private, nonprofit institutions. Ten years later, Congress and the Eisenhower Administration took a second significant step by amending the New Deal's Aid to Dependent Children program to permit federal reimbursement of one-half of the costs of various "rehabilitation" services provided to the mothers of dependent children, a precursor to what would ultimately be broader federal support for a range of social services. Here, again, a significant portion of these funds likely found their way to local nonprofit service organizations with which state and local governments were accustomed to partnering.[13]

The War on Poverty and Great Society programs of the 1960s did not displace the nonprofit sector but brought the federal government into a more robust partnership with it.

The "Great Society" and the "Rights" Revolution

But it remained for the election and tragic assassination of John F. Kennedy in the early 1960s for the nation to muster the political will to overcome long-standing conservative opposition and launch a major assault on the country's lingering problems of poverty, hunger, and ill health. This period also witnessed an upsurge of citizen activism in pursuit of various "rights"— civil rights, women's rights, consumer rights, environmental rights, students' rights, gay rights, and many more. Both developments—the expansion of social protections and the rights revolution—had enormous implications for the country's nonprofit organizations, though these are implications that are not well understood.

THE GREAT SOCIETY AND THE EXPANSION OF FEDERAL SOCIAL WELFARE INVOLVEMENT

Most significantly, the Great Society era did more than simply expand the federal government's role in the social welfare and education arena, as is widely believed. Rather, it massively expanded the long-standing partnership between government and nonprofit organizations and produced a massive enlargement of the nonprofit sector in the process. In other words, the War on Poverty and Great Society programs of the 1960s adhered closely to the template of government-nonprofit cooperation that was already a central feature of the country's existing, but much more limited, social welfare system. Their great accomplishment was not to displace the nonprofit sector but to bring the federal government and its substantial resources into a much more robust partnership with it. More particularly, the changes of this period included:

- **Human service programs:** The creation of a host of new poverty-alleviation, employment and training, social service, and housing programs targeted on overcoming poverty. More than 500 new programs were created during the mid-1960s, many of them competitive project grants open to nonprofit providers, and others grants to state and local governments that in turn contracted with nonprofits to deliver the services.[14]

- **Health care for the elderly:** The establishment of Medicare, offering federal reimbursement for medical and hospital care for the elderly.

- **Health care for the needy:** The creation of the Medicaid program, a joint federal-state program providing reimbursement for health care and nursing home care for the disadvantaged.

- **Pre-school and other education and research aid:** The launching of a network of nonprofit "Community Action Agencies" to help empower the poor and offer preschool education opportunities for disadvantaged children; the creation of the Title I program to funnel financial aid to disadvantaged schools; and the expansion of health and other scientific research.

- **Broadened welfare coverage:** The transformation of the Aid to Dependent Children program into Aid to *Families with* Dependent Children and the addition of further social services to help such families transition into self-sufficiency.

Subsequent changes in the early 1970s extended these benefits further. Included here were:

- **Inflation protection for retirees:** The introduction in 1972 of an automatic cost-of-living increase in the basic Social Security program to adjust benefit levels automatically to inflation.

- **Food aid:** The expansion of the federal "food stamp" program providing coupons to indigent families and individuals for the purchase of food.

These changes fundamentally reshaped key features of the American social welfare system, albeit in ways that were fully consistent with earlier patterns. In particular, the system came to have the following distinguishing features:

- **Rapid growth in spending.** Between 1965 and 1980, government spending on social welfare and education accelerated significantly in the United States, as shown in Figure 5.1. Such spending grew by nearly seven-fold in current dollars, and nearly three-fold in inflation-adjusted dollars, during this fifteen-year period. In the process, it expanded from 9 percent of gross domestic product (GDP) in 1965 to 16 percent in 1980.[15] During the first part of this period, 1965–1975, the principal source of growth was actual program expansion triggered by the creation of a host of new federal programs. Between 1975 and 1980, the principal source of growth was inflation, which boosted pension and health payments considerably.

- **Federal preeminence.** Around 1968, federal government spending on social welfare and education surpassed state and local government spending for the first time, as Figure 5.1 shows. What is more, the federal government widened its lead subsequently, reaching just over two-thirds (67 percent) of the total by 1980. In the process, federal spending on social welfare and education went from 5 percent of GDP to nearly 11 percent. State and local spending increased as well, but at a somewhat slower rate.[16]

- **Substantial growth of welfare and social service spending.** Significant growth took place in government spending on welfare and social services, including employment and training services, addiction prevention, counseling, foster care, child protective services, housing aid, and related services. This expansion was driven by a conscious "services strategy" that viewed persistent poverty as remediable through improved education, health, counseling, job training, and associated rehabilitation services—precisely the kinds of services many nonprofit organizations were equipped to supply. Government spending on welfare and social services thus jumped substantially more than three-fold between 1965 and 1980 in real dollar terms, thus exceeding the overall growth rate of social welfare spending.

- **Predominance of pensions and health.** While the Great Society unquestionably boosted spending on welfare and social services, which significantly target the poor, what mostly accounted for the great surge of spending that occurred between 1965 and 1980 were the social insurance and health programs, particularly Social Security and Medicare, which significantly target the middle class. Together, as Figure 5.3 shows, these two sets of programs absorbed 60 percent of the growth in total government social welfare spending between 1965 and 1980, and with education included this total comes to 86 percent. By contrast, the welfare, social service, and housing programs that have received the bulk of the attention accounted for less than 15 percent of the total growth.

The reasons for this were several:

- First, the welfare and social service programs started from a much smaller base. As of 1965 they accounted for less than 9 percent of all government social welfare and education spending. Substantial percentage gains therefore did not translate into huge absolute amounts of growth.

FIGURE 5.3: Shares of Government Social Welfare Expenditure Growth, by Field, 1965–1980

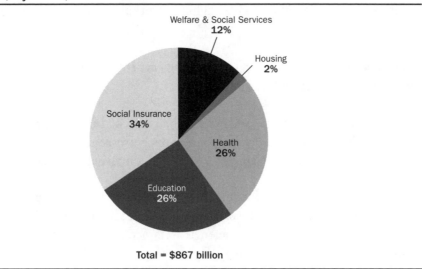

Total = $867 billion

Source: See Figure 5.1.

- Second, most of the "War on Poverty" programs were pilot efforts and few were fully funded.

- Third, demographic changes were boosting the elderly population by a substantial amount, increasing the draw on the entitlement programs for the elderly, especially Social Security and Medicare, but also the nursing home coverage of Medicaid.

- Finally, a combination of technological changes and lack of sufficient cost controls in the Medicare program plus programmatic changes such as the introduction of a cost-of-living adjustment in the Social Security program boosted expenditures on these programs even further.

By contrast, as a share of total government social welfare spending, spending on the welfare and social service programs especially targeted on the poor barely budged from the 8.7 percent of all government social welfare spending it represented in 1965 to 10.7 percent in 1980.

THE RIGHTS REVOLUTION

Side by side with the growth of federal social welfare expenditures during the 1960s and 1970s, and in many senses contributing directly to it, was a broad-based "rights revolution," a political and social awakening of significant groups in the society laying claims to rights they felt owed them as citizens but not yet fully accorded: civil rights, women's rights, ethnic rights, children's rights, the rights of the disabled, the rights of the mentally challenged, environmental rights, rights to workplace safety, consumer rights, gay rights, and dozens more.[17]

IMPLICATIONS FOR NONPROFIT ORGANIZATIONS: EXPANSION OF THE GOVERNMENT–NONPROFIT PARTNERSHIP

Not surprisingly, the developments outlined here had important implications for the evolution of the nation's private, nonprofit sector. In a word, far from displacing the nonprofit sector, they triggered a massive expansion of it.

There were several reasons for this. For one thing, as we have seen, the patchy character of the public social welfare system even after the New Deal reforms of the 1930s meant that private agencies retained a significant place in the American social welfare structure despite these reforms. When public aid expanded in the 1960s, therefore, it was only natural to draw on the existing nonprofit delivery system to meet the new demands, especially given the long history of such cooperation. Secondly, continuing conservative opposition to an expanded government bureaucracy, especially an expanded federal bureaucracy, made it politically impossible to add substantially to the federal workforce to handle the expanded human service functions. What is more, nonprofits had a substantial foothold in a number of fields and resisted any direct government role. Private hospitals, for example, insisted on reliance on the existing private hospitals to provide the medical care to be funded by Medicare, and insisted as well on a payment system that respected the normal fee-for-service model with which hospitals were comfortable.

The upshot was a substantial expansion of "third-party" or "indirect" government, particularly at the federal level. The central feature of this pattern of government operations is the reliance on the part of governmental authorities on various third parties—states, cities, industrial corporations, hospitals, universities, and, increasingly in the 1960s, private nonprofit organizations—to deliver publicly funded services.[18]

The private, nonprofit sector became a major beneficiary of this mode of government operation during the 1960s, as federal support to the nonprofit sector, already firmly established through such programs as Hill-Burton and the funding of universities to conduct health and scientific research, virtually exploded. For example:

- **Medicare**, the massive new federal health insurance program for the elderly created in 1965, essentially reimburses hospitals for care they provide to the elderly but leaves to the recipient the choice of which hospital to use. Because the preponderance of hospital beds are in private, nonprofit hospitals, as Chapter 6 will show, these institutions have received the preponderance of the benefits.

- **Private, nonprofit universities** benefited from expanded federal support for medical and other research, as well as from new programs of scholarship aid and loan guarantees for post-secondary education.

- **New social service and community development programs** provided grants-in-aid to state and local governments, which in turn often contracted with local nonprofit organizations to provide such services as "meals on wheels" to the elderly, day care, residential care, adoption assistance, and the like.

As of 1980, therefore, approximately 25 percent of all government spending in the fields where nonprofit organizations were active flowed to such organizations. Expressed in constant 2009 dollars, the federal government alone provided $123.2 billion in support to the private nonprofit sector that year, as shown in Table 5.1.[19] State and local governments, in turn, provided additional amounts from their own resources. As a consequence, government accounted for 30 percent of overall nonprofit revenue as of 1977, and in some fields, such as social services, it constituted over half. By comparison, total private charitable giving to these organizations that same year, expressed in 2009 dollars, totalled $81.7 billion, which was only 17 percent of total nonprofit income.[20] No wonder the influential Commission on Private Philanthropy and Public Needs (the Filer Commission) concluded in the mid-1970s that government had become "a major 'philanthropist,' the major philanthropist in a number of the principal, traditional areas of philanthropy."[21]

TABLE 5.1: Federal Government Support to Nonprofit Organizations, 1980 (Billions of 2009 Constant Dollars*)

Field	Amount	%
Health	$75.9	61%
Social services	19.9	16%
Education, research	17.1	14%
Community development	7.0	6%
Foreign aid	2.4	2%
Arts, culture	0.9	1%
Total	$123.2	100%

*Adjusted for inflation using deflator for personal consumption expenditures.
Source: Salamon and Abramson (1982), p. 43.

The rights revolution of the 1960s and 1970s added further impetus to the nonprofit sector. Nonprofit organizations functioned as the ideal cauldrons for the identification, nurturing, and promotion of new rights. The number of organizations thus skyrocketed as new groups formed to advance each of the various rights and, in many cases, to deliver the services that achievement of the rights made possible. By 1977, the United States boasted 276,000 501(c)(3) organizations, and by 1989 this number had increased to nearly 466,000, an increase of nearly 16,000 organizations per year. Not only did this transform the nonprofit economy, but it also transformed the U.S. polity as nonprofit organizations pressed new citizen demands on government.[22]

The 1980s: The Decade of Retrenchment

THE RETRENCHMENT

After a decade and a half of rapid growth, government social welfare spending entered a period of retrenchment in the latter 1970s and the 1980s. The initial impetus for this was a desire on the part of the Carter administration to avoid growth in the federal deficit. But this gave way in the early 1980s to a much more basic assault by the Reagan administration on at least a portion of the Great Society program structure. Between 1977 and 1982, therefore, the inflation-adjusted value of federal spending dropped 31 percent in the social services field, where many of the Great Society programs were concentrated (see Table 5.2). In addition, federal spending on education was reduced by 35 percent; and even spending on income assistance for the poor, which is driven by "entitlement" formulas, declined by 8 percent. Although it was hoped that state and local governments would offset these reductions, in fact the value of state and local government spending declined also in these fields. Outside of health and pensions, therefore, federal social welfare spending declined by 17 percent in inflation-adjusted terms, and state and local spending declined by 7 percent, for an overall decline of 10 percent between 1977 and 1982.[23]

TABLE 5.2: Changes in Government Social Welfare Spending, Fiscal Year 1982 versus Fiscal Year 1977 (Constant Dollars*)

	% change, 1977-82:		
Area	Federal	State/Local	Total
Pensions	13%	29%	16%
Health	27%	23%	26%
Education	-35%	-6%	-10%
Housing	16%	44%	19%
Income assistance	-8%	-18%	-10%
Social services	-31%	-14%	-25%
Total	**9%**	**4%**	**7%**
Total w/o pensions & health	**-17%**	**-7%**	**-10%**

* Based on implicit price deflators for services component of personal consumption expenditures.
Source: Compiled from data in *Social Security Bulletin*, Vol. 51, No. 4 (April 1988), pp. 23–26 and Vol. 46, No. 8, pp. 10–12. Implicit price deflators from *Economic Report of the President* (February 1998).

Although Congress resisted at least a portion of the further cuts proposed in the balance of the decade, the significant tax cut it enacted in 1981 as part of the "Reagan revolution" seriously deepened the federal deficit and placed a limit on future growth. The result was a considerable slowing in the growth of government social welfare spending. Thus, as reflected in Figure 5.4, despite the entitlement character of many of the new social welfare programs, the average annual rate of growth of overall government social welfare spending was cut from 6.8 percent per year between 1965 and 1980 to 1.9 percent per year, or barely enough to keep pace with the growth of population, during 1980–1990. And for federal spending alone, the drop in the rate of growth was even sharper, from 8.2 percent per year during the 1965–1980 period to 1.5 percent over the 1980–1990 decade.

These figures obscure, however, the considerable variations that existed among program areas. Generally speaking, the discretionary programs absorbed most of the cutbacks while the entitlement programs were barely touched. As Figure 5.5 suggests:

- **Cuts concentrated in programs for the poor**. Income assistance and social service programs targeted mostly on the poor and low-income populations barely benefited at all from the limited growth in government social welfare spending between 1977 and 1989. To the contrary, these programs experienced actual cuts, or severe slowing of growth, during this period. As a result, as of 1989, spending on income assistance programs was still 15 percent below its 1977 value in inflation-adjusted terms, and spending on other social services was down by 28 percent. This was largely

FIGURE 5.4: Average Annual Growth of Government Social Welfare Spending, 1965–1980 versus 1980–1990

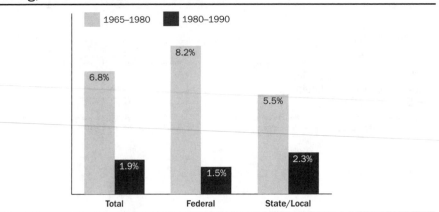

Source: See Figure 5.1.

due, moreover, to spending decisions at the federal level: federal funding of income assistance as of 1989 was 16 percent below its 1977 value, and federal funding of social services was down a massive 40 percent.

- **Limited education gains**. Education spending also suffered from the cutbacks of the 1980s. Such spending barely kept pace with inflation during most of this period, growing by only about 1 percent per year until the very end of the decade. In fact, after adjusting for inflation, the federal contribution to education spending by 1989 was 36 percent below what it had been in 1977, and it was only growth at the state and local level that produced a net gain. While representing 27 percent of government social welfare spending as of 1977, therefore, education absorbed a disproportionately smaller 14 percent of spending growth between 1977and 1989.

- **Continued growth in health spending**. While federal social service, income assistance, and education spending declined, however, federal *health* spending, the beneficiary of the two enormous health care entitlement programs—Medicare and Medicaid—continued its steep rise throughout this period of supposed retrenchment. Fueled by escalating health costs and the aging of the population, such spending grew by 61 percent between 1977 and 1989 even after adjusting for inflation. Indeed, as Figure 5.5 shows, although accounting for only 18 percent of government social welfare spending when this period began, health care absorbed a disproportionate 46 percent of the spending growth.

FIGURE 5.5: Selective Retrenchment, 1977–1989: Shares of Spending, 1977, versus Shares of Spending Growth, 1977–1989

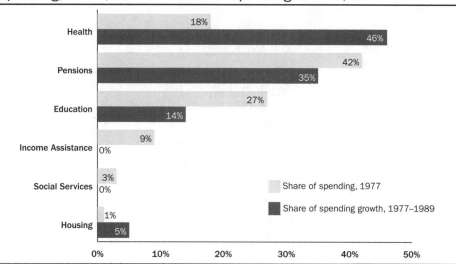

Source: See Figure 5.1 and Table 5.2.

- **Significant growth in pension expenditures**. Despite a steady decline in veterans' payments, pension expenditures also experienced continued growth during this period, rising by some 19 percent after adjusting for inflation. This was due to the automatic cost-of-living increases built into the Social Security program in 1972, coupled with the continued growth of the elderly population. Pensions and health care—both serving a broad middle-class population—thus absorbed over 80 percent of the growth that occurred during this period.

- **Housing program expansion**. Alone among the programs at least moderately targeted on the poor, housing assistance experienced significant growth during this period. This reflects in part the low base from which it started and, in part, the commitments that had been entered into long before the Reagan administration came to power.

In short, the decade of the 1980s not only reduced the overall growth of government social welfare spending; it also reversed the tilt toward lower-income citizens that was a central hallmark of the Great Society programs of the previous decade. The overall effect was thus to shift the center of gravity of the social welfare system more towards the middle class and away from the poor, and more towards health and away from other human services.

The 1980s shifted the center of gravity of the social welfare system more towards the middle class and away from the poor, and more towards health and away from other human services.

IMPLICATIONS FOR NONPROFIT ORGANIZATIONS

These changes had significant implications for the newly burgeoning nonprofit sector. To be sure, health organizations continued to grow, boosting their income by an average of 5.8 percent per year between 1977 and 1982, which included the sharpest period of the Reagan cutbacks. The story was far different for other key segments of the nonprofit sector, however. Social service organizations in particular saw the growth in their government support drastically reduced. Through much of the decade of the 1980s, government support to social service organizations barely kept pace with inflation, and at least in the early portion of this period overall growth stalled.

Perhaps even more significant than the actual impacts, however, were the psychological ones. After coming to look to the federal government as a welcome partner in addressing serious social and economic problems, nonprofit leaders had to come to terms with the reality that this partner was not totally reliable as a long-term source of support. With charitable giving constrained as well, nonprofit social service agencies began examining fee-based sources of support. As a consequence, such support tripled between 1982 and 1992, swelling from 13 percent of nonprofit social service organization income in 1982 to nearly 20 percent in 1992. Through it all, moreover, the number of nonprofit organizations continued to grow, a residue, perhaps, of the citizen activism of the 1960s and 1970s. Thus, after languishing somewhat at an average growth rate of 3.1 percent per year between 1977 and 1982, the growth of nonprofit organizations surged between 1982 and 1989, producing an annual average increase of 5.4 percent in the number of registered nonprofits over the entire 1977–1989 period.[24]

Into the Twenty-First Century: Recovery, Restructuring, and Disasters

In the years since 1990, three broad sets of developments have shaped the context within which the nonprofit sector has operated in the United States.

PARTIAL RECOVERY

In the first place, following the retrenchment of the 1980s, social welfare policy in the United States experienced at least a partial recovery in the ensuing twenty years, although further retrenchment seems in prospect as the first decade of this new century gives way to the second. Thus, as reflected in Figure 5.1, overall government spending on social welfare and education turned markedly upward in the latter 1980s and into the 1990s and beyond, even after adjusting for inflation. More specifically, as Figure 5.6 shows, such spending grew by an annual average of 3.2 percent over the twenty years between 1990 and 2009, well below its 6.8 percent per year rate between 1965 and 1980, but well above its 1.9 percent per year rate between 1980 and 1990.

This growth was largely driven by social welfare spending at the federal level, which rose by 4 percent per year on average, compared to a more limited average growth rate of 2.6 percent among state and local governments. Interestingly, the average rate of increase in government social welfare and education spending was higher during the twelve years that Republicans occupied the White House than in the eight years that Democrats did, as

Figure 5.6 also shows. The presidency of Republican George Bush Senior was particularly noteworthy in this regard, with overall social welfare spending spiking upward by an average of 4.6 percent per year compared to the 1.7 percent rate of the preceding Reagan years and the 2.3 percent rate in the subsequent Clinton years. This was due in important part to a significant series of expansions of coverage under the Medicaid program between 1988 and 1992.

RESTRUCTURING

Not only did government social welfare spending resume its growth, however; it also changed its basic structure. Most important for the nonprofit organizations of special interest to us here are three features of the resulting restructuring:

Medicalization. In the first place, health care further extended its rapid ascendance as the dominant component of government social welfare spending, displacing education as the second most important component by 1991 and social insurance as the largest component by 2001. Indeed, starting with 26 percent of all government social welfare spending as of 1990, the health field captured 43 percent of the growth in government social welfare spending that occurred between 1990 and 2009, achieving an average annual

FIGURE 5.6: Average Annual Change in Government Social Welfare Spending, 1990–2009, by Level of Government and Presidential Party (Constant 2009 Dollars)

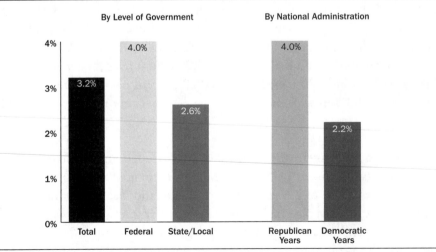

Source: See Figure 5.1.

growth rate of 4.7 percent, as shown in Figure 5.7, well above the growth rate of other components of the social welfare field. By contrast, growth in the core social service and income assistance programs lagged badly behind, with real growth rates just barely above 2 percent, well behind the annual average growth of the population. As a result, these programs captured only 6 percent of the growth, as shown in Figure 5.8, reducing their share of the total to barely 8 percent by 2009.

FIGURE 5.7: Average Annual Change in Government Social Welfare Spending, 1990–2009, by Field

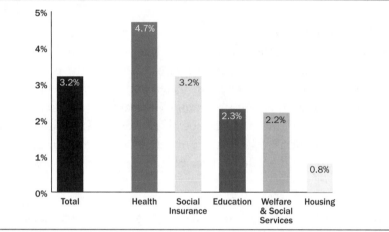

Source: See Figure 5.1.

FIGURE 5.8: Shares of Growth in Government Social Welfare Spending, by Field, 1990–2009

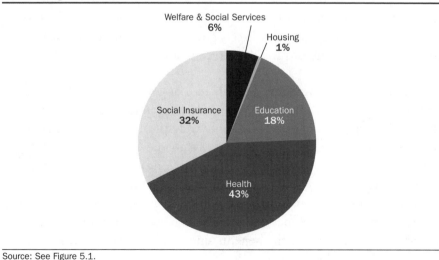

Source: See Figure 5.1.

This outcome was largely a product of the entitlement character of the two major federal health care programs, Medicare and Medicaid, which makes it difficult to control their spending levels.[25] But it was also a product of a number of policy changes that extended coverage under these programs to wider portions of the population and additional types of services. Thus, Medicare reimbursement was made available for home health care, hospice care, skilled nursing care, and kidney dialysis in addition to hospital care. Meanwhile, the income cut-off for Medicaid eligibility was raised on successive occasions; and care for the developmentally disabled, clinic care, family planning, child welfare services, and rehabilitation services were added to the list of conditions for which Medicaid support was mandated.[26]

This did not happen in a vacuum, of course. Rather, advocates for these different forms of assistance, frustrated by their inability to secure support through the existing discretionary programs, redefined the problems they were concerned about as health-related and sought coverage under the health-related entitlement programs, Medicare and Medicaid. In the process, Medicaid became a virtual social service "block grant" as numerous types of formerly social service programs came within the purview of Medicaid funding and Medicare became a more general-purpose health support program.

Marketization. This shift in the structure of government social welfare spending affected not only the substantive focus of such spending, it also altered the basic *form*. The social service programs of the Great Society era were "producer-side subsidies," that is, they delivered their benefits directly to the providers of the services through such tools as grants and contracts. By contrast, the major health entitlement programs are "consumer-side subsidies," that is, they give consumers of services a voucher in the form of a Medicare or Medicaid card that directs government reimbursement for eligible services to whichever provider a recipient chooses.[27]

What is more, vouchers were not the only tool of government action embodying this consumer-side mechanism that expanded greatly during this period. The tax system came into more widespread use as well, thanks in important part to conservative resistance to any new program that did not take the form of a tax cut. Special tax deductions or tax credits, some of them "refundable," were therefore enacted to help offset the costs of day care, foster care, low-income housing, and numerous other socially desirable activities.[28] Here, again, the market became the mechanism for distribution of government-advantaged social benefits since the choice of providers was left in the hands of individual taxpayers.

The Welfare Reform Windfall. A final significant shift in the structure of government social welfare funding resulted from the welfare reform law enacted in 1996. This law essentially transformed the New Deal's Aid to Dependent Children program of entitlement grants to support low-income children in single-parent families into a capped, or fixed, federal grant that was set for six years, during which states were required to move welfare recipients into paying jobs. As an incentive, states were permitted to use the capped grants not only for benefit payments to recipients, but also to pay for training and supportive services needed to help welfare recipients secure permanent employment. When the economy rebounded in the latter 1990s, reducing the welfare rolls, states were left with a fiscal windfall that they were free to use for a variety of supportive services. As a consequence, spending for social services increased even though budgets for the overt social service programs were frozen or cut.[29]

Despite the cutbacks of the early 1980s, nonprofit organizations have registered substantial growth over the past thirty years.

THE DECADE OF DISASTERS

Finally, the first decade of the twenty-first century, initially heralded as a time of great hope, proved to be an especially traumatic one for the nation. Along with some spectacular technological breakthroughs came a series of disasters that demonstrated the nation's vulnerabilities. Included here were the September 11, 2001, terrorist attack, the ensuing wars in Iraq and Afghanistan, a series of tax and spending policies that transformed a promising budget surplus into a deep deficit, the Katrina hurricane that devastated New Orleans and the Gulf Coast, the BP oil spill that cast serious doubt on the commitment of business to safety and the environment, and the 2008 financial crisis that deepened the nation's sense of helplessness and triggered a recession whose effects lingered for years.

IMPLICATIONS FOR THE NONPROFIT SECTOR

Not surprisingly, these changes in government policy and in the broader context of nonprofit operations have had some significant implications for the country's nonprofit organizations. Generally speaking, the sector has shown considerable resilience. But it has also been exposed to significant strains. More specifically, three outcomes of particular importance deserve mention.

Overall Growth. In the first place, despite the cutbacks of the early 1980s, nonprofit organizations have registered substantial growth over the past thirty years.[30]

This growth was already evident in the early part of this period, between 1977 and 1996. Thus:

- Between 1977 and 1996, nonprofit revenues swelled by 96 percent after adjusting for inflation, for an average annual growth rate of 3.6 percent. By comparison, during this same period the U.S. gross domestic product grew by a significantly smaller 62 percent, or about 3.0 percent per year (see Figure 5.9). Put somewhat differently, nonprofit revenues increased 50 percent faster than did the overall U.S. GDP.

- What is more, this growth was not restricted only to nonprofit health organizations. Rather, while nonprofit health organizations boosted their revenue by 109 percent between 1977 and 1996, nonprofit arts organizations grew by 114 percent and nonprofit social service organizations by 117 percent.[31]

But the growth in nonprofit revenue has accelerated in more recent years. Thus, between 1997 and 2007:

FIGURE 5.9: Average Annual Growth in Nonprofit Revenues and U.S. GDP, 1977–1996 and 1997–2007 (Constant 2007 Dollars)

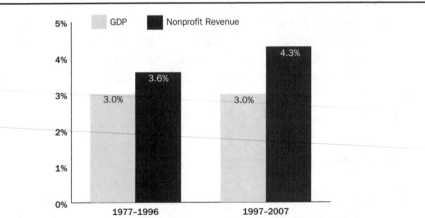

Source: See Figure 5.1 and Chapter 5, endnote 30.

- Nonprofit revenues grew by another 53 percent after adjusting for inflation, for an average growth rate of 4.3 percent per year, well above the 3.6 percent in the earlier 1997–2007 period, as shown in Figure 5.9. During this period as well, moreover, the growth of the nonprofit sector outpaced the growth of the U.S. economy as a whole. Thus, compared to the 53 percent increase in nonprofit revenues between 1997 and 2007, the U.S. GDP grew by a smaller 32 percent, or about 3.0 percent per year.

- As Figure 5.10 shows, moreover, this recent growth, too, was not restricted to any one component of the nonprofit sector. Although the category of "other" organizations, embracing environmental, international, and other assorted organizations, appears to have surged ahead of other fields, this is likely a reflection of the small base against which these percentages are computed. More generally, the growth pattern of most fields of nonprofit activity hovered around 50 percent during this 1997–2007 decade, and the one laggard, culture and recreation, still had a growth rate that beat that of the U.S. GDP.

- While the *rate* of growth among the different components of the nonprofit sector was quite uniform, however, the share of the growth captured by the different segments differed markedly, reflecting the divergent scale of these segments. Thus, as Figure 5.11 shows, health care nonprofits generated 57 percent of the growth of the nonprofit sector between 1997 and 2007, roughly equivalent to the share of the total with which they started the period. Education organizations accounted for 21 percent of the growth, followed by social service providers, with 14 percent. The remaining

FIGURE 5.10: Changes in Nonprofit Revenues, by Field, 1997–2007 (Constant 2007 Dollars)

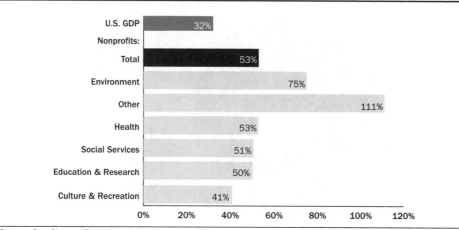

Source: See Chapter 5, endnote 30.

organizations, embracing culture and recreation, environment, and other, accounted for the remaining 8 percent.

Growth Fueled Mainly by Increased Fee Income. That nonprofit organizations were able to achieve these gains in revenue in the face of dramatic shifts in government policy was due in important part to their ability to capitalize on the social and demographic shifts increasing the demand for their services in recent decades, as well as to the continuing inflation in health care costs. Thus, for example, the lengthening of life expectancy and growth in the labor force participation rates of women since the 1960s have increased the need for nursing home care and child day care, two fields in which nonprofits have been active.

Reflecting these developments, the principal source of increased revenue fueling the significant growth of the nonprofit sector between 1997 and 2007 was commercial income (service fees, investment income, and income from sales of products). Overall, nonprofit revenue from commercial sources surged 64 percent between 1997 and 2007 after adjusting for inflation. As Figure 5.12 shows, this source alone accounted for nearly 60 percent of the sector's revenue growth during this period.

This substantial reliance on fee income is not a new development for the country's nonprofit sector, of course. Commercial sources accounted for a substantial 55 percent of nonprofit revenue growth in the 1977 to 1996

FIGURE 5.11: Shares of Nonprofit Growth, by Field, 1997–2007

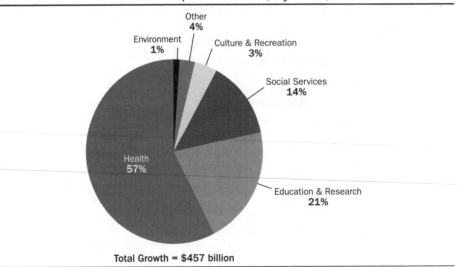

Total Growth = $457 billion

Source: See Chapter 5, endnote 30.

period as well. What is noteworthy about the more recent period, however, is how widespread the reach of commercial sources has become within the sector. Such sources have long dominated the revenue base of education and health organizations, especially hospitals, and played a major role in the financing of arts and culture. But as Figure 5.13 shows, they have come to play an enormous role as well in the field of social services, accounting for 40 percent of the growth that nonprofit social service organizations achieved during the 1997–2007 decade. Since these are the organizations that have historically been most available to the poor, this *marketization* of the social service field has especially important potential implications for the operation of the nonprofit sector.[32]

Also growing rapidly during recent years has been private philanthropy. Philanthropic income to nonprofit organizations also grew by 64 percent in real dollar terms during the 1997–2007 period. Because it started from a fairly small base, however, private philanthropy accounted for only 12 percent of overall nonprofit revenue growth during this period. Nevertheless, for some types of nonprofits, such as those engaged in environmental protection and international assistance, or culture and the arts, private giving has been the major, or a major, source of revenue growth, accounting for 66 percent of the growth of the former and 44 percent of the growth of the latter.

FIGURE 5.12: Sources of Nonprofit Growth, 1997–2007

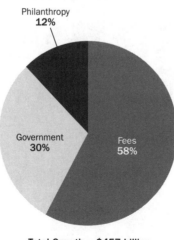

Philanthropy
12%

Government
30%

Fees
58%

Total Growth = $457 billion

Source: See Chapter 5, endnote 30.

Government revenue has grown somewhat more slowly than overall nonprofit revenue in recent years. Thus, between 1997 and 2007, government support to nonprofit organizations, including through Medicaid and Medicare, increased by 38 percent, well below the rates of growth achieved by fees and philanthropy. This was largely due, however, to the constraints introduced into the financing of health care by the shift in reimbursement methods under the huge Medicare and Medicaid programs as well as other cost-control measures. Outside of health care providers, the growth in government support to nonprofit organizations during the 1997–2007 period has been substantial—149 percent for environmental organizations, 82 percent for education organizations, 69 percent for social assistance organizations, and 61 percent for international assistance organizations. This attests to the success many nonprofit organizations achieved in adapting to the changes in the structure of government funding streams by repackaging traditional social services as behavioral health services and securing government support through the expanding health programs. As a result, government accounted for 30 percent of the overall growth in nonprofit revenue, and 41 percent of the growth of social service providers.

FIGURE 5.13: Sources of Nonprofit Revenue Growth, by Field, 1997–2007

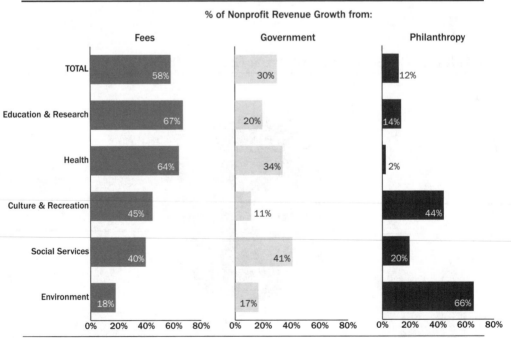

Source: See Chapter 5, endnote 30.

Growing Competition from For-Profit Providers. Finally, as they have
sought to take greater advantage of the growing commercial markets for their
services, nonprofit organizations have encountered increased competition
from for-profit providers that have also recognized the revenues these
markets offer. For-profit firms have also been enticed into fields once largely
dominated by nonprofit organizations by the growth of government funding
and the shift in the structure of government funding streams towards
consumer-side subsidies identified earlier. Such consumer-side subsidies give
an advantage to providers with marketing skills and experience, precisely
the skills with which for-profits have a distinct edge. Coupled with the
advantages private businesses enjoy in generating capital by virtue of their
ability to access the equity markets by issuing stock, the result has been
a striking growth of for-profit penetration in many traditional fields of
nonprofit activity. For example:

- Between 1977 and 1992, for-profit firms captured 80 percent of the
  growth in *day care centers* and 70 percent of the growth in day care
  employment even though they started the period with only 57 percent of
  the former and 46 percent of the latter. The for-profit share of day care
  employment thus increased from 46 percent in 1977 to almost 62 percent
  by 1997 and nearly 63 percent by 2007, as reflected in Table 5.3.

TABLE 5.3: Growth of For-Profit Competition in Fields of
Nonprofit Activity

Field	For-profit % of private employment		
	1977	1997	2007
Day Care	46.1%	61.8%	62.5%
Individual and Family Services	8.5%	9.2%	30.5%
Home Health Care	29.0%	71.8%	77.1%

Source: U.S. Census Bureau, *Economic Census*, 1977, 1997, and 2007.

- In the field of *home health*, the growth curve was even steeper. As of the
  late 1970s, home health care was a heavily nonprofit industry, with for-
  profits accounting for under 30 percent of the employment. But then, in
  the early 1980s, in an effort to reduce escalating health costs resulting from
  over-use of expensive hospital facilities, home health care was made eligible
  for Medicare reimbursement. The resulting surge of funding triggered
  a corresponding surge of for-profit expansion. For-profits consequently
  captured close to 90 percent of the growth that this field experienced
  and ended up by 1997 with 72 percent of the employment. And this

growth continued into 2007, boosting the for-profit share of home health employment to 77 percent.

• More recently, for-profits have moved more extensively into another formerly nonprofit-dominated field—individual and family counseling—boosting their share of employment from under 10 percent in 1997 to over 30 percent ten years later.

As later chapters will show, similar trends are evident in other fields as well. The result has been to put a significant squeeze on many nonprofit providers.

Summary

The American social welfare system is thus a complex "mixed economy" of federal, state, and local governmental, private for-profit, and private nonprofit activity. Although sizable governmental expenditures are made for social welfare, much of this goes for old-age pensions, veterans' payments, health care for the elderly, and public schools. Expenditures for the poor and the disadvantaged, by contrast, represent only a fraction of the total, albeit still a sizable amount.

Alongside the governmental system, moreover, stands a private nonprofit one that rivals it in size. Private philanthropy plays an important part in supporting this nonprofit system, but income from government and fees plays a larger part.

From earliest times, nonprofit organizations cooperated actively with government and received governmental support that importantly supplemented the charitable revenues they were able to generate. For the most part, this support came from state and local authorities and was constrained by the limited resources these authorities had at their command. As the distress produced by rapid urbanization and industrialization mounted in the latter nineteenth and early twentieth centuries, pressures mounted for a more active federal role in relieving the resulting distress. But these pressures were resisted by conservative forces that fastened on national consciousness a convenient myth of privatism that posited an inherent conflict between government and the nonprofit sector and denied the validity of government-nonprofit cooperation.

Not until the 1960s, in the midst of a widespread "rights revolution," therefore, was it possible to break through this resistance and bring the federal government into the partnership between government and the nonprofit sector at the state and local level. The result, far from displacing the nonprofit sector, gave it new life and unleashed the most massive expansion in its history. At the same time, the breakthrough was partial and vulnerable to a series of setbacks—first in the 1980s and later in the mid-1990s. In response, nonprofit managers pursued two broad strategies: first, they pushed for changes in the programmatic definition of "health" that allowed a wide range of human service programs to qualify for assistance under the federal government's popular Medicare and Medicaid program; and second, they actively pursued commercial sources of support.

Neither of these strategies was without problems. Yet together they allowed the nonprofit sector to grow, and grow quite substantially, though in ways that have raised questions in the minds of many people about the real rationale for the special tax and other privileges that nonprofits enjoy, and that have brought increased competition into the fields in which nonprofits operate. Both of these topics will be explored more fully below.

What these observations make clear, among other things, is that the American nonprofit sector cannot be understood at the aggregate level alone. To make sense of what is going on, it is necessary to move from the sector overview provided in this section to a more in-depth look at the separate components into which the sector is divided. It is to this task that we therefore now turn, beginning with the largest component, health.

ENDNOTES

1. Ronald Reagan, *Papers of the President of the United States: President Ronald Reagan*, Speech of September 24, 1981. Accessed at: www.reagan.utexas.edu/archives/speeches/1981/92481d.htm.

2. See, for example: David Rothman, *The Discovery of the Asylum: Social Order and Disorder in the New Republic* (Boston: Little, Brown, 1971).

3. On this early federal government support for social welfare provision in the United States, see: Theda Skocpol, *Social Policy in the United States: Future Possibilities in Historical Perspective* (Princeton: Princeton University Press, 1995).

4. The discussion here draws heavily on: Lester M. Salamon, *Partners in Public Service: Government-Nonprofit Relations in the Modern Welfare State* (Baltimore: Johns Hopkins University Press, 1995), 54–86.

5. John S. Whitehead. *The Separation of College and State: Columbia, Dartmouth, Harvard and Yale, 1776–1876.* (New Haven: Yale University Press, 1973), 3–16.

6. Rosemary Stevens, "A Poor Sort of Memory: Voluntary Hospitals and Government Before the Depression," *Milbank Fund Quarterly/Health and Society* 60:4 (1982), 551–84; David Rosner, "Gaining Control: Reform, Reimbursement, and Politics in New York's Community Hospitals, 1890–1915," *American Journal of Public Health* 790 (1980), 533–42.

7. Amos G. Warner, *American Charities: A Study in Philanthropy and Economics* (New York: Thomas Y. Crowell, 1894), 337; Frank Fetter, "The Subsidizing of Private Charities," *American Journal of Sociology* (1901–2), 376.

8. A study of 200 private organizations for orphan children and the friendless in New York State in the late 1880s thus showed that twice as much of their support came from government as from private donations. Similarly, private charity accounted for only 15 percent of the income of private charities in the District of Columbia as of 1899. Warner, *American Charities*, 337; Fetter, "Subsidizing Private Charities," 376.

9. Waldemar A. Nielsen, *The Endangered Sector* (New York: Columbia University Press, 1979), 47, 14.

10. The discussion in this section draws on material in Lester M. Salamon, *Welfare: The Elusive Consensus—Where We Are, How We Got Here, and What's Ahead* (New York: Praeger Publishers, 1977).

11. Ann Kallman Bixby, "Public Social Welfare Expenditures, Fiscal Years 1965–87," *Social Security Bulletin* 53:2 (February 1990), 22.

12. Unless otherwise noted, government spending data throughout this chapter are drawn from: U.S. Bureau of Economic Analysis, *National Income and Product Accounts*, Table 3.16: Government Current Expenditures by Function, 1959–2009 (last revised September 13, 2010), accessed at: www.bea.gov/national/nipaweb/SelectTable.asp?Selected=N.

13. U.S. Department of Health and Human Services, "A Brief History of the AFDC Program," accessed at: aspe.hhs.gov/hsp/afdc/baseline/1history.pdf.

14. For a discussion of many of these programs and the systems through which they operated, see: Sar Levitan and Robert Taggart, *The Promise of Greatness* (Cambridge: Harvard University Press, 1976); and James L. Sundquist and David W. Davis, *Making Federalism Work* (Washington, DC: The Brookings Institution, 1969).

15. The social welfare share of GDP reported here differs from that reported in Chapter 4 because the OECD data used for the comparison to other countries in Chapter 4 excludes education from social welfare expenditures whereas the data here include education. With education excluded, the social welfare share of U.S. gross domestic product as of 1980 would be just over 11 percent rather than the 16 percent cited in the text.

16. State and local spending on social welfare and education rose from 5 percent of GDP in 1965 to 7.4 percent in 1980.

17. See, for example, Cass R. Sunstein, *After the Rights Revolution: Reconceiving the Regulatory State.* (Cambridge: Harvard University Press, 1990).

18. For further elaboration of this concept of "third-party government," see: Lester M. Salamon, "Rethinking Public Management: Third-Party Government and the Changing Forms of Government Action," *Public Policy* 29 (1981), 255–275; and Lester M. Salamon, ed., *The Tools of Government: A Guide to the New Governance* (New York: Oxford University Press, 2002).

19. Lester M. Salamon and Alan J. Abramson, *The Federal Budget and the Nonprofit Sector* (Washington, DC: The Urban Institute Press, 1982), 62. Adjusted to 2009 dollars using the deflator for personal consumption expenditures as reported in Bureau of Economic Analysis, National Income and Product Accounts, Table 1.14. On the growth of government contracting with nonprofit organizations, *See also*: Salamon, *Partners in Public Service: Government-Nonprofit Relations in the Modern Welfare State*; and Steven R. Smith and Michael Lipsky, *Nonprofits for Hire: The Welfare State in the Age of Contracting* (Cambridge: Harvard University Press, 1993).

20. Computed from data in Virginia A. Hodgkinson, et al., *Nonprofit Almanac 1996–1997: Dimensions of the Independent Sector* (San Francisco: Jossey Bass, 1996), 191, Table 4.2.

21. Commission on Private Philanthropy and Public Needs. *Giving in America: Toward a Stronger Voluntary Sector* (Washington, DC: Commission on Private Philanthropy and Public Needs, 1975), 89.

22. See, for example: Jeffrey M. Berry, *The New Liberalism: The Rising Power of Citizen Groups* (Washington, DC: Brookings Institution Press, 1999).

23. The data reported here are based on a more detailed data base than is available through the National Income and Product Accounts and therefore permits a more refined picture of social welfare spending by field. Unfortunately this data base, compiled by the Social Security Administration and published in successive editions of the *Social Security Bulletin*, was discontinued in the mid-1990s, necessitating reliance in subsequent sections on more aggregated estimates. For the earlier data base, see: Ann Kallman Bixby, "Social Welfare Expenditures, 1963–83," *Social Security Bulletin* 49:2 (February 1986), pp. 12–21; Ann Kallman Bixby, "Public Social Welfare Expenditures, Fiscal Years 1965–87," *Social Security Bulletin* 53:2 (February 1990), 10–26; and Ann Kallman Bixby, "Public Social Welfare Expenditures, Fiscal Year 1994," *Social Security Bulletin* 60:3 (1997), 40.

24. Based on data from the Internal Revenue Service *Exempt Organization Master File*, accessed through Virginia Hodgkinson et al., *Nonprofit Almanac 1996–1997*.

25. The key characteristic of "entitlement programs" is that their funding is automatically driven by the number of people who meet the eligibility requirements and are seeking support for eligible services. Once these eligibility features are set, the government is legally obliged to cover the eligible costs for the eligible recipients. By contrast, in so-called "discretionary programs," no entitlement is established and the government can limit the budget made available. Significant efforts were put in place to slow the growth in Medicare costs during this period by moving from a cost-based reimbursement system to a prospective payment system in which reimbursements were set in advance and hospitals given an incentive to keep the cost below the pre-set reimbursement rate.

26. Lester M. Salamon, *The Resilient Sector* (Washington, DC: The Brookings Institution Press, 2003), 40–43; Teresa A. Coughlin, Leighton Ku, and John Holahan, *Medicaid Since 1980: Costs, Coverage, and the Shifting Alliance between the Federal Government and the States* (Washington: The Urban Institute Press, 1994).

27. For an analysis of the characteristics of these different "tools of government" and the consequences they can have, see: Salamon, *The Tools of Government*.

28. A "refundable" tax credit essentially delivers a cash benefit to an eligible individual whose tax liabilities fall below the benefit level of a tax credit program. Thus, if an individual's benefit under a particular tax credit is $2,500 but the individual's tax liabilities are only $500, the remaining $2,000, or some portion of it, would be provided to the individual in the form of a payment from the Treasury. The most prominent example of a refundable tax credit is the Low Income Tax Credit, which serves as an income supplement to the working poor.

29. Between 1994 and 1999, the number of people on "welfare" fell by one-half, from 14.2 million to 7.2 million. In addition, the portion of those remaining on the rolls requiring full cash grants also declined because more of them were supplementing their income with work. Because states were guaranteed federal grants under the new Temporary Assistance for Needy Families (TANF) program at their peak levels of the early 1990s, and were also obligated to maintain their own spending on needy families at 75 percent of their previous levels, this translated the pre-existing Aid to Families with Dependent Children cash assistance program into what the U.S. Congress' Committee on Ways and Means termed "a broad human services funding stream." U.S. Congress, Committee on Ways and Means, *2000 Green Book: Background Materials and Data on Programs within the Jurisdiction of the Committee on Ways and Means*. 106th Congress, 2d Sess. (October 6, 2000), 354, 376, 411.

30. Estimates of nonprofit revenue in this section are drawn from two broad sets of sources: For the period 1977 through 1996 from author's estimates based on data in Virginia Hodgkinson et al., *Nonprofit Almanac 1996–1997*, 190–191; unpublished data supplied by Independent Sector; and U.S. Bureau of the Census, *Service Annual Survey: 1996*. For these estimates, social and fraternal organizations have been deleted from civic, social, and fraternal; and social services n.e.c. grouped

with civic. Inflation adjustment is based on the implicit price deflator for the services component of personal consumption expenditures as reported in the *Economic Report of the President* (February 1998), p. 290. For the period 1997–2007, estimates have been developed from Special Tabulations available from the Internal Revenue Service, Statistics of Income, supplemented by data from the U.S. Census Bureau, *Service Annual Survey*, 2006, on government voucher payments (Medicare and Medicaid) to nonprofit organizations. Reported nonprofit "program service revenue" (i.e., market sales) has been adjusted for both health and social service organizations to take account of government voucher payments recorded as market sales or fees in IRS data. Even so, the fee portion of nonprofit revenue may still be overstated somewhat due to the fact that government contract and voucher payments are treated as program service revenue on the Form 990 filed by nonprofits and used by the Internal Revenue Service in its data. For further detail, see Chapter 3, endnote 18.

31. Based on data presented in Lester M. Salamon, *America's Nonprofit Sector: A Primer*, 2nd ed. (New York: Foundation Center, 1999), 68.

32. For further detail on this phenomenon, see: Lester M. Salamon, "The Marketization of Welfare: Changing Nonprofit and For-Profit Roles in the American Welfare State," *Social Service Review* 67:1 (March 1993), pp. 17–39. The data reported here exclude Medicare and Medicaid payments from "program service revenue," where it is listed in IRS data. Instead, such payments are included in the government sources of support.

PART TWO
Key Subsectors

6

Health Care

Of all the components of the nonprofit service sector, the largest by far, at least in terms of expenditures, is health care. As Chapter 3 indicated, nonprofit health providers absorbed just over 60 percent of all nonprofit revenues in 2007 and over 25 percent of all private charitable contributions. This reflects the tremendous scale of the health care field. But it also reflects the substantial role that nonprofit organizations continue to play in this field.

The purpose of this chapter is to explore this nonprofit role in the health field and to put it into context in relation to the roles of government and for-profit providers. To do so, we begin by looking more closely at the overall scale, character, and sources of health care expenditures in the United States. We then zero in on the four subfields where nonprofit organizations are particularly prominent: 1) hospital care, 2) in-home or outpatient clinic care, 3) nursing home care, and 4) health insurance. In each of these subfields, we seek to determine what role nonprofit organizations play, how this compares with the roles of government and for-profit organizations, and what the major trends have been in recent years.

Perhaps the central conclusion that emerges from this analysis is that nonprofit organizations play a vital part in the delivery of health services in the United States. At the same time, their position has been under serious challenge in recent years.

Overview: National Health Spending

BASIC CONTOURS

Health has emerged in recent years as one of the largest and fastest-growing components of national spending. As Chapter 4 made clear, fully one-third of all government social welfare spending goes for health care. But an even larger amount of private spending goes into this field as well. In fact, as of 2008, health care absorbed $2.339 trillion in the United States, or 16.2 percent of the country's gross domestic product.[1]

RECENT GROWTH

Health expenditures are not only large, but they have also been growing rapidly. As Figure 6.1 shows, total health spending grew approximately seven-fold between 1965 and 2008, after adjusting for inflation, roughly twice as fast as the nation's overall gross national product. As a result, health expenditures went from about 6 percent of gross national product in 1965 to over 16 percent by 2008.[2]

FIGURE 6.1: Growth in U.S. Health Care Spending, 1965–2008 (in Billions of 2008 Constant Dollars)*

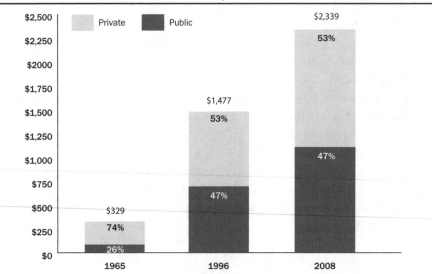

*Based on implicit price deflator for services component of personal consumption expenditures.
Source: Centers for Medicare and Medicaid Services, National Health Expenditure Data, 2008.

Although health expenditures have grown rapidly over this nearly forty-year period, the pace of growth seems to have slowed somewhat since the 1990s. This is partly a result of the size of the base against which the rate of change is now measured, and partly a result of the so-called "managed care revolution," the widespread replacement of fee-for-service insurance by managed care insurance plans that impose more severe limits on the amounts that health care providers can charge for various services and the replacement of cost-based reimbursement systems in the government-financed insurance programs with prospective payment schemes that set fixed rates for particular procedures. After expanding at an average rate of 10 to 13 percent per year (before adjusting for inflation) during the 1970s and 1980s, therefore, health spending growth dropped to 4 to 5 percent per year in the mid-1990s. However, this improvement was short-lived and health expenditure growth accelerated again at a 6 to 9 percent per year rate in the late 1990s and through the middle years of the new century's first decade before declining to 4 percent as the country headed into a recession in 2008.

Fully one-third of all government social welfare spending goes for health care, but an even larger amount of private spending goes into this field as well.

SOURCES OF GROWTH

A major factor making the growth in health spending possible between 1965 and 1996, as Figure 6.1 shows, was the expansion of government support that resulted from the creation in 1965 of the federal Medicare and Medicaid programs, which provided government financing of health care for the aged and the poor. As a consequence, government health care spending grew eight-fold between 1965 and 1996, after adjusting for inflation, compared to a three-fold increase in private health spending. In the process, government spending on health went from 26 percent of the total in 1965 to 47 percent of a much larger total in 1996, and millions of people gained improved access to health care. Between 1996 and 2008, however, private spending on health care climbed more than public spending in absolute terms so that the 53-to-47 split between private and public spending established as of 1996 remained in place 12 years later. This reflects some containment of the growth in spending on Medicare and Medicaid over the past decade.

THE ROLE OF PHILANTHROPY

Although the nonprofit sector plays a major role in the health field, as will be documented more fully below, very little of the revenue in this field comes from private philanthropy. In particular, of the $2.338 trillion in health care spending in 2008, only $21.64 billion, or less than 1 percent, came from private philanthropic giving.[3] Such giving is somewhat more important in financing certain sub-fields, such as medical research and construction, but even here it is far from the dominant source.

Hospital care represents the largest single component of health care spending in the United States, and also the one where nonprofit organizations are most prominent.

The Role of Nonprofit Providers in Health Care

While private philanthropy may constitute a relatively limited part of overall health *finance*, however, the private, nonprofit sector nevertheless plays a very significant role in health care *delivery*. To understand this role, however, it is necessary to divide the health sector into its component parts and look more closely at the four components where nonprofit organizations have historically been especially important: hospital care, outpatient and home health care, nursing home care, and health insurance.

HOSPITAL CARE

Overview: Scale and Sources of Funding. Hospital care represents the largest single component of health care spending in the United States, and also the one where nonprofit organizations are most prominent. As Figure 6.2 shows, nearly one-third of all health spending goes for hospital care—a total of $718.4 billion in 2008. By comparison, private practitioners (dentists and physicians) received 25 percent of total health expenditures, clinics and home health care providers 12 percent, and nursing homes 6 percent.[4]

Unlike health care as a whole, government is the dominant source of funding for hospitals, as shown in Figure 6.3. At the same time, at 57 percent, the government share of hospital spending is down significantly from the

FIGURE 6.2: Where Health Care Spending Goes, 2008

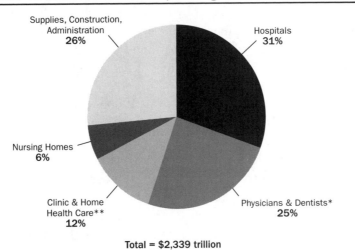

Supplies, Construction,
Administration
26%

Hospitals
31%

Nursing Homes
6%

Clinic & Home
Health Care**
12%

Physicians & Dentists*
25%

Total = $2,339 trillion

*Physicians & Dentists includes "professional services."
**Clinic & Home Health Care includes outpatient care, home health care, "other personal health care," and "government public health activities."
Source: Centers for Medicare and Medicaid Services, National Health Statistics, Table 2, 2008; see Chapter 6, endnote 4.

FIGURE 6.3: Sources of Health Care Spending, 2008*

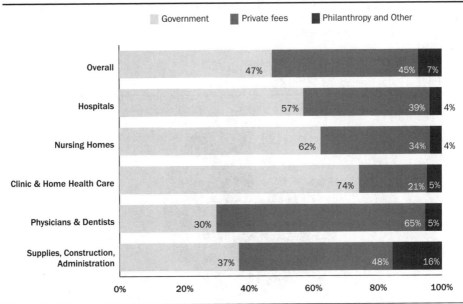

■ Government   ■ Private fees   ■ Philanthropy and Other

Overall: 47% | 45% | 7%
Hospitals: 57% | 39% | 4%
Nursing Homes: 62% | 34% | 4%
Clinic & Home Health Care: 74% | 21% | 5%
Physicians & Dentists: 30% | 65% | 5%
Supplies, Construction, Administration: 37% | 48% | 16%

0%   20%   40%   60%   80%   100%

Source: Centers for Medicare and Medicaid Services, National Health Expenditures, Table 4; see Chapter 6, endnote 5.
*Some figures may not add up to 100 percent due to rounding.

62 percent level it reached in the mid-1990s. Of this government funding, the federal government contributes by far the lion's share—81 percent of all government funding of hospitals, or 46 percent of all hospital revenue. State and local governments provide the remaining 19 percent of government support of hospitals, which translates into 11 percent of hospital costs.[5]

The rest of hospital funding—43 percent in 2008—comes from private sources, of which 39 percent takes the form of private fees and insurance payments and just under 4 percent private philanthropy and miscellaneous sales. Corresponding with the decline of the government (especially federal government) share of hospital funding, the share coming from private fees and insurance payments has increased over the past twelve years, rising from 34 percent in 1996 to 39 percent in 2008. Since the overall total increased substantially during this period, this meant a substantial escalation in the absolute levels of private support for hospitals.

Nonprofit versus Government and For-Profit Roles in the Hospital Industry. This sizable hospital spending supports a relatively small number of quite large institutions. As of 2008 there were 5,962 hospitals in the United States as recognized by the American Hospital Association. Of these, as Figure 6.4 shows, the overwhelming majority (over 80 percent) were general medical and surgical hospitals, the type with which most people are familiar. But 19 percent were specialty hospitals focusing on such specialties as psychiatric treatment, rehabilitation services, and treatment of children.[6]

FIGURE 6.4: Types of Hospitals, 2008

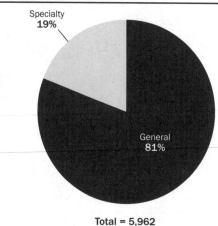

Specialty
19%

General
81%

Total = 5,962

Source: American Hospital Directory, Special Tabulations, 2008.

Nonprofit hospitals. While government provides most of the hospital spending, *nonprofit institutions* deliver most of the hospital services, at least most of the *general hospital* services. As reflected in Figure 6.5, just over half (50.5 percent) of all hospitals in the country are organized as nonprofits. These nonprofit hospitals account for an even larger 61 percent of the country's hospital beds and 69 percent of all hospital revenues. This suggests that the nonprofit hospitals are generally larger than their government or for-profit counterparts.

Nonprofits are especially prominent among the country's general hospitals, which form the heart of the nation's hospital industry. Despite a flurry of for-profit hospital formation and conversions of nonprofit institutions in the 1980s, 56 percent of these institutions remain private, nonprofit organizations as of 2008, and they account for 66 percent of the general hospital beds and 70 percent of the general hospital revenues. By contrast, only 25 percent of the specialty hospitals are nonprofit organizations, and they account for 26 percent of the specialty hospital beds.

FIGURE 6.5: Relative Roles of Nonprofit, For-Profit, and Government Hospitals, 2008

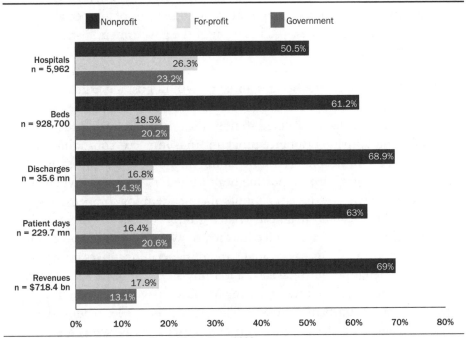

Source: American Hospital Directory, Special Tabulations, 2008.

For-profit hospitals. While nonprofits dominate the hospital scene, at least with respect to general hospitals, they are hardly the only providers of hospital care. To the contrary, both the for-profit and government sectors are also actively involved, though the former has been expanding its role and the latter contracting. Thus, as Figure 6.5 shows, for-profit firms now operate 26 percent of all hospitals, though a somewhat smaller 19 percent of all hospital beds. Most for-profit hospitals (61 percent) are general hospitals, many of them nonprofit conversions. But for-profits have been especially active in establishing specialty facilities, 55 percent of which, accounting for 38 percent of specialty hospital beds, are now under for-profit control. For-profits are therefore now the single largest providers of specialty hospital care, measured both by their share of institutions and their share of beds. Of these for-profit specialty hospitals, 44 percent are long-term care facilities, 30 percent are psychiatric hospitals, and 26 percent are rehabilitation facilities.

Government-owned hospitals. Another 23 percent of all hospitals are operated by *governmental authorities*, chiefly at the state and local levels (see Figure 6.5). Most of these are general hospitals, many of them in central city areas, where they have long functioned as the last-resort source of hospital care for indigent persons. However, government has also long been quite prominent in the specialty hospital field, particularly in the operation of psychiatric hospitals. As of 2008, public authorities were operating 228 specialty hospitals across the country, or 20 percent of all specialty institutions, and 193 of these—85 percent of the government institutions—were psychiatric facilities.

Hospital Trends. Despite the substantial growth in hospital expenditures, the hospital sector has been under enormous strain over the past several decades as pressures have mounted to limit the growth of health care costs. Both public and private insurance programs thus imposed constraints on reimbursements for hospital costs. Beginning in 1983, for example, the federal Medicare program supporting health care for the elderly switched from a retrospective cost-based reimbursement system for compensating hospitals to the so-called "diagnosis-related group," or DRG, system under which hospitals are paid a given fee for each of over 400 medical procedures they might perform. This has created strong financial incentives for hospitals to reduce the length of hospital stays and limit their cost of care so as to keep the cost of specific procedures under the Medicare payment maximum.[7] Private insurance companies quickly followed Medicare's lead, adopting various arrangements designed to limit reimbursements as well. These pressures reduced the number of hospital beds needed.

Reflecting these pressures, the total number of hospitals declined by 9 percent in the United States between 1980 and 1996 and the number of hospital beds declined by about 22 percent—a net reduction of over 600 hospitals and over 300,000 hospital beds. This pattern then continued into the first decade of the new century, leading to a further 6 percent net reduction in the number of hospitals between 1996 and 2008, and an additional 16 percent decline in the number of hospital beds (see Figure 6.6). Between 1980 and 2008, therefore, the total number of hospitals declined by about 1,000 and the total number of hospital beds declined by about 440,000.[8]

Not all segments of the hospital industry have been affected equally by these pressures, however. To the contrary, the overall figures obscure some very dramatic differences in the outcomes for different types of hospitals and for different types of providers. In particular, general hospitals bore most of the brunt of the reductions while specialty hospitals actually grew by 28 percent between 1980 and 1996 and by another 4 percent between 1996 and 2008. Thus, the number of general hospitals declined from 6,131 in 1980 to 4,830 as of 2008, a decline of roughly 1,300 hospitals. During this same

FIGURE 6.6: Hospital Trends, by Ownership, 1996–2008

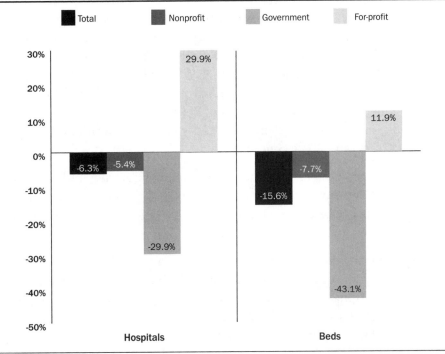

Source: Chapter 6, endnote 8.

period, the number of specialty hospitals increased from 857 in 1980 to 1,132 in 2008. These divergent patterns naturally had different implications for the different types of providers. In particular, as Figure 6.6 shows:

- *Sharp decline of government hospitals.* The recent contraction in the hospital industry has been especially marked among government institutions, which fell from 2,585 institutions in 1980 to 1,384 in 2008, a drop of nearly 50 percent. Two major developments lie behind this result.

  – First, squeezed by rising health costs, reduced Medicaid reimbursements, and limited fee income due to the historic focus of their institutions on lower-income patients, many cities and counties were forced to close their *general* hospitals. Between 1980 and 1996, the number of government-owned and -operated general hospitals thus declined by one-fourth, as 544 of the 2,167 publicly owned general hospitals were forced to close their doors, reducing the number of beds in government-owned hospitals by over 40 percent. This contraction has continued into more recent times as an additional 467 government-operated hospitals were shuttered between 1996 and 2008, bringing the total down to 1,156 institutions.

  – Second, in addition to the pressures on government-run *general* hospitals, the movement that started in the 1970s to "de-institutionalize" the mentally ill and other long-term ill persons previously treated in large psychiatric and other specialty hospitals led to the closing of sizable numbers of these publicly operated *specialty* hospitals, particularly in the mental health field. Thus the number of government-run specialty hospitals declined by nearly 20 percent between 1980 and 1996 and fell further between 1996 and 2008, bringing the total down to 228 as of 2008, from over 400 in 1980. As a result, the government share of specialty hospitals fell from 31 percent in 1996 to only 20 percent in 2008.

  – Taken together, therefore, the total number of government hospitals declined by 30 percent just in the recent 1996 to 2008 period, and the number of beds they controlled dropped 43 percent, as shown in Figure 6.6.

- *Consolidation of nonprofit presence.* Though somewhat less pronounced, the past thirty years have also witnessed a shrinkage in the presence of nonprofit hospitals. Thus, between 1980 and 1996 at least 375 nonprofit general hospitals, or about 12 percent of the total, ceased operations, merged, or were taken over by for-profit institutions. This trend continued in more recent years, though at a distinctly slower pace, as another 173 hospitals, accounting for 47,300 beds, ceased operations, were converted into for-profit institutions, or were merged into for-profit conglomerates between 1996 and 2008. This amounted to a 5 percent decline in the number of nonprofit hospitals and a nearly 8 percent decline in the number of nonprofit hospital beds.

These developments reflect the fact that nonprofit hospitals have been exposed to the same cost-containment pressures and resulting excess capacity as the government hospitals. In addition, because, as nonprofits, they lack access to the stock market to raise capital, they face special challenges in remaining on the cutting edge of technology, including the computer technology needed to manage costs given the new reimbursement systems. This has induced a number of nonprofit boards to accept buy-out offers from for-profit chains. At the same time, because of their established position in the general hospital field and their access to tax-privileged bond financing, nonprofits in the general hospital arena have been able to hold their own far better than their counterparts in some other fields.

Because of the general contraction in the hospital field, however, the nonprofit share of the number of general hospitals has stayed fairly constant, and their share of the beds and revenues has risen slightly. What is more, nonprofits managed to hold their own in the specialty hospital field, growing modestly in the number of facilities and beds, but, as we will see, at rates well below those of the for-profit institutions.

• *For-profit expansion.* While both government and nonprofit hospitals declined in numbers over the past several decades, for-profit ones have surged. After increasing their share of hospitals from 13 to 19 percent between 1980 and 1996, for-profits increased the number of hospitals they control by 30 percent and the number of beds they control by 12 percent between 1996 and 2008, as shown in Figure 6.6.

For-profits have been particularly aggressive in the field of specialty care, the most dynamic component of the hospital industry over the last quarter-century. For-profit providers moved actively into this field, carving out a new niche of short-term specialty care institutions (for example, eye clinics, orthopedic hospitals) while long-term specialty institutions (for example, psychiatric institutions), most of them publicly run, were closing. Thus, while the number of publicly operated specialty hospitals declined between 1980 and 1996, the number of for-profit specialty hospitals increased by 296, or 157 percent, more than offsetting the decline in specialty government hospitals. From 1996 to 2008, for-profits added another 136 specialty hospitals while government and nonprofit specialty hospitals declined by 86.

Moreover, for-profit businesses experienced some of the only growth in the general hospital field, adding 254 institutions and 47,000 beds between 1980 and 2008 while government and nonprofit institutions lost 303,000.

In short, the shift toward managed care and the general pressures on hospital bottom lines are not only reducing the overall number of hospitals and hospital beds; they are also producing significant shifts in the basic structure of the hospital industry, toward a proliferation of specialty hospitals, a substantial departure of public institutions, and a significant expansion of for-profit involvement, particularly in the expanding specialty hospital arena.

Managed care and the pressures on hospital bottom lines are producing shifts toward specialty hospitals, a departure of public institutions, and an expansion of for-profit involvement.

CLINIC AND HOME HEALTH CARE

Overview. The second-largest component of the health field in which nonprofit organizations have a substantial role is outpatient care other than in doctors' offices. Included here is a wide assortment of health care providers outside of hospitals and traditional doctors' offices, such as clinics, home health care organizations, kidney dialysis centers, government public health activities, and health care delivered in unconventional provider sites like schools and community centers.[9]

As reflected in Figure 6.2, this component of the health care field accounted for 12 percent of all health expenditures in 2008, or $284.6 billion in all. Of this total, nearly one-fourth goes for *government public health activities*, which include local public health screening and the federal government's Public Health Service and Centers for Disease Control. An even larger share (29 percent) goes for a variety of *outpatient clinics* (for example, kidney dialysis centers, drug treatment centers, rehabilitation centers). These institutions bear a strong resemblance to the short-term specialty facilities that are gaining ground within the hospital industry, except that they are tailored to "outpatient" care. Another 23 percent of this portion of health care spending goes for *home health care* (that is, skilled nursing or medical care provided in the home). Finally, the remaining 24 percent goes for *other personal health care*, such as school- and community center–based health services.

Like hospital care, clinic and home health care spending is mostly financed by government. As Figure 6.3 showed, government provides nearly three-quarters of all spending in this field. This is due in significant part to the fact that this field includes direct public health activities as well as school and community health services. But it also reflects the broadening of Medicare coverage, beginning in the 1980s, to include home health services and not just hospital care, which created a considerable surge in the home health care industry.

Nonprofit Role. Nonprofit organizations play a significant role in the provision of outpatient care, though they have faced considerable competition from for-profit providers. As a result, as Figure 6.7 shows, nonprofit organizations represent just under a third of the roughly

FIGURE 6.7: Nonprofit Share of Private Clinic and Home Health Care Field, 2007

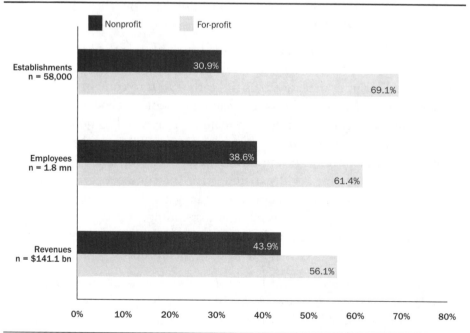

Source: Chapter 6, endnote 8.

58,000 outpatient care establishments identified by the U.S. Census Bureau in its 2007 Economic Census. The nonprofit facilities seem to be larger on average than the for-profit ones, however, so that they account for 39 percent of the employees and 44 percent of the revenues. The nonprofit role varies considerably among the different components of the outpatient care field, however. Among clinics, for example, nonprofits account for 43 percent of the establishments, 50 percent of the revenues, and 60 percent of the revenues. In the home health component of the outpatient care field, however, nonprofits account for only 13 percent of the establishments and a third of the revenues.[10]

Nonprofit organizations play a significant role in the provision of outpatient care, though they have faced considerable competition from for-profit providers.

Recent Trends. Clinic and home health care have been extremely dynamic fields over the past 30 years, and nonprofit providers have hardly been immune from the resulting shifts. Two major developments have been apparent: first, an early period of innovation and explosive growth followed by a more recent maturation; and second, a significant shift from nonprofit to for-profit dominance.

- *Early rapid growth and recent maturation.* Much of today's sizable clinic and outpatient care industry is a recent development, the product of efforts that began in the late 1970s and early 1980s to contain hospital and fee-for-service medical costs by treating patients outside of hospitals and traditional doctors' offices. One major step in this direction was the broadening of Medicare coverage in the mid-1980s to embrace reimbursement for home health care services, triggering a massive expansion in the home health care industry. As a consequence, between 1975 and 1996, spending on outpatient care grew three times faster than the already rapidly growing overall health spending, and spending on home health care grew fifteen times faster. Even public health spending exceeded the growth rate of overall health expenditures.[11]

This early investment in home health and clinic care seems to be paying dividends in more recent years, contributing to an overall slowing in the rate of growth of health spending. One reflection of this is the fact that clinic and home health spending has increased at a slower rate than overall health spending, thus exerting downward pressure on the overall rate of health cost escalation. In particular, as shown in Figure 6.8, while total health spending grew by 50 percent between 1997 and 2008, spending on clinics, home health, and other outpatient care grew by just under 40 percent, and even this was due largely to a 75 percent spike in spending on health care delivered through schools and other community settings. Spending on clinic care, by contrast, increased by a much smaller 20 percent, and on home health by 35 percent.[12]

- *Increased for-profit competition.* The surge of spending that accompanied the increased emphasis on outpatient care from the 1970s through 1990s had enormous impacts on the structure of the outpatient care industry, and these impacts are still quite visible. In particular, for-profits poured into this field and quickly overwhelmed the nonprofit providers. Thus, between 1977 and 1992 the number of for-profit outpatient clinics and related health service establishments jumped from around 5,000 to close to 25,000, a 400 percent increase. During the same period, the number of people employed by for-profit facilities swelled from just around 70,000 to more than 600,000, while revenues increased a comparable 800 percent. While nonprofit providers also benefited from the growth in this field,

FIGURE 6.8: Recent Trends in Clinic and Home Health Care Expenditures, 1997–2008 (Constant 2008 Dollars)

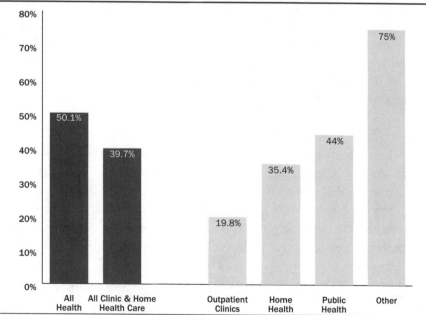

Source: Centers for Medicare and Medicaid Services, Table 2: Selected Calendar Years 1960–2008; see Chapter 6, endnote 12.

they did so far less extensively. As a consequence, they lost their once-dominant position in this industry, dropping from 55 percent of the establishments and 64 percent of the employees in 1977 to 33 percent of the establishments and 45 percent of the employees by 1992. By 1996, in fact, nonprofit providers of home health and allied health services accounted for only 29 percent of the revenues in this field, well below the 63 percent share they enjoyed in 1977.[13]

Very likely contributing to this rapid restructuring was the superior access to capital enjoyed by newly formed for-profit home health and other outpatient care networks by virtue of their ability to issue stock and thereby build the facilities needed to serve the burgeoning demand. Because of their nonprofit status, nonprofits are unable to raise capital by issuing shares of stock, severely limiting their ability to compete in expanding markets.

For-profit expansion was especially robust in the home health field, a field that nonprofits had pioneered in the 1960s and 1970s. Once Medicare made home health care eligible for reimbursement in the 1980s, it set off a rapid expansion of for-profit involvement. By 1997, therefore, for-profits operated 83 percent of the home health establishments and accounted for 72 percent of home health employees. As shown in Figure 6.9, moreover, this trend continued into recent years. Thus, between 1997 and 2007, the total number of home health establishments grew by 16 percent but the number of nonprofit establishments declined by another 11 percent and the number of nonprofit home health employees by 16 percent. By contrast, for-profit establishments swelled by another 22 percent and the number of for-profit home health employees by 10 percent. As a consequence, for-profits ended this period, as noted above, with 87 percent of the establishments, 71 percent of the employees, and 67 percent of the revenues.[14]

Nonprofits held their own considerably better in the clinic care area. As of 1997, nonprofits retained 43 percent of the clinics and accounted for 65 percent of outpatient clinic employees. Between 1997 and 2007, nonprofits were able to boost their share of facilities by 38 percent, roughly equivalent to the growth of for-profit establishments. However, the for-profit establishments were larger and boosted their employees and revenues at rates that far exceeded those achieved by the nonprofits (47 percent versus 19 percent in the case of employment and 64 percent versus 16 percent in the case of revenues). As a consequence, the nonprofit share of clinic employment slipped from 65 percent in 1997 to 60 percent in 2007.[15]

In short, as medical care has moved out of large, general-purpose hospitals and long-term care institutions into outpatient care facilities or home health arrangements, nonprofits have encountered stiff competition from for-profit establishments and have lost significant portions of their market share even as the overall size of the fields expanded dramatically.

NURSING HOME CARE

Overview. Nursing home care is the third major component of the health field where nonprofit organizations are active. As noted in Figure 6.2, nursing homes absorbed about 6 percent of all health spending in 2008, a total of some $138 billion. Of this, just over 60 percent came from government and about 38 percent from private sources, of which 34 percent took the form of private fees and 4 percent of philanthropy (see Figure 6.3). Most of the government revenue comes from the Medicaid program, but Medicare has also expanded coverage for sub-acute care in skilled nursing facilities as part of the general push to reduce the length of more expensive hospital stays.[16]

FIGURE 6.9: Trends in Nonprofit and For-Profit Roles in Outpatient Health Care, 1997–2007

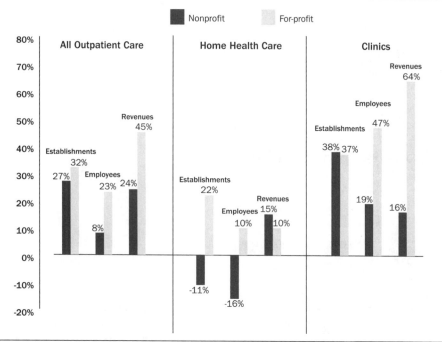

Source: U.S. Census Bureau, *Economic Census*, 1997, 2007; See Chapter 6, endnote 14.

Nonprofit versus Government and For-Profit Roles. Unlike the hospital and outpatient clinic portions of the health field, for-profit dominance has long been a distinguishing feature of the nursing home industry, stretching back to at least the 1950s. But ebbs and flows have occurred since then, and nonprofits have played an important role in fostering innovation and in providing a safety net when economic circumstances have induced for-profits to exit the field.

According to the latest data, nonprofits accounted for 19 percent of nursing home establishments as of 2007, as shown in Figure 6.10.[17] Nonprofit nursing homes tend to be larger in scale than their for-profit counterparts, however. Reflecting this, nonprofits accounted for a disproportionate 29 percent of nursing home employees and 31 percent of private nursing home revenues.

As is true of other components of the health field, the nursing home field contains a variety of types of entities, and the nonprofit role varies somewhat among the different types. Thus, the most numerous of these facilities, accounting for 44 percent of the establishments but 67 percent of the employees, are nursing care facilities, that is, homes offering skilled nursing

FIGURE 6.10: Nonprofit Share of Nursing Home Industry, 2007*

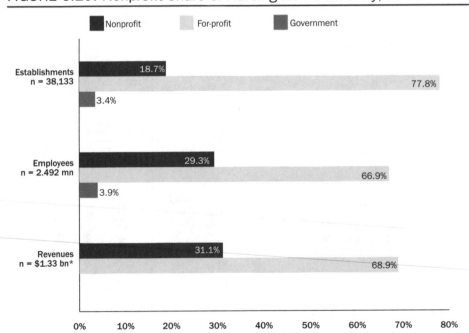

*Data on government establishments and employees cover 2004. Revenue data available on private institutions only.
Source: U.S. Census Bureau, *Economic Census*, 2007, and Centers for Disease Control, *Nursing Home Health Survey*, 2004; see Chapter 6, endnote 17.

services. As Figure 6.11 shows, nonprofits account for 19 percent of these establishments, though they are somewhat larger establishments, employing 25 percent of the employees and receiving 25 percent of the revenues. The second most numerous type of nursing home are what the Census refers to as "homes for the elderly," providing some nursing assistance but less than the skilled nursing facilities. These entities account for 40 percent of all nursing homes but a much smaller 12.5 percent of the nursing home employees. As Figure 6.11 shows, nonprofits are also the junior providers in this component of the nursing home field, accounting for only 16 percent of the facilities though they employ 21 percent of the employees. The final, and newest, component of the nursing home field, accounting for 16 percent of the facilities and 19 percent of the employees, are continuing care retirement communities, which offer a combination of residential care and supported living arrangements. Nonprofits comprise a considerably larger part of this component of the nursing home industry, with 30 percent of the facilities but a much larger 57 percent of the employees and 59 percent of the revenues.

Key Trends. Several key trends have characterized the nursing home field over the past nearly forty years, though none of these has been wholly unidirectional. Rather, ebbs and flows have been evident, and these have importantly influenced the evolving shape of the field.

FIGURE 6.11: Nonprofit Share of Private Nursing Homes, by Type, 2007

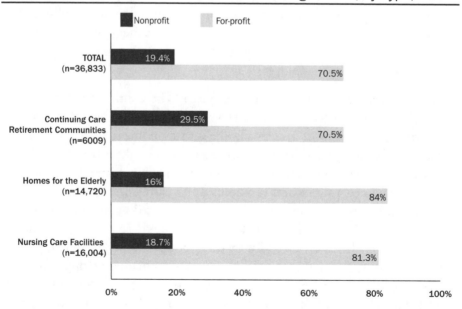

Source: U.S. Census Bureau, *Economic Census*, 2007; see Chapter 6, endnote 17.

- *Expanded government support.* In the first place, the nursing home field has been significantly affected by shifts in government policy. The early growth of this field was aided by provisions in the 1935 Social Security Act for limited support of nursing home care for the elderly. Federal construction subsidies followed in the 1950s with an amendment to the Hill-Burton Act, which made nursing homes eligible for tax-advantaged bond financing that had formerly been available only for hospitals. The major breakthrough, however, was the passage of the Medicaid program, which made significant federal and matching state support available for nursing home care for the indigent elderly. Then, in 1992, provision was made for coverage of skilled nursing home care for a much broader portion of the elderly population under the massive Medicare program. Each of these innovations prompted expansions in the scope, and often the structure, of the nursing home field, most recently boosting nursing home spending by some 20 percent in inflation-adjusted terms between 1997 and 2008 and raising government support from 60 percent of the total as of 1997 to 64 percent by 2008.[18]

- *Proliferation of types of providers.* Shifts in government policy have also often been associated with changes in the composition of the nursing home field. Early homes were places of residence for persons unable to care for themselves. With the opening of Medicare reimbursement for temporary stays in facilities providing significant medical care, skilled nursing homes emerged as a growth field in the industry. Finally, in more recent years, as the aging of the population has been leaving greater numbers of people in situations requiring a smooth transition from assisted living to full-scale nursing care, a new breed of "continuing care retirement communities" has emerged. As of 2007, as noted above, such facilities accounted for one out of five nursing home employees.

- *For-profit expansion with nonprofit persistence.* These shifts in policy have in turn interacted with market forces to shape the balance between nonprofit and for-profit presence in the nursing home industry. While the overwhelming trend has been toward for-profit takeover of the field, however, the dynamics have hardly been unidirectional, and nonprofits have maintained a significant foothold. Thus, early nursing homes were nonprofit in structure, often developed and operated by organizations with a religious affiliation and designed to care for elderly co-religionists who could not be adequately cared for by their families. With the opening of public funding through the Social Security Act, a marketing opportunity was created for commercial firms, and for-profit operators took substantial advantage of it. By the mid-1950s, therefore, over 70 percent of nursing homes were for-profit establishments, many of them little more than

boarding houses for the elderly.[19] The availability of construction subsidies
for nonprofit homes allowed nonprofits to gain ground temporarily
during the 1950s, but the passage of the Medicaid program set off another
growth frenzy on the part of for-profit firms. With expenditures increasing
by more than 100 percent in inflation-adjusted terms, for-profits took
advantage of their superior access to the equity markets to expand their
role, boosting their share of nursing home beds to 72 percent by 1971.

In what would become a recurrent boom-and-bust pattern, however, the
for-profit nursing home industry experienced a shake-out beginning in the
latter 1970s and continuing into the 1980s and early 1990s as Medicaid
lowered its reimbursement rates, and Medicare reimbursement policies
encouraged expanded use of home health care and other outpatient facilities
that dimmed the prospects for the optimistic stock offerings that had been
floated by for-profit nursing home chains. While economic conditions led to
a significant slowing in the growth of for-profit homes, however, nonprofit
homes, responding to social and religious needs rather than purely economic
incentives, expanded their capacity.[20]

Between 1997 and 2007, the latest act in this drama of nonprofit/for-profit
competition in the nursing home field appears to have unfolded in response
to the opening of Medicare reimbursement for skilled nursing care and
the emergence of the latest "new thing" in the nursing home field, namely
"continuing care retirement communities." As in the past, new funding sources
and new types of entities have favored for-profit providers, who have far more
ready access to capital. Thus, as shown in Figure 6.12, while the number of
nursing homes has increased by 18 percent between 1997 and 2007, most of
this increase accrued to the for-profit segment of the industry. Nonprofits did
manage to increase their employment and their revenues during this period,
but at rates that lagged behind those of for-profit operators.[21]

Table 6.1 provides even more insight into the dynamics at work. What it
reflects is a continuing decline in the absolute number of nonprofit facilities
among the established types of nursing home facilities—the skilled care
facilities and homes for the elderly. While the nonprofit workforce and
revenues nevertheless expanded during this period, they did so at rates below
those of the for-profit providers. As a result, as Table 6.1 shows, nonprofits
suffered further losses in their market share. By 2007, therefore, the nonprofit
share of homes for the elderly had declined to 16 percent, from 21 percent as
of 1997, and the nonprofit share of revenues and employees in such facilities
had declined to 21 and 22 percent, respectively, from roughly 30 percent a
decade earlier.[22]

FIGURE 6.12: Recent Trends in Private Nursing Home Industry, 1997–2007

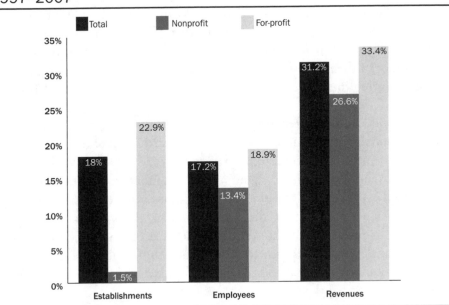

Source: U.S. Census Bureau, *Economic Census*, 1997, 2007; see Chapter 6, endnote 14.

TABLE 6.1: Trends in Nonprofit versus For-Profit Nursing Homes, by Type, 1997–2007

	Nonprofit share, 1997 versus 2007					
Type	Establishments		Employees		Revenues*	
	1997	2007	1997	2007	1997	2007
Homes for the Elderly	21.2%	16.0%	29.7%	20.7%	30.6%	22.3%
Continuing Care Retirement Communities	42.8%	29.5%	71.2%	57.0%	74.2%	59.4%
Nursing Care Facilities	19.8%	18.7%	25.5%	24.7%	25.5%	24.5%
TOTAL	**22.6%**	**19.4%**	**31.5%**	**30.4%**	**32.3%**	**31.1%**

Source: 2007 and 1997 *Economic Census*. See Chapter 6, endnote 14.
*Inflation adjusted.

A similar pattern was evident as well in the new, rapidly growing continuing care component of the nursing home field. Here as well, nonprofits have surrendered their commanding lead of a decade earlier, as for-profits have added establishments, employees, and revenues at a far faster rate than nonprofits. As a consequence, the nonprofit share of establishments has declined from 43 percent in 1997 to 30 percent in 2007, its share of employees from 71 percent to 57 percent, and its share of revenues from 74 percent to 59 percent. Whether nonprofit involvement in this component of the nursing home field will go the way of its involvement in other components remains to be seen. Given the bust in the housing market that began in 2008, however, it seems likely that nonprofits will continue to play the role they have been playing for decades in the nursing home field: as the steady providers of care who stay the course even when economic circumstances cause the for-profit providers to stumble.

Nonprofit organizations were the early vehicle for the creation and spread of pre-paid health insurance, which revolutionized the financing of hospital care.

HEALTH INSURANCE

In addition to contributing significantly to the delivery of health services, nonprofit organizations have also historically played a crucial role in health insurance. Most importantly, nonprofit organizations were the early vehicle for the creation and spread of pre-paid health insurance, which revolutionized the financing of hospital care by spreading the risks among entire communities, thereby bringing such care within the financial reach of middle- and working-class families. Begun in 1929, the resulting Blue Cross and, subsequently, Blue Shield insurance programs spread rapidly across the country in the 1940s and 1950s.[23]

More recently as well, the nonprofit form has been used to pursue new health financing experiments. Thus the health maintenance organization (HMO) phenomenon, which has revolutionized health care finance in recent years, got its start through a nonprofit organization, Kaiser Permanente. In its original "pure" form, HMOs were pre-paid group plans in which groups of physicians agreed in advance to be paid a fixed fee for medical services provided to a group of patients, rather than on a fee-for-service basis as in traditional medical practice. Kaiser Permanente, the originator of this concept, still operates as a nonprofit organization and claims 8.6 million members nationwide who are served by 35 hospitals, 454 other medical offices, 15,129 physicians, and 164,098 employees.[24]

As with many other facets of the nonprofit role in the health sector, however, in recent years nonprofit health insurers have encountered significant competition from for-profit providers, often abetted by public policy. In the first place, private insurance companies launched an assault on the Blue Cross and Blue Shield "community rating" plans by offering insurance plans targeted on less risky, and therefore less costly, subsets of a community's population. This disrupted the Blue Cross/Blue Shield business model, which was based on spreading health care risks across as broad a swath of the eligible population as possible in order to keep overall rates low. In response, Blue Cross/Blue Shield organizations were forced to raise their rates to cover the remaining, higher-risk populations. Over time, this contributed to the expansion of the uninsured population as marginal purchasers of health insurance found themselves unable to cover the higher costs. Worse yet, as nonprofit Blue Cross/Blue Shield organizations took on more of the character of their for-profit competitors, Congress responded by revoking their tax-exempt status. This, in turn, accelerated a trend of conversions of nonprofit plans into for-profit status, often through insider deals executed at questionable prices.[25]

During this same period, a series of shifts in federal policy eliminated the tax and other advantages enjoyed by nonprofit HMOs. No sooner had Congress passed a law in 1973 to provide grants and loans to promote the development of what was then a nonprofit-dominant HMO industry than the Internal Revenue Service began issuing rulings denying tax exemption to HMOs on grounds that they served only a limited set of "members" and therefore did not meet the "broad public benefit" test required for nonprofit status. With the ascendance of the Reagan Administration in 1981, moreover, funding for nonprofit HMOs was terminated and emphasis placed on encouraging private investor funding, which required for-profit status for the resulting entities. Within five years, by 1986, the for-profit share of HMOs had skyrocketed from 18 percent to 60 percent, and by 2003 it stood at 72 percent.[26] By this time, however, consolidation had proceeded so far in the health insurance industry that it became impossible to differentiate HMOs from other multi-purpose, mostly for-profit, health insurers. Whether the state-level "insurance exchanges" mandated by the Obama administration's Patient Protection and Affordable Care Act of 2010 will restore a meaningful nonprofit role in the health insurance field remains to be seen. But it is notable that policymakers turned again to the nonprofit form to launch an innovation intended to reverse the ill effects of past developments in the health insurance field.

For-profits have long dominated the nursing home industry ... but nonprofits have played an important role in fostering innovation and in providing a safety net.

Conclusion

The health care sector is thus the largest component of the American social welfare system outside of old-age pensions. It is, moreover, a complex sector, containing many different types of institutions and multiple sources of funds. The primary access to this complex system for most people is through private practitioners operating as for-profit businesses. But much of the institutional care is provided through nonprofit organizations. Although for-profit firms have recently made enormous inroads here as well, nonprofits still account for over 60 percent of the hospital care, 45 percent of the outpatient clinic and home health care, and nearly 30 percent of the nursing home care. Moreover, although nonprofits have recently been all but squeezed out of the health insurance field, they may be poised for a comeback thanks to the role accorded them in the recently passed health insurance law, which calls for the creation of a new network of nonprofit or state-run health insurance "exchanges" mandated to ensure access to insurance at competitive prices for individuals or employees of small businesses. Nonprofits thus form a vital part of the nation's health care delivery system and have demonstrated durability in the face of rather dramatic recent changes.

The public sector also plays a major role in the nation's health care system, but less as a deliverer of services than as a financer of them. Indeed, government involvement in the delivery of health services has declined sharply in recent years. By contrast, nearly half of overall health expenditures are financed with public funds. And in the fields of hospital, clinic, and nursing home care, where nonprofit organizations are most involved, the public sector accounts for an even larger 60 percent of the expenditures.

In short, the health field provides an excellent example of the "mixed economy" that lies at the heart of the American social welfare system, with nonprofit, for-profit, and governmental institutions all playing vital roles, often in close collaboration with one another. At the same time, as pressures for cost reductions have intensified, the position of the nonprofit providers in this mixed economy has come under particular stress, and that of the for-profit providers has grown. What this will mean for the quality, cost, and accessibility of services over the long run, however, remains very much open to debate.

ENDNOTES

1. U.S. Department of Health and Human Services, Centers for Medicare and Medicaid Services, *National Health Expenditure Data*, 2008, "Table 1: National Health Expenditures Aggregate, Per capita Amounts, Percent Distribution, and Average Annual Percentage Growth, by Source of Funds: Selected Calendar Years 1960–2008"; available at www.cms.gov/ NationalHealthExpendData/downloads/tables.pdf. The government portion of national health expenditures reported in this source for 2008 differs slightly from the 2009 estimate presented in Chapter 4 due to slight differences in the definition of health activities between the Bureau of Economic Analysis National Income and Product Accounts and the National Health Expenditures data source. The BEA estimate puts total government health spending at $1.029 trillion as of 2009 vs. the NHE estimate of $1.107 trillion as of 2008.

2. All data in this paragraph and the two following, except for 1965, from: Centers for Medicare and Medicaid Services, National Health Expenditure Data, 2008, Table 1. 1965 data from U.S. Department of Health and Human Services, Health Care Financing Administration, "National Health Expenditures, 1987," *Health Care Financing Review* 10:2 (Winter 1988), 112. Inflation factors based on implicit price deflators for services component of personal consumption expenditures as reported by the Bureau of Economic Analysis (last updated December 22, 2009).

3. *Giving USA: 2009*, 4.

4. Data derived from: U.S. Department of Health and Human Services, Centers for Medicare and Medicaid Services, Office of the Actuary, National Health Statistics Group, Table 2: National Health Expenditures Aggregate Amounts and Average Annual Percentage Change, by Type of Expenditure: Selected Calendar Years 1960–2008, accessed at: www.cms.gov/ NationalHealthExpendData/downloads/tables.pdf.

5. U.S. Department of Health and Human Services, Centers for Medicare and Medicaid Services, Office of the Actuary, National Health Statistics Group, Table 4: National Health Expenditures, by Source of Funds and Type of Expenditure: Calendar Years 2003–2008. Accessed at: www.cms. gov/NationalHealthExpendData/downloads/tables.pdf.

6. Derived from special tabulations of data from the 2008 American Hospital Survey produced by the American Hospital Association. Unless otherwise noted, all data in this section are from this source and from earlier editions of AHA's *Hospital Statistics*.

7. For further detail on the DRG system and its origins, see: Rick Mayes, "The Origins, Development, and Passage of Medicare's Revolutionary Prospective Payment System," *Journal of the History of Medicine and Allied Sciences* 62:1 (January 2007), 21–55.

8. See endnote 6 for source of 2008 data. Data on earlier years from AHA Hospital Statistics, AHA Abridged Guide on Diskette 1996/7, and Lester M. Salamon, *America's Nonprofit Sector: A Primer*, 2nd ed. (Foundation Center, 1999).

9. Also included are payments provided through home and community-based waivers in the Medicaid Program. This category does not include "other professional health services," which are categorized in the National Health Expenditures data as services delivered through specialty offices, such as chiropractors, podiatrists, and physical and speech therapists. Although other professional health services also include private-duty nurses, these professional services are grouped here with physician and dental care.

10. Data here drawn from 2007 Economic Census, Sector 62: ECO 76211: Health Care and Assistance: Industry Series, Preliminary Summary Statistics for the United States: 2007. Accessed at: factfinder.census.gov/servlet/IBQTable?_bm=y&-geo_id=&-ds_name=EC0762I1&-_lang=en.

11. U.S. Department of Health and Human Services, Health Care Financing Administration, "National Health Expenditures, 1997," *Health Care Financing Review* 20:2 (Winter 1998); Salamon, *America's Nonprofit Sector* (1999), 85–86.

12. Data derived from: Centers for Medicare and Medicaid Services, Office of the Actuary, National Health Statistics Group; Table 2: National Health Expenditures Aggregate Amounts and Average Annual Percentage Change, by Type of Expenditure: Selected Calendar Years 1960–2008. Accessed at: www.cms. gov/NationalHealthExpendData/downloads/tables.pdf.

13. U.S. Department of Commerce, *Current Business Reports: Service Annual Survey* 1996 (1998).

14. U.S. Bureau of the Census, *2007 Economic Census*, Sector 62: EC0762I1: Health Care and Social Assistance: Industry Series: Preliminary Summary Statistics for the United States: 2007, accessed at: factfinder.census.gov/servlet/IBQTable?_bm=y&-geo_id=&-fds_name=EC0700A1&-_skip=100&-ds_name=EC0762I1&-_lang=en; and *1997 Economic Census*, Health Care and Social Assistance Geographic Area Series, accessed at: www.census.gov/prod/ec97/97s62-us.pdf.

15. See endnote 14 above.

16. Medicare support for nursing home care occurs where Medicare patients are released from hospitals but are still in need of subacute care. Many nursing homes have converted excess space into subacute care units to accommodate such patients, earning Medicare reimbursement in the process. To be eligible, however, the facility must qualify as a "skilled nursing facility." U.S. Department of Health and Human Services, "National Health Expenditures, 1995," *Health Care Financing Review* (Fall 1996), 189; *See also*: seniorjournal.com/NEWS/Medicare/2008/8-01-18-SenCitNeed2Know.htm.

17. Data on nonprofit and for-profit nursing homes from: U.S. Bureau of the Census, *2007 Economic Census*, Sector 62: EC0762I1: Health Care and Social Assistance: Industry Series: Preliminary Summary. Available at: factfinder.census.gov/servlet/IBQTable?_bm=y&-geo_id=&-ds_name=EC0762I1&-_lang=en. Data on government nursing homes from: Centers for Disease Control, 2004 Nursing Home Health Survey, Tables 1 and 2, accessed at: www.cdc.gov/nchs/data/nnhsd/nursinghomefacilities2006.pdf#01. Data on government homes available only for 2004. Revenue data covers private homes only.

18. Centers for Medicare and Medicaid Services, Office of the Actuary, National Health Statistics Group, Table 4: National Health Expenditures, by Source of Funds and Type of Expenditure: Calendar Years 2003–2008. Accessed at: www.cms. gov/NationalHealthExpendData/downloads/tables.pdf.

19. Bradford H. Gray and Mark Schlesinger, "Health," in *The State of Nonprofit America*, ed. Lester M. Salamon (Washington, DC: The Brookings Institution Press, 2002), 89.

20. See: Genevieve W. Strahan, "An Overview of Nursing Homes and their Current Residents: Data from the 1995 National Nursing Home Survey," *Advance Data* 280 (January 23, 1997).

21. See endnote 14 above.

22. See endnote 14, this chapter, for sources.

23. For a useful discussion of the origins of Blue Cross and Blue Shield, see: Rosemary Stevens, *In Sickness and in Wealth: American Hospitals in the Twentieth Century* (New York: Basic Books, 1997), 171–199.

24. Kaiser Permanente, *Annual Report: 2009*. Accessed at: xnet.kp.org/newscenter/annualreport/by_the_numbers.html.

25. Bradford H. Gray, *The Rise and Decline of the HMO: A Chapter in US Health-Policy History* (Washington, DC: The Urban Institute, 2006), 327–8; Judith E. Bell. "Saving their Assets: How to Stop the Plunder at Blue Cross and Other Nonprofits," *The American Prospect* (May–June, 1996), 60–66.

26. Gray, "The Rise and Decline of the HMO," 313, 315.

7

Education

If health is the largest component of the American nonprofit sector, education is the second-largest. One out of every five dollars of nonprofit revenue flows to nonprofit education institutions, as Figure 3.4 showed. What is more, nonprofit institutions play important roles in all four major segments of the education field: 1) higher education, 2) elementary and secondary education, 3) vocational education, and 4) library services.

But what exactly is this role, and how does the nonprofit sector compare to government and the for-profit sector in this field?

To answer these questions, this chapter looks first at the basic scale and composition of educational expenditures in America and then examines the nonprofit role in each of the major spheres of educational activity.

Education Spending

OVERVIEW

Scale and Uses. Americans spent $1.13 trillion on education in the 2007/08 academic year, about half as much as on health, but still a significant 8 percent of the gross domestic product.[1]

As Figure 7.1 shows, the bulk of this spending (53 percent) went for elementary and secondary education. Higher education absorbed another 41 percent. Approximately 5 percent went for vocational education, and the balance (about 1 percent) went to libraries.

One out of every five dollars of nonprofit revenue flows to nonprofit education institutions.

Sources of Spending. Unlike the situation in the health sphere, where private fees are the dominant source of revenue, in the education sphere most of the spending originates with government. As of 2007, just over 60 percent of total education spending in the United States came from government, 90 percent of it from the state and local level (see Figure 7.2).[2] By comparison, private fees and payments accounted for 34 percent of the total and private philanthropy for only about 4 percent.

FIGURE 7.1: Where Education Spending Goes, 2007–2008 (Billions of 2007 Dollars)

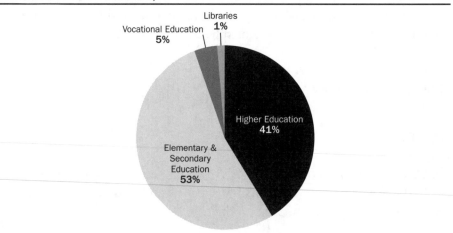

Libraries 1%
Vocational Education 5%
Higher Education 41%
Elementary & Secondary Education 53%

Total = $1,129 billion

Source: See Chapter 7, endnote 1.

As Figure 7.2 makes clear, however, this situation is largely a reflection of the major role that government plays in the financing of elementary and secondary education in the United States. Thus, 90 percent of all elementary and secondary education funds come from government. By contrast, government provides only 32 percent of the funding for higher education, while 62 percent comes from tuition and fees and the remaining 6 percent from philanthropy.[3]

Growth. Education spending has not experienced anywhere near as rapid a rate of growth in recent years as has health spending, though it has managed to increase faster than the overall growth of the U.S. economy. Thus, while the U.S. gross domestic product grew by 46 percent in real terms between 1995 and 2007, education spending grew by a slightly more robust 52 percent, as shown in Figure 7.3.[4] As a share of gross national product, therefore, education spending edged up from 7.0 percent in 1995 to 8.4 percent in 2007. This reversed a trend in the period from 1975 to 1995, when education expenditures lagged behind the overall growth of the economy and declined as a share of gross domestic product.

FIGURE 7.2: Sources of Education Spending, 2006–2007 (Millions of 2009 Dollars)

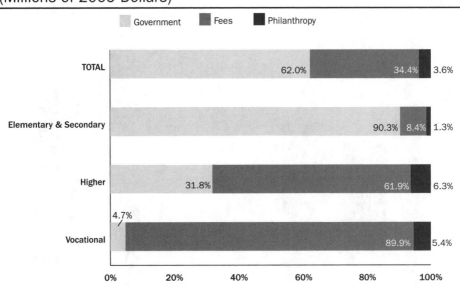

Source: *Digest of Education Statistics, 2009*; U.S. Bureau of the Census, *Economic Census*, 2007; Internal Revenue Service, Statistics of Income Tabulations; U.S. Bureau of Economic Analysis, National Income and Product Accounts, Table 3.16. Also see Chapter 7, endnote 2.

As Figure 7.3 shows, what has kept education spending from growing more robustly is its dependence on government support. In the recent 1995–2007 period, as in the prior 1975–1995 period, government support for education has not kept pace with the overall growth in the economy. Thus, while the economy grew by 46 percent between 1995 and 2007, government funding of education increased by only 37 percent. Government support of education thus declined as a share of the country's GDP.

Faced with this limited growth of government support, education institutions turned to two other sources: private philanthropy and fees and charges. The latter was clearly the more substantial, both relatively and absolutely, increasing by 88 percent during this twelve-year period. As a consequence, fees went from providing 28 percent of educational expenditures in 1995 to providing 34 percent by 2007. Philanthropy also increased a robust 65 percent during this period. However, since it started from a much smaller base its overall impact was less substantial, though its impact on nonprofit institutions was greater.

FIGURE 7.3: Change in Education Spending, 1995–2007, by Source*

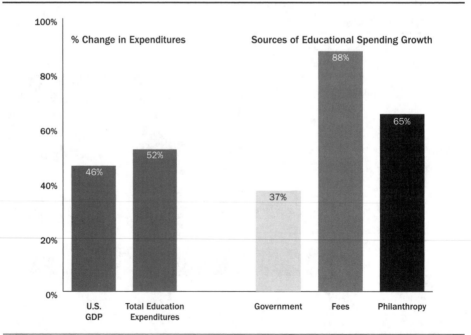

Source: *Digest of Education Statistics, 2009.*

The Nonprofit Role in Education

Although philanthropy plays a relatively minor role in the financing of education, as in the case of health the nonprofit sector nevertheless plays a significant role in the delivery of education. Overall, as Figure 7.4 shows, nonprofit organizations absorb 22 percent of all education spending, or just over one in every five dollars. Moreover, in some fields, such as higher education, the nonprofit share is considerably larger than this. To understand the role that nonprofit organizations play in the nation's education system, therefore, it is necessary to examine each of the four major subfields of education in turn.

HIGHER EDUCATION

The most important of these subfields as far as nonprofit organizations are concerned is higher education. As Figure 7.1 showed, just over 40 percent of all education spending goes into higher education, a total of $465 billion in academic year 2006/07.

Overview. Nonprofit organizations are a major presence in the higher education field in America.

FIGURE 7.4: Share of Education Spending Flowing to Public, For-Profit, and Nonprofit Institutions, 2004

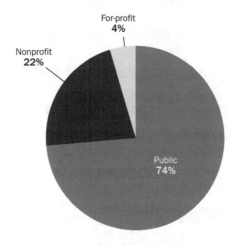

For-profit
4%

Nonprofit
22%

Public
74%

Total = $1,115.8 billion

Source: *Digest of Education Statistics, 2009* and U.S. Bureau of the Census, *Economic Census*, 2007.

- Nearly 40 percent of all higher education institutions are private nonprofit organizations, as shown in Figure 7.5.[5] Nonprofit prominence is even more striking when we restrict our attention to four-year colleges. More than 56 percent of all four-year colleges and universities in the United States are nonprofit organizations.

- Unlike many other countries, whose premier universities are frequently government institutions, many of the most distinguished colleges and universities in the United States are private, nonprofit institutions. This includes Harvard, Yale, Princeton, Duke, Stanford, Johns Hopkins, Dartmouth, Brown, Vanderbilt, Rice, Swarthmore, Williams, Vassar, and many others.

- While nonprofit higher education institutions are quite numerous, they also tend to be smaller than their public counterparts, particularly since the public institutions include a disproportionate share of two-year institutions. With 37 percent of all higher education institutions, nonprofit schools thus account for only 20 percent of all higher education *enrollments*, as Figure 7.5 also shows.

FIGURE 7.5: The Nonprofit Role in Higher Education, 2007–2008

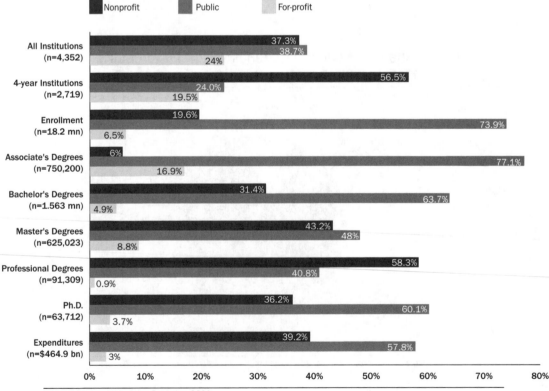

Source: *Digest of Education Statistics, 2009.*

- The nonprofit institutions play a much larger role in the granting of higher education degrees, however. This is understandable given the fact that many of the public institutions are two-year colleges that do not issue baccalaureate degrees. For another, the nonprofit institutions traditionally have had especially strong graduate and professional programs. As a result, the private nonprofit institutions account for about a third of all baccalaureate degrees issued in the United States, 36 percent of all Ph.D. degrees, 43 percent of all master's degrees, and close to 60 percent of all professional degrees (for example, medical degrees, law degrees) (see Figure 7.5).

- Reflecting this substantial role, nonprofit higher education institutions absorb close to 40 percent of all higher education expenditures (see Figure 7.5). All in all, therefore, they play a much more substantial role than the enrollment figures alone would suggest.

Sources of Funds. As noted above, the pattern of funding of higher education in the United States differs considerably from that for other levels of education. In particular, fees and charges play a significantly more important role in the funding of higher education than they do for elementary and secondary education, where government is the dominant source of support.

What Figure 7.6 makes clear is that this distinctive higher education funding pattern applies to the nonprofit institutions almost as fully as it does to the for-profit ones. Thus, as Figure 7.6 shows, more than three-fourths of the revenue fueling nonprofit higher education comes from tuition and other fees and charges. Government is a distant second as a source of support, providing 12 percent of the revenue. Private gifts, grants, contracts, and endowment earnings together account for the remaining 11 percent of support. Even for the private nonprofit institutions, therefore, private philanthropy is only the third most important source of support.[6] The comparable figures for the for-profit institutions were 94 percent from fees and just under 6 percent from government.

The public institutions of higher education, by contrast, rely more heavily on government support, though even here government's contribution is somewhat smaller than might be assumed. Just over half of the revenue of the public institutions now comes from fees also, with government accounting for a smaller 46.5 percent of support. The remaining 3 percent comes from gifts and grants.

These figures are, of course, aggregates that disguise the considerable diversity that exists among nonprofit higher education institutions. Based on National Center for Education Statistics data, it is possible to differentiate at least six different categories of nonprofit higher education institutions.[7] As Table 7.1 shows, these different types of nonprofit higher education institutions differ markedly in the share of resources they command and the funding structure that supports their activity. In the first place, a small group of major research universities representing only a little more than 1 percent of the institutions capture nearly half (46.6 percent) of the total nonprofit higher education revenues. What is more, these institutions have a very distinctive funding structure, with relatively high levels of government and philanthropic support and correspondingly lower levels of reliance on tuition and other earned income. Most significantly, they receive a quarter of their revenue from government, largely in the form of research grants for medical and other research—another example of the significant partnership between government and the nonprofit sector in our country. In fact, a striking 71 percent of all government funding of private, nonprofit higher education flows to this subset of institutions.

FIGURE 7.6: Sources of Revenue of Nonprofit Higher Education Institutions Compared to Public and For-Profit Institutions

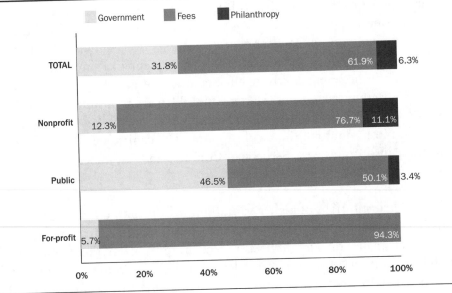

Source: *Digest of Education Statistics, 2009.*

TABLE 7.1: Distribution of Nonprofit Higher Education Institutions
and Revenues, 2007/08, by Type of Institution

Type of Institution	Share of:		Share of revenue from:			
	Institutions	Revenues	Government	Philanthropy	Fees	TOTAL
Major research university	1.2%	46.6%	24.8%	14.6%	60.6%	100%
Research and doctoral	3.0%	13.4%	10.5%	13.1%	76.4%	100%
Master's	14.6%	16.4%	5.7%	9.9%	84.4%	100%
Baccalaureate	25.9%	13.7%	5.0%	22.6%	72.4%	100%
Specialized	31.2%	9.7%	16.3%	18.2%	65.5%	100%
Two-year	24.1%	0.2%	10.9%	11.6%	77.5%	100%
TOTAL	100.0%	100.0%				

Source: *Digest of Education Statistics*, 2009, Table 356.

At the other end of the spectrum are the liberal arts colleges, designated here as "baccalaureate" institutions because they primarily offer baccalaureate degrees. Only 5 percent of their funding comes from government, forcing them to rely more heavily on charitable donations from their alumni and tuition payments from their students. The most fee-dependent institutions are those specializing in master's degrees and associate degrees (the two-year institutions), both of which are more professionally oriented in their offerings.

Even this does not fully clarify the funding picture of nonprofit higher education, however, because these institutions (or at least some of them) do not only benefit from government research funding; a significant portion of the tuition they receive is actually subsidized by government grants or loan guarantees to students. The partnership between government and the nonprofit sector identified as a salient feature of the American social welfare system is therefore far more in evidence in this sphere than the figures on direct support to the institutions may suggest. Just as in the case of Medicare and Medicaid payments to hospitals discussed in the previous chapter, this assistance has allowed tuition-dependent private, nonprofit colleges and universities to attract a much more economically and socially diverse student body than was possible earlier in their histories and thus to survive, and in some cases to thrive, in a difficult higher education marketplace.

Recent Trends. The current structure of American higher education is
a product of changes that have occurred largely since the Second World
War. Prior to this, the nonprofit sector had an even larger role in the higher
education sphere than it does now. As late as 1950, for example, almost two-
thirds of all higher education institutions were private nonprofits, and these
institutions held half of all the higher education students.[8]

Beginning in the 1950s and accelerating in the 1960s, however, state and
local governments made major investments to build comprehensive systems
of public higher education, embracing both two- and four-year institutions.
As a consequence, enrollment in American higher education increased
dramatically—by 40 percent in the 1950s and by another 120 percent in
the 1960s. Public higher education naturally claimed the lion's share of this
increase, boosting its enrollments by 60 percent in the 1950s and 170 percent
in the 1960s. By 1980, therefore, close to 80 percent of all students enrolled
in higher education in the United States were in public institutions,
compared to 20 percent in private ones.

Since 1980, two trends have dominated the nonprofit higher education
scene: first, consolidation of the nonprofit position following the dramatic
challenge from the rapid rise of less expensive public universities; and second,
the emergence of a significant new challenge in the form of a rapidly growing
for-profit presence in the higher education arena.

The consolidation process began in the 1970s and has continued in more
recent years. Most significantly, nonprofit institutions have found ways to
boost their revenues without correspondingly increasing their enrollments.
Thus, for example, nonprofit higher education institutions were able to boost
their revenues by 65 percent in inflation-adjusted terms between 1975 and
1995 while increasing enrollments only 16 percent, and then to double down
on this performance in the more recent 1996–2007 period by increasing
revenues another 45 percent while enrollments increased a more modest
24 percent (see Figure 7.7). Although this recent growth lagged slightly
behind the comparable figure for public higher education institutions, as
shown in Figure 7.7, it exceeded the 40 percent growth rate of the overall
economy during this period.[9]

The key to the success for, but also the constraint on, nonprofit revenue
growth during this period has been the ability of these institutions to capture
increased tuition revenue. Thus, 76 percent of the growth in nonprofit higher
education institution revenue between 1975 and 1995 came from tuition and

other commercial income, compared to 9 percent from government support and 15 percent from philanthropy. In the more recent 1996–2007 period, the share that tuition and other commercial income contributed to growth was an even higher 80 percent, compared to 10 percent from government and 9 percent from philanthropy.

One factor doubtless contributing to the ability of nonprofit (and public) higher education institutions to capture increased revenue through expanded tuition payments, especially after the mid-1970s, has been the expanded availability of the government grant and loan guarantee programs identified earlier. At the same time, however, as the data for the more recent period show, the considerable debt these programs are creating for students and their families may have begun to take a toll on nonprofit higher education prospects, as reflected in a slowdown in the rate of revenue growth.

As with other facets of the nonprofit higher education scene, the success that nonprofit higher education institutions achieved in recent years varied considerably by type of institution. As Figure 7.8 shows, the relative handful

FIGURE 7.7: Recent Trends in Higher Education, 1995/96–2006/07*

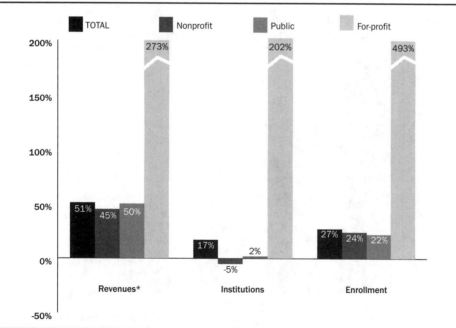

*Revenue change data for public and nonprofit institutions cover 1996/97–2006/07; revenue data for for-profit institutions cover 1997/98–2006/07. All other data cover 1995/96–2006/07.
Source: *Digest of Education Statistics*, various tables. See Chapter 7, endnote 9.

.jor research universities fared best, boosting their total revenue by
:rcent between 1995 and 2007.[10] Fees and philanthropic support
weɪ⸗ the major drivers of this growth, the former growing by 56 percent in
real terms and the latter by 143 percent. At the other extreme, the smaller
baccalaureate institutions actually lost ground financially during this period
and were unable to keep pace with inflation. Some were even forced to shut
down, as Figure 7.8 shows.

The ability of nonprofit higher education institutions in the aggregate to hold
their own in recent years is all the more noteworthy in light of the recent
emergence of a new competitive threat in the form of the rapid explosion
of for-profit higher education. Starting with only 5 percent of all higher
education institutions as of 1980, for-profit firms accounted for 40 percent of
the new higher education institutions created between 1980 and 1995, and
this growth has accelerated in more recent years. Thus, between the 1997/98
and 2006/7 school years, for-profit higher education providers boosted
their revenues nearly four-fold, from under $4 billion in inflation-adjusted
dollars to $14 billion. During this same period, these providers expanded
their number of institutions by over 200 percent and their enrollments
by 493 percent, as revealed in Figure 7.7. With a mere 1 percent of the

FIGURE 7.8: Revenue Change Among Nonprofit Higher Education Institutions, 1995/96–2007/08, by Type of Institution

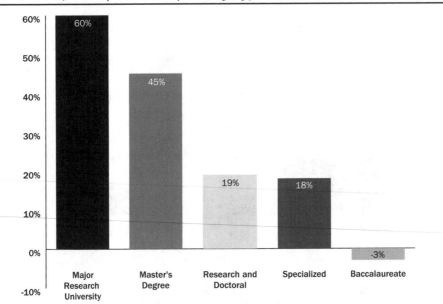

Source: *Digest of Education Statistics, 2009*, Table 356; *1999*, Table 336. Also see Chapter 7, endnote 10.

higher education students when this period began, for-profits thus attracted 25 percent of the growth of higher education enrollments between 1996 and 2007. And to accommodate this growth, they accounted for 100 percent of the net growth in the number of higher education institutions.[11]

No longer restricted to non-degree programs, for-profit institutions are posing a competitive challenge at all levels of higher education. Thus in 2007 they granted 76,000 baccalaureate and nearly 54,000 master's degrees.

The striking success of this new arrival on the higher education scene reflects important changes in the country's demographics and in the technology of education, changes that both the public and nonprofit sectors have been slow to recognize and respond to. These include the trend toward lifelong learning, the growing pattern of mixing education with work, and the increased sophistication of distance-learning technologies. Equally crucial, however, has been the expanded availability of federal student financial assistance, which finances a considerable portion of the tuition at these schools. This, in turn, has raised some questions about the marketing techniques of some private, for-profit schools and about the disproportionate default rates their graduates have sustained on their federally backed student loans. How these issues are addressed, and how quickly the public and nonprofit institutions respond to the market demand the for-profits have identified, will determine whether nonprofits will be able to withstand this latest challenge to their important niche in the higher education field.

ELEMENTARY AND SECONDARY EDUCATION

Overview. If the major locus of nonprofit activity in the education field is at the higher education level, nonprofits also hold an important position at the elementary and secondary education level, which is the level at which most of the nation's education expenditures are made. Indeed, as Figure 7.1 noted, elementary and secondary education absorbs more than half of all education spending in the United States.

Unlike the higher education level, however, government clearly plays the dominant role at the elementary and secondary level and has at least since the latter nineteenth century. This is so, moreover, with respect to both the financing and the delivery of such education. Thus, nine out of every ten of the dollars spent on elementary and secondary education in the country comes from government. Beyond this, as Figure 7.9 shows, 75 percent of all elementary and secondary school facilities are operated by government agencies, and these institutions account for nearly 90 percent of the enrollments and 92 percent of the expenditures.[12]

Although government—usually local government—clearly plays the dominant role in the elementary and secondary education field in the United States, it hardly occupies this field by itself. To the contrary, a vibrant set of private, nonprofit education institutions also exists. In fact, as of 2007, one out of every four elementary and secondary schools in the country was a nonprofit institution—some 33,740 schools in all. These schools enrolled 5.9 million students, or about 11 percent of all elementary and secondary school students.[13] Included here are some well-known and prestigious secondary schools such as Phillips Exeter Academy, Andover, and the network of Friends schools as well as many of the pre-school Montessori schools.

Regional Variations. Considerable variations exist in the scale of enrollment in private schools across the United States. In Delaware, for example, one out of every five elementary and secondary school students (21 percent) attends a private school. In nearby Maryland, this figure is over 16 percent, and in Pennsylvania it is over 15 percent. In South Carolina, however, this figure

FIGURE 7.9: Nonprofit Share of Elementary and Secondary Education, 2007

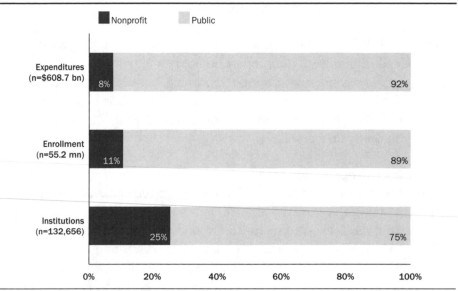

Source: *Digest of Education Statistics, 2007*, Tables 27, 35, 62.

is just over 9 percent and in nearby Alabama it is 10 percent.[14] Generally speaking, the proportion of students in private schools is lowest in the South and the West and highest in the Northeast and parts of the Midwest.

As of 2007, one out of every four elementary and secondary schools in the country was a nonprofit institution.

Religious Affiliation. One reason for the variations in the extent of private elementary and secondary education is the close connection historically between such private education and religion. As Figure 7.10 shows, three out of every four private elementary and secondary schools are religiously afffiliated, and 81 percent of the students in private elementary and secondary education are in religiously affiliated ones.[15] Of the 81 percent of all students in religiously affiliated schools, over half (43 percent of all students) are in

FIGURE 7.10: Religious Affiliation of Private Elementary and Secondary Schools, 2007*

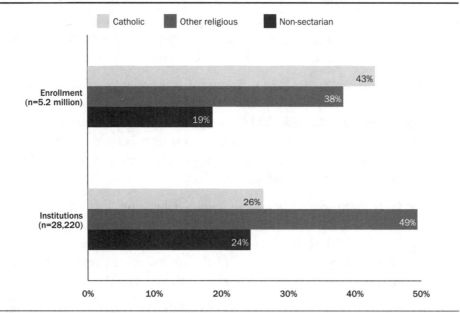

*Figures may not total 100 percent due to rounding.
Source: *Digest of Education Statistics, 2009*, Table 60.

Catholic schools and the rest are in schools with other religious affiliations. The other religious schools are more numerous, however, accounting for 49 percent out of the 75 percent of all private elementary and secondary schools with a religious affiliation. The areas of the country with large Catholic populations thus tend to have the largest concentrations of students in private elementary and secondary schools, though the rise of religious fundamentalism has increased the number of "Christian" schools as well, altering long-standing patterns of private school prevalence.

Recent Trends. Not only have private, nonprofit organizations retained an important foothold in the elementary and secondary education field, but that foothold has been growing, at least until relatively recently. Because of the strong tradition of public education, private elementary and secondary schooling did not become a broad phenomenon until after the Second World War. As of 1939, for example, private elementary and secondary schools enrolled only about 2.6 million pupils out of the 28 million in school, and the vast majority of these were in Catholic schools. From the early 1950s onward, however, private elementary and secondary education took off, at least in some regions of the country, and broadened its demographic base. By 1980, 5.3 million students were attending private elementary and secondary schools, and the share attending Catholic schools had fallen to 58 percent from over 70 percent previously.

During the 27 years between 1980 and 2007, the overall enrollment of private schools varied in a fairly narrow range between 5.3 and 6.3 million students. These seemingly stable enrollment numbers disguise a considerable amount of internal change, however. In particular:

- Catholic education underwent a significant consolidation as social changes undercut its enrollment and funding difficulties challenged its economic viability. Between 1960 and 2007, the number of Catholic schools declined by 43 percent and the number of students enrolled in such schools declined by 57 percent, dropping the number of institutions by 2,200 and the number of students by 836,000.[16]

- Despite this sharp consolidation of Catholic education, the overall enrollment in private elementary and secondary schools actually increased by roughly 600,000 students during the 1960-2007 period, a net increase of 11 percent, as shown in Figure 7.11. What is more, a surge occurred in the formation of new schools, as Figure 7.11 also shows.

- Much of this growth seems to have occurred during the 1980s and 1990s, when dissatisfaction with public education was particularly intense in the United States.

- Also at work, very likely, was the growth of fundamentalist religion in some parts of the country and a movement toward other religious private education as a protest against Supreme Court decisions outlawing prayer in the public schools. The number of non-Catholic religiously affiliated schools thus surpassed the number of Catholic-affiliated schools in the early 1990s and continued to increase into the new century, though the number of students in such schools remained below the reduced numbers in Catholic schools.[17]

- More recently, a relatively new development has emerged to offset the continuing decline in the once-dominant Catholic component of the private-school field: the rise of the "charter school" movement as part of the effort to reform the U.S. education system. Charter schools are special schools organized by parents or others to offer creative approaches to elementary or secondary education free of some of the restrictions of regular public schools. Charter schools are "chartered" by local school districts or state authorities but often incorporate as nonprofit organizations. Students attending such schools receive a stipend paid by the regular public school at a rate set to approximate the per-pupil cost in

FIGURE 7.11: Recent Trends in Elementary and Secondary Education, 1980–2007

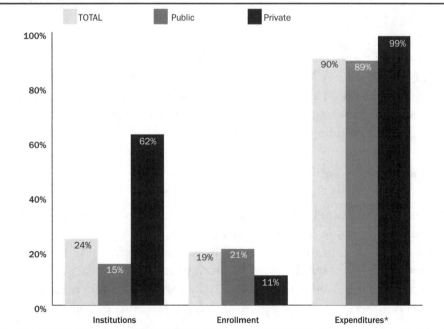

*Constant 2007 dollars.
Source: *Digest of Education Statistics, 2009*, Tables 27, 35, 62.

regular public schools, but the schools are free to raise additional support from private sources. Estimates of the number of such schools vary, but a recent (2008) estimate put the number at 4,100, though it is not known what portion of these are separately incorporated as nonprofits.[18]

A relatively new development is the rise of the charter school movement as part of the U.S. education reform effort.

In some communities, such as Washington, D.C., the growth of charter schools has been enormous. Nearly 70,000 students attended the Washington public elementary and secondary schools as of 1999, and 10,000 attended charter schools. By the beginning of the 2008 school year, public school enrollment had dropped to 46,100 and charter school enrollment was at a peak of 26,000.[19] The rise of charter schools may be doing as much to help stimulate the growth of public education as of private education, of course, since many of these institutions remain public. But enough may be in the private arena to have offset continuing declines in the students enrolled in Catholic education and at least hold private school enrollments constant between 1995 and 2007. It may also help explain the appearance of 1,700 nonsectarian private schools between 1999 and 2007.[20]

In short, the private nonprofit sector has thus served in the elementary and secondary education field the important function it has performed in other areas of life: providing a "safety valve" through which people with different values and opinions or different concepts about what works could act on them without disrupting the overall social fabric of the nation.

VOCATIONAL EDUCATION

Overview. In addition to the formal, academic institutions discussed earlier, nonprofit organizations also play a significant role in the provision of non-degree vocational education. Much public-sector involvement in vocational education takes place within larger institutions such as secondary schools and community colleges and is therefore partially covered in prior sections of this chapter. But there also exist a significant number of other establishments, most of them private, providing such training. Included here are a variety of correspondence and trade schools, such as data-processing schools, business and secretarial schools, commercial arts schools, practical nursing schools, fine arts schools, cosmetology and barber schools, and many others. Data available on the private-sector involvement in this field through the Economic Census make it clear that this has become a sizable industry with revenues that had reached nearly $45 billion as of 2007.[21]

Nonprofit Role. As Figure 7.12 makes clear, for-profit firms are clearly the dominant element in this industry. As of 2007, such firms accounted for over four-fifths of the establishments, three-fourths of the employees, and just over 70 percent of the revenues, a pattern that was already firmly established by the early 1990s.

Despite the commanding for-profit lead, however, nonprofit organizations retain a significant presence in this field. Nonprofits are particularly evident in the "educational services" portion of this field, where they account for 28 percent of the institutions, 46 percent of the employees, and 60 percent of the revenues. Included here are non-instructional services that support educational development, such as guidance counseling, testing and test preparation services, student exchange programs, and the like. Nonprofits hold a roughly 20 percent share in both the "technical and trade schools" and

FIGURE 7.12: Nonprofit Share of Vocational Education, 2007

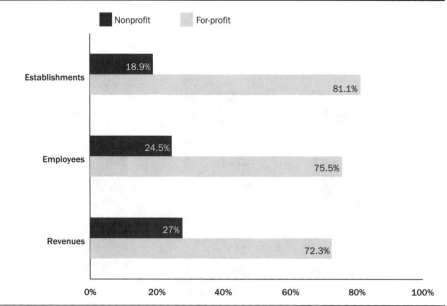

Source: U.S. Bureau of the Census, *Economic Census*, 2007.

"other schools and instruction" components of this industry, which include such areas as exam preparation and tutoring, fine arts, language, and sports instruction schools as well as cosmetology, flight training, and other technical training. By contrast, they account for only 13 percent of the business-oriented computer and management training establishments and 16 percent of the revenues in this field.

Recent Trends. Nonacademic vocational and specialized training has been one of the most dynamic growth fields within education in recent years. As Figure 7.13 makes clear, between 1997 and 2007 the revenues of private providers of vocational and other specialized education increased by 62 percent after adjusting for inflation.[22] This exceeded the growth rate of all education spending as well as the growth rate of gross domestic product, which increased by about 34 percent over the same period.[23] This comes on the heels of prior growth during the period 1982 to 1992, when the revenues of this component of the education scene grew by 78 percent after adjusting for inflation. This is all the more striking in view of the earlier finding that education spending in general has barely kept pace with the overall growth of the economy.

FIGURE 7.13: Recent Trends in Vocational Education, 1997–2007

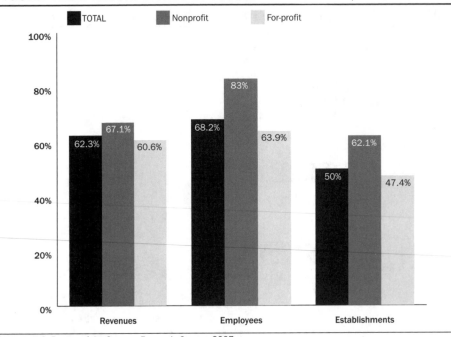

Source: U.S. Bureau of the Census, *Economic Census*, 2007.

Nonprofit involvement in this component of the education field is a story of decline and resurgence. In the early 1980s, nonprofits accounted for 29 percent of what was at the time a much smaller set of vocational education establishments in the country and 28 percent of their revenues. While nonprofit and for-profit providers both experienced growth over the next decade, however, for-profits captured a disproportionate share of this growth so that the nonprofit share of the establishments declined from 29 percent in 1982 to 17.5 percent as of 1997.

One explanation for the growth of nonprofit presence in vocational education may be the increased emphasis on workforce preparation in the 1996 welfare reform law.

During the most recent decade for which data are available, 1997–2007, nonprofits have turned the tables on for-profits, exceeding the growth rate of for-profits along each of the three different dimensions along which growth can conveniently be measured; that is, number of establishments (62 percent nonprofit growth versus 47 percent for-profit), revenues (67 percent nonprofit growth versus 61 percent for-profit), and employment (83 percent nonprofit growth versus 64 percent for-profit). Especially striking were the nonprofit gains in the field of business and computer training, where nonprofits started with only 8 percent of both establishments and employees but captured 32 percent of the growth in the former and 90 percent of the growth in the latter, doubling their share of employment in this sphere of vocational education from 8 to 16 percent.

One possible explanation of this significant growth of nonprofit presence in the vocational education field may be the increased emphasis on remedial education, counseling, and workforce preparation resulting from the 1996 welfare reform law, which, as we will see more fully in Chapter 8, has brought significant new resources into workforce preparation and training. Whatever the reason, it seems clear that nonprofit providers are continuing to make important contributions in this field of education as well.

LIBRARIES

One final component of education worth exploring is the provision of library services. To a significant extent, such services have already been covered in our earlier discussion of higher education and elementary education because most higher education and secondary schools have their own libraries.

However, there are also close to 20,000 free-standing libraries.[24] Most of these (88 percent) are public institutions, reflecting the same philosophy that motivated the creation of the system of public elementary and secondary education—the desire to improve the general educational level of the population. Like public education, moreover, these libraries are almost all run by local governments, although a limited amount of federal support is available to them.

Having survived the challenge from less expensive public universities in the 50s through the 70s, nonprofit higher education is confronting a new challenge from a burgeoning for-profit presence.

Beyond these public libraries and school libraries, however, there are also close to 2,500 private libraries in the United States employing close to 30,000 people. These libraries had some $1.854 billion in revenue as of 2007 and represent about 12 percent of all nonschool libraries. We assume that most of these institutions are nonprofits, though earlier censuses identified a small number of for-profit private libraries as well.[25] Even so, if the private college and university libraries were included, it is probably reasonable to conclude that nonprofit organizations operate at least a third of all adult libraries in the United States.

Conclusion

The past several decades have been a period of tremendous transitions for nonprofit organizations in the educational arena, but these organizations have more than survived the succession of challenges they have faced and retained or strengthened their important positions in all of the major components of the educational field. Once the dominant providers of higher education, nonprofit institutions ceded this position to public institutions in the period following World War II, but they have remained a critical force in this field, importantly aided by public policies that have broadened the student populations able to afford private-institution tuitions and strengthened the research base of these institutions.

Despite the long tradition of tax-supported, free public elementary and secondary education in this country, nonprofits have also established a significant role in the elementary and secondary education field, initially as providers of high-quality, elite, or religiously (mostly Catholic) affiliated education, but more recently as providers of more broadly based, nonsectarian education as well. Historically, the government-nonprofit partnership so prevalent in other fields of activity has been less in evidence in the elementary and secondary education field, but that may be in the process of changing thanks to the charter school movement, which is creating new types of private nonprofit, as well as public, schools funded jointly by government and private funds.

As in the health field, recent years have witnessed a growing for-profit presence in the education arena as well. For-profit firms have secured a commanding position in the growing field of vocational and special education and have also been a rapidly expanding presence in higher education. Nonprofit education providers are therefore confronting competitive pressures on two fronts at once.

These and other pressures arising from the economic downturn of 2008 and beyond are already hampering the operation of some nonprofit education providers, particularly among the smaller liberal arts colleges. But with their reputations for quality and independence, and their proven resilience in the face of past challenges, it seems likely that nonprofit organizations in the education field will find ways to continue to provide the important measure of diversity and choice that has sustained them up to now.

ENDNOTES

1. No single source of data is available on education spending or nonprofit educational institutions. Therefore, several different sources had to be pieced together to provide the cumulative portrait offered here. The principal source of the data on educational spending in this section is the U.S. Department of Education, Center for Education Statistics, *Digest of Education Statistics, 2009* (Washington, DC: U.S. Government Printing Office, 2010), henceforth *Digest of Education Statistics*. The *Digest* covers public and private elementary and secondary education (though it does not distinguish between nonprofit and for-profit schools); and public, private nonprofit, and private for-profit degree-granting higher education institutions. Because the *Digest* does not report data on non-degree-granting higher education or libraries, other sources had to be

consulted for these institutions. Data on vocational education, both for-profit and nonprofit, and private libraries were secured from: U.S. Bureau of the Census, *Economic Census, 2007.* Data on public libraries were drawn from the Institute of Museum and Library Services, Public Library Survey: harvester.census.gov/imls/data/pls/index.asp#fy2008KsInfo. Data reported here represent expenditures of education institutions and may therefore include research and other non-educational expenditures.

2. Data on sources of education spending here were assembled from a variety of sources, no one of which provides a complete picture. Data on public elementary and secondary schools were drawn from the *Digest of Education Statistics, 2009,* Table 173. With regard to private elementary and secondary schools, the Digest provided the total expenditures but no breakdown by source. Further, it did not break down "private" elementary and secondary education institutions between nonprofit and for-profit. Nor is this information available from the *Economic Census.* Accordingly, several assumptions had to be applied. First, because for-profit involvement in elementary and secondary education is still limited, we assumed that only 5 percent of private elementary and secondary education expenditures were made by for-profit institutions. Second, we assumed that nonprofit private elementary and secondary schools received from philanthropy proportionally half as much as nonprofit higher education institutions (i.e., 5.5%). Data on sources of revenue of degree-granting public, nonprofit, and for-profit higher education institutions were assembled from the *Digest of Education Statistics,* Tables 352, 356, and 358. Data on nonprofit and for-profit vocational education were drawn from U.S. Census Bureau, *Economic Census, 2007,* Sector 61, ECO 76113. The breakdown of government spending on education was drawn from the U.S. Bureau of Economic Analysis, National Income and Product Accounts, Table 3.16.

    The estimate of nonprofit education institution expenditures here, drawn largely from the *Digest of Education Statistics,* differs somewhat from the estimate of the revenues of nonprofit education and research organizations reported by the Internal Revenue Service in its Statistics of Income Special Tabulation used as the basis for the discussion in Chapter 3. The *Digest* reports total nonprofit education organization expenditures of $242.6 billion in the 2006/07 academic year, of which $25.4 billion comes from philanthropy. The IRS data used in Chapter 3 report $282.6 billion in nonprofit education and research organization revenues as of 2007, of which $39.5 billion is reported as coming from philanthropy. There are several possible explanations of these apparent differences: (a) the fact that the IRS is reporting revenues and the *Digest* expenditures may explain part of the difference since organizations, especially large ones such as universities, often have higher revenues than expenditures and carry funds over into subsequent years or into endowment; (b) the IRS data also cover research institutions such as think tanks, which are not covered in the *Digest* statistics; and (c) it is highly possible that some portion of the additional philanthropic support is going into endowments or building campaigns rather than into annual expenditures.

3. These figures do not take account of the contribution to the cost of higher education that the federal government provides through its loan guarantee programs for college tuition. The revenue generated from such loan guarantees shows up as tuition and fees.

4. For the sources of 2007 data, see endnote 3 above. Data on sources of support of elementary, secondary, and higher education for 1994/95 are from *Digest of Education Statistics, 1997,* Table 33. However, the Digest does not distinguish between fees and private philanthropy. Data on philanthropic giving to education was secured from *Giving USA 1997* and Council for Aid to Education, *1996 Voluntary Support of Education* (prepared by David R. Morgan) (New York: Council for Aid to Education, 1997), 3, 8. Government support for vocational education was secured from the *Social Security Bulletin,* various editions. The balance of support for vocational education in 1994/95was assumed to come from fees.

5. Data in this section are drawn from the *Digest of Education Statistics,* Tables 265, 266, 187, 362, 365, 367.

6. Data in this section are drawn from the *Digest of Education Statistics*, Tables 352, 356, and 368.

7. The National Center for Education Statistics actually identifies seven types of institutions, but we have grouped two categories—"Research, high" and "Doctoral/research"—together here for ease of presentation since they share a number of crucial characteristics. It should be noted that the National Center was not able to categorize all nonprofit higher education institutions so the totals reported on do not correspond to the totals in other tables in this section. See: *Digest of Education Statistics, 2009*, Tables 234 and 356.

8. *Digest of Education Statistics, 1990*, 12, Table 3; and 228, Table 216.

9. Estimates of the change in revenues of different components of the higher education universe are complicated by different accounting conventions between public, nonprofit, and for-profit institutions. For example, data on public institutions is mostly available on a "Current Fund" basis, whereas private nonprofit higher education data are reported on a "Total Revenue" basis. Changes in data-gathering methods also complicate time-series analyses. Thus, for example, official education statistics did not begin breaking out for-profit higher education from nonprofit until the mid-1990s when, as we will see below, for-profit higher education began emerging as a significant force. Data availability issues thus arise in making comparisons. In Figure 7.7, public revenue is reported on a current fund basis and nonprofit on a total revenue basis. Both of these cover the period 1996/97 through 2006/07. For-profit data are reported on a total revenue basis but only for the period 1997/98 through 2006/07. The for-profit figures therefore likely understate the disparity between nonprofit and for-profit revenue growth rates. Data on public institutions for 1996/97 derived from the *Digest of Education Statistics, 2005*, Table 329; data for 2006/07 from the *Digest of Education Statistics, 2009*, Table 352. Data on private nonprofit institutions for 1996/97 derived from the *Digest of Education Statistics, 2005*, Table 329; those for 2006/07 from the *Digest of Education Statistics, 2009*, Table 355. Data on private for-profit institutions for 1996/97 derived from the *Digest of Education Statistics, 2003*, Table 342; those for 2006/07 from the *Digest of Education Statistics, 2009*, Table 358.

10. 2006/07 data from: *Digest of Education Statistics, 2009*, Table 356; 1995/96 data from: *Digest of Education Statistics, 1999*, Table 336. Adjusted for inflation using the services component of personal consumption expenditures.

11. *Digest of Education Statistics, 2009*, Tables 187, 265, 5. As just one example of the growth of these institutions, Kaplan University, now a subsidiary of The Washington Post Company, boosted its enrollment from 62,600 students in 2006 to 110,020 in 2009. See The Washington Post Company Annual Report, 2007 and 2009.

12. *Digest of Education Statistics, 2009*, Tables 62, 27, 35.

13. *Digest of Education Statistics, 2009*, Tables 3, 62. This source provides the only data on private elementary and secondary education available. However, no breakdown is provided between nonprofit and for-profit private elementary and secondary education institutions. Since such a breakdown is provided in the case of higher education, we assume that the number of for-profit institutions at this level is fairly limited and cannot be easily detected in the sample surveys that provide the source data for the Digest. Accordingly, we treat the "private" data reported in the *Digest* as a good approximation of the nonprofit presence in this field. Readers should be aware that this may overstate the nonprofit role somewhat, however.

14. *Digest of Education Statistics, 2009*, Tables 62 and 34.

15. Data are not available on the religious orientation of all private schools. Therefore, the percentages reported here are computed against the 28,800 schools for which such data are available and may not apply to the somewhat larger population of all nonprofit elementary and secondary schools. *Digest of Education Statistics, 2009*, Table 59.

16. *Digest of Education Statistics, 2009*, Table 61.

17. *Digest of Education Statistics, 2009*, Table 59.

18. See: Center for Education Reform, *Annual Survey of Charter Schools 2008* (Washington, DC: Center for Education Reform, 2008).

19. "Fixing D.C.'s Schools: The Charter Experiment," *A Washington Post Investigation*. Available at www.washingtonpost.com/wp-srv/metro/specials/charter/.

20. *Digest of Education Statistics, 2009*, Table 59.

21. Included within this industry are organizations classified under four North American Industrial Classification System codes: 6114—Business schools and computer and management training; 6115—Technical and trade schools; 6116—Other schools and instruction; and 6117--Educational support services. Unless otherwise noted, data reported here were drawn from the U.S. Census Bureau, *Economic Census,* 2007, Sector 61: EC0761A1: Educational Services: Geographic Area Series, Summary Statistics: 2007 (Released 6/29/2010).

22. Data in this section from U.S. Census Bureau, *Economic Census,* 2007, Sector 61: EC0761A1: Educational Services: Geographic Area Series, Summary Statistics: 2007 (Released 6/29/2010).

23. GDP amounts taken from the Bureau of Economic Analysis, Economic Accounts, "Current-dollar and 'Real' GDP levels 1929–2008." Available at www.bea.gov/national/index.htm#gdp. Inflation adjustment based on services component of Personal Consumption Expenditures.

24. Data on private libraries from U.S. Census Bureau, *Economic Census,* 2007: Sector 51: EC0751A1: Information: Geographic Area Series: Summary Statistics for the United States, States, Metro and Micro Areas (NAICS 51912); data on public libraries from Public Library Survey, FY2008, Public Library Data Files, Institute of Museum and Library Services.

25. The 2007 Census provides no breakdown of these libraries between nonprofit and for-profit. However, the 1992 Census of Service Industries identified 232 private for-profit libraries in existence as of that date. Assuming that the same proportion holds, this would translate into 350 for-profit libraries as of 2007. See: U.S. Bureau of the Census, *Census of Service Industries*, 1992, Table 1a and 1b. SIC code 823 includes "establishments primarily engaged in providing library services, including the circulation of books and other materials for reading, study, and reference."

8

Social Services

For all their complexity, the fields of health and education are still generally comprehensible to most people. Although there may be uncertainties over the precise definition of an "outpatient clinic," there are few people who do not have some clear idea of what a hospital or a university is.

Not so with the third major field of nonprofit activity: social services. The term itself is ambiguous, and the range of organizations typically grouped under it exceedingly diverse.

Yet, more people probably have contact with nonprofit social service agencies than with any other type, if for no other reason than that they are so numerous. According to the U.S. Census Bureau, 106,000 nonprofit social service organizations were functioning in the United States as of 2007, and this does not include the thousands of small self-help and mutual organizations.[1] As previous chapters have shown, this compares with 3,008 nonprofit hospitals, 1,700 nonprofit colleges and universities, and about 37,000 nonprofit nursing homes.

What do these organizations do? What is the "social services" field, and what role do nonprofit organizations play in it? How has this role changed in recent years? This chapter seeks to answer these questions.

Overview: The Social Service Field

DEFINITION

Although the term "social services" is somewhat amorphous, the basic concept behind it is fairly straightforward. Social services are essentially forms of assistance, other than outright cash aid, that help individuals and families to function in the face of social, economic, or physical problems or needs. Included are day care services, adoption assistance, family counseling, residential care for the physically or mentally handicapped, vocational rehabilitation, disaster assistance, refugee assistance, emergency food assistance, provision of housing and shelter, substance abuse treatment, and many more.[2]

OVERALL SCALE

Although the social services field has expanded considerably since the 1960s—the product of some major economic and demographic changes as well as the launching of a number of new government programs—the scale

FIGURE 8.1: Spending on Social Services versus Health and Education, 2007

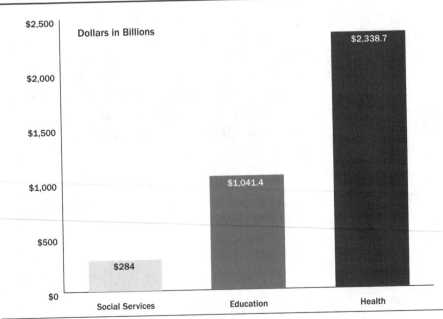

Source: See Chapter 8, endnote 3.

of this field still lags far behind that of either health or education. Thus, compared to the $2.3 trillion in spending on health and the $1.0 trillion in spending on education identified in previous chapters, total social service spending barely comes to $284 billion, or about one-eighth the scale of health spending and one-fourth the scale of education spending (see Figure 8.1).[3]

SOURCES OF SOCIAL SERVICE SPENDING

As shown in Figure 8.2, the largest single source of social service spending is government. As of 2007, this source accounted for an estimated 51 percent of total social service spending in the United States. The second-largest source of such spending is fees and charges, which accounted for 38 percent of the total as of 2007. By contrast, private giving from all sources—individuals, foundations, and corporations—accounted for a considerably smaller 11 percent of social service spending.

The substantial role that fees and service charges play in the financing of social services reflects the changing character of the social service market in recent years. The aging of the population, the increased labor force participation of women, and the proliferation of drug abuse and related forms of addiction have increased the demand for residential care, counseling, day care, and related social services on the part of populations that can pay for

FIGURE 8.2: Sources of Social Services Spending, 2007

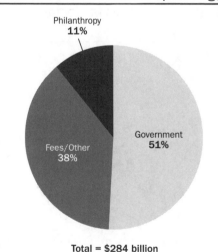

Total = $284 billion

Source: See Chapter 8, endnote 3.

such services, either directly or through expanded health insurance programs.[4] Also at work has been some constraint on the growth of government social service spending, though, as we will see, social service providers have found ways to tap into health care spending to sustain and grow their public-sector support. Meantime, philanthropy has remained a junior partner in the financing of this most basic of "charitable" services.

Nonprofit, Government, and For-Profit Roles

Despite the dominant role of fees and government support in the funding of social services, private, nonprofit organizations still play the dominant role in the actual delivery of such services. At the same time, government agencies and for-profit companies also play important—and, in the case of for-profit companies, growing—roles.

THE NONPROFIT ROLE

Overall Scale. As noted earlier, there were approximately 106,000 nonprofit organizations providing social services in the United States as of the late 2000s.[5] Of these, the most numerous were providers of individual and family services (37 percent), residential care for special populations (25 percent), and child day care (20 percent), as shown in Figure 8.3. The balance are providers of emergency food and community housing (12 percent) and vocational rehabilitation (6 percent).[6]

FIGURE 8.3: Distribution of Nonprofit Social Service Agencies, by Subfield, 2007

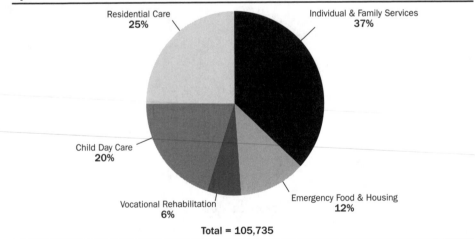

Residential Care
25%

Individual & Family Services
37%

Child Day Care
20%

Vocational Rehabilitation
6%

Emergency Food & Housing
12%

Total = 105,735

Source: See Chapter 8, endnote 5.

Despite the dominant role of fees and government support in funding social services, private nonprofit organizations play the dominant role in delivering such services.

These 106,000 organizations employ an estimated 2.1 million employees in all, and this does not take account of the more than one million full-time-equivalent volunteer workers that these organizations also enlist in their work. Individual and family services agencies also rank highest in terms of employment, with 38 percent of nonprofit social service paid workers and a comparable share of revenues. Residential care facilities and day care centers are next-largest, with 26 percent and 15 percent of nonprofit social service employment, respectively. Even the 5 percent of all nonprofit social service organization employees working for the 14,000 nonprofit housing, emergency shelter, and nutrition agencies translates into a sizable workforce of 165,000 people, however.[7]

As Figure 8.4 shows, these nonprofit agencies play a very significant role in the provision of social services in the United States. In particular, they account for:

FIGURE 8.4: Nonprofit versus For-Profit Roles in Social Services, 2007

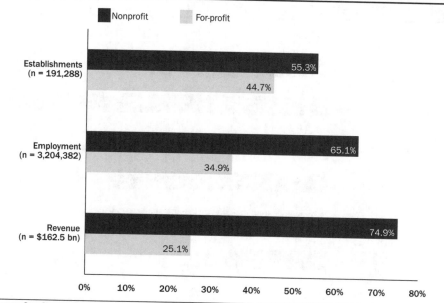

- 55 percent of the private social service agencies;

- 65 percent of all private social service employment; and

- 75 percent of all private social service revenue.

Governments at federal, state, and local levels also play important roles in the social services field, but mostly as sources of funding rather than direct providers of services. Even with the estimated 550,000 government social welfare workers included, therefore, nonprofits still command a substantial 56 percent share of employment in this field.[8]

Variations by Subfield. Although nonprofit organizations play a major role in all facets of the social service field, there are significant variations among the subfields. As shown in Figure 8.5, nonprofit organizations play a particularly dominant role in the provision of emergency food and shelter, where they represent 95 percent of the active entities even without considering the numerous informal religious and other groups providing these services. Nonprofits also account for a sizable three-fourths of the agencies providing vocational rehabilitation services. A sizable nonprofit role is also evident in the large individual and family services and residential care fields, though here for-profits have established an important foothold in recent years, as we will see more fully below. Finally, nonprofits play a far less

FIGURE 8.5: Nonprofit versus For-Profit Share of Private Social Service Organizations, by Subfield, 2007

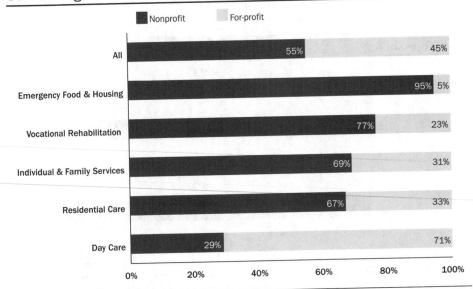

Source: U.S. Census Bureau, *Economic Census*, 2007.

substantial role in the day care field, where over 70 percent of the providers are for-profit firms, often single proprietorships.

This picture of substantial nonprofit involvement is even more pronounced in financial terms because nonprofit providers tend to be larger than their for-profit counterparts. Thus, as of 2007, the nonprofit share of private social service agency revenue stood at:

- 98 percent in the case of emergency food and housing organizations;

- 84 percent in the case of vocational rehabilitation agencies;

- 81 percent in the case of individual and family services agencies;

- 75 percent in the case of residential care; and

- 40 percent in the case of day care.

In short, the nonprofit sector plays an immense role in the provision of social services.

Social service spending lags far behind that of either health or education.

Self-Help, Mutual Assistance, and Faith-Based Charity. In addition to the more formal organizations described above, a host of informal organizations are also active in the social services field, although the scope of this activity is more difficult to gauge. One aspect of this is the work of *self-help groups.* The more structured of these, such as Alcoholics Anonymous, are probably captured in the statistics presented above, but others are much more informal and unstructured, consisting of individuals and families who share a common experience, such as loss of a child or the presence of a physical or emotional disability, and who meet together for mutual support. The National Institute of Mental Health identifies three distinct types of such groups: first, groups for people with a physical or mental illness; second, recovery groups for people with problems such as alcoholism, drug addiction, or the like; and third, groups for certain minorities, such as the handicapped. As many as half a million such groups are estimated to exist in the United States; web sites providing listings of such groups and instructions on how to form and operate them have proliferated.[9]

In addition to the self-help groups there are numerous other organized, but largely informal, forms of social assistance that also are unlikely to be captured in the official data. According to one recent study, for example, as many as 42 percent of congregations somehow help to feed the hungry, 16 percent distribute clothing, 12 percent serve the homeless, and 11 percent have staff devoting at least quarter time to social service activities.[10] More generally, grassroots organizations, a number of them religiously affiliated or faith-based, have surfaced in numerous communities across the country to cope with problems of homelessness, hunger, and inadequate job preparation.[11] While many of these are included in the data cited above, others are not. According to one recent survey, for example, 27 percent of a sample of small faith-based human service organizations in Illinois, and 13 percent of other human service agencies, were not included in the Internal Revenue Service listings that form the base for much of our statistical knowledge of the nonprofit sector.[12] In short, the nonprofit contribution to social service provision extends well beyond the contours of the formal agencies described above.

For-profit firms have increasingly surfaced as major providers of social services.

GOVERNMENT AGENCIES

Although nonprofit organizations are the major providers of social services, government agencies also play a significant role in this field. As we have seen, government is a major financier of social services. But government agencies also help to deliver certain kinds of social services, even though most government-funded services are delivered by others. Thus, as we have seen, some 500,000 government employees are engaged in various "public welfare" activities. Most of these manage the cash assistance programs (for example, Temporary Assistance to Needy Families, formerly Aid to Families with Dependent Children) at the local level, provide "casework" to client families, and oversee contractual arrangements with private providers to deliver social services to target populations. Public employees also manage the foster care system that places children without suitable homes in foster care settings. Altogether, about 15 percent of the employees in the social service/public welfare field work for government agencies—a significant proportion, but well below what the level of public spending in this field might suggest, since so much of the public-sector support goes to support the provision of services by nonprofit (and for-profit) organizations.

FOR-PROFIT PROVIDERS

As already noted, for-profit firms have increasingly surfaced as major providers of social services. Such firms accounted for nearly half of all social service agencies and 24 percent of all social service employment as of 2007, as Figure 8.4 showed.

For-profit providers are concentrated in particular segments of the social service field, and in these segments their presence is even larger. Thus, 60 percent of for-profit social service agencies are day care centers, and in this field for-profits constitute over 70 percent of the private providers, as Figure 8.5 showed. Nonprofits play a smaller role in the field of individual and family services, though as we shall see they have recently gained important ground in this field as well.

A relatively new development in the social service arena has been a type of entity called a "social enterprise," which mixes nonprofit and for-profit operations.

SOCIAL ENTERPRISES

Finally, a relatively new development in the social service arena has been the appearance of a new type of entity called a "social enterprise," which mixes nonprofit and for-profit operations in a particularly integrated way. To be sure, as already noted, receipt of income from fees-for-service is a long-established feature of nonprofit operations. In fact, fees constitute over half of overall nonprofit income and 45 percent of the income of nonprofit social service organizations. In addition, there is a long history of nonprofit involvement in so-called unrelated business activities, that is, businesses designed to generate income to help support the organizations' mission-related functions.

What differentiates "social enterprises" from these other types of fee-related nonprofit operations is that they utilize market-oriented businesses not simply to generate income but to carry out their charitable missions. For example, rather than training disadvantaged individuals and sending them out cold into the private labor market, some nonprofit training agencies have begun creating their own small business ventures to help reintegrate their disadvantaged or structurally unemployed clientele into the mainstream economy. The venture is not a sideline or a mere revenue source but an integral component of the agency's program, directly related to the pursuit of its mission. Thus, Asian Neighborhood Design employs low-income individuals in a furniture manufacturing business; Barrios Unidos employs Latino youth in a screen printing business; and Community Vocational Enterprises employs people with psychiatric disabilities in janitorial, food service, clerical, and messenger service businesses—all with the goal of using the business to teach job skills and promote self-reliance.[13]

The emergence of these hybrid nonprofit/for-profit entities has led to considerable experimentation with new organizational forms. While many of the resulting entities remain as nonprofits, some have taken a for-profit form, either as free-standing entities or as subsidiaries of nonprofits. More recently, some states have established laws creating an entire new legal category under which such organizations can incorporate as "low-profit limited liability" companies, or "L3Cs." This designation is intended to facilitate access to so-called "program-related investments" by foundations. Such investments take the form of loans or other types of financial transactions on which some type of return is expected.[14]

FIGURE 8.6: Sources of Nonprofit Social Service Organization Revenue, 2007

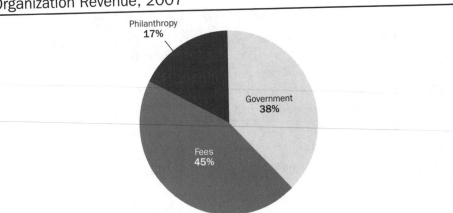

Philanthropy
17%

Government
38%

Fees
45%

Source: Internal Revenue Service microdata files, 2007; and U.S. Census Bureau, *Economic Census*, 2007; see Chapter 3, endnote 18.

Where Do Nonprofit Social Service Agencies Get Their Revenues?

Gaining a clear picture of the revenue base of nonprofit social service organizations is complicated by the considerable diversity of this set of organizations. Overall, as Figure 8.6 shows, the major source of nonprofit social service income is *fees and charges*. Such commercial income accounts for a substantial 45 percent of total nonprofit social service organization income. This is due in important part, however, to the inclusion within the social services field of low-income housing and community development organizations, some of which manage low-income housing projects or other economic development projects on which they collect rent or other income. As Table 8.1 shows, this subset of nonprofit social service organizations has a quite different revenue structure from the remaining social assistance organizations. In particular, close to 60 percent of their revenue comes from fees and charges compared to 41 percent for the remaining social assistance organizations. Even so, at 41 percent, fees constitute an important component of the revenue of these other social service organizations as well.[15] This reflects the growth in demand for social services throughout the population, the significant fee support for day care services, and the eligibility of many other types of social services, such as drug addiction treatment, for reimbursement under private health insurance plans.

TABLE 8.1: Revenue Sources of Nonprofit Social Service Organizations, by Major Subfields, 2007

Subfield	Share of Total Revenue (%)			
	Government	Fees	Philanthropy	Total
Housing, jobs	25%	59%	16%	100%
Social assistance	42%	41%	17%	100%
Total social services	**38%**	**45%**	**17%**	**100%**

Source: See Figure 8.6.

The second-largest source of overall nonprofit social service organization income, and the largest one for all but the housing and community development organizations, is *government*, as Figure 8.6 and Table 8.1 also show. Almost 38 percent of overall nonprofit social service agency income, and 42 percent for all but the housing and community development organizations, comes from government sources. This reflects the success that nonprofit social service providers have had in accessing the expanding pool of government health spending, particularly through the federal-state Medicaid program, which now supports care for the developmentally disabled and other special-needs groups of the population as well as other social services. Reflecting this, public-sector support is especially significant to the residential care and family and children's service agencies.

Private charitable contributions from individuals, foundations, and corporations account for a considerably smaller 17 percent of nonprofit social-service-organization income. This is well above the 10 percent share that private giving represents of total nonprofit service and expressive organization revenue as reported in Chapter 3, but it is still well below what many people believe about the financing of these nonprofit human service organizations.

Little reliable information is available about the sources of for-profit social service agency revenue. Almost certainly, fees and service charges comprise a significant portion. Beyond this, for-profit providers have increasingly entered the competition for government support. The welfare reform legislation of 1996, for example, created new demands for work-readiness and related social service assistance that for-profit firms have increasingly sought to meet.

Recent Trends

The emergence of a sizable for-profit presence in the social services field is but a part of a broader set of changes that has affected this field over the recent past. Broadly speaking, these changes can be grouped under three major headings: overall growth, "medicalization," and "marketization."

OVERALL NONPROFIT GROWTH

In the first place, nonprofit social services has been a growth industry. Thus, while the overall U.S. economy as measured by gross domestic product grew by 32 percent after adjusting for inflation between 1997 and 2007, the revenues of nonprofit social service organizations grew by 51 percent, as shown in Figure 8.7. Significant growth has also occurred in nonprofit employment. Between 1977 and 1997, for example, employment in nonprofit social service organizations more than doubled, from 676,000 employees to 1.6 million. The growth rate moderated slightly in the subsequent decade, in part due to the limited growth in the vocational rehabilitation field. Nevertheless, nonprofit social service organizations added 400,000 new workers between 1997 and 2007, an increase of

29 percent. As shown in Figure 8.7, employment growth was most robust among housing and emergency feeding organizations, which boosted their employment by 57 percent between 1997 and 2007. The major drivers of nonprofit social service employment growth, however, in absolute, if not always in percentage, terms were residential care and family service agencies, the former boosting employment by nearly 50 percent and accounting for 38 percent of all nonprofit social service employment growth in the decade, and the latter boosting employment by 24 percent and accounting for one-third of the growth.[16]

MEDICALIZATION

What makes this growth especially intriguing is that it occurred during a period of relative constraint in basic welfare and social service spending. As previewed in Chapter 5, government spending on welfare and social services in the United States barely kept pace with inflation between 1997 and 2007, rising only 8 percent in inflation-adjusted terms over the entire decade. Yet

FIGURE 8.7: Changes in Nonprofit Social Service Organization Revenues and Employment, by Field, 1997–2007

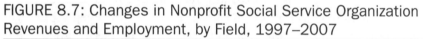

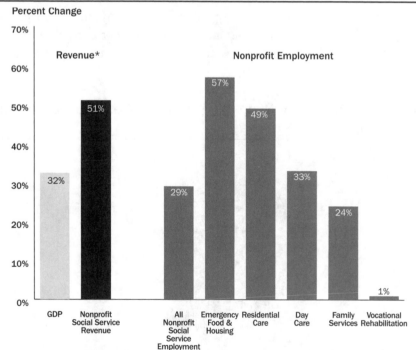

*Inflation-adjusted.
Source: See Chapter 8, endnote 16.

nonprofit receipts from government soared 57 percent over this period. Indeed, as Figure 8.8 shows, government funding alone accounted for over 40 percent of the growth that nonprofit social service agencies achieved during this period, and, with the housing and community development organizations excluded, this figure reached 51 percent.[17]

How was this possible? How could nonprofits boost their support from government so robustly at a time of limited growth of government social welfare spending?

The answer to this apparent puzzle, it seems, lies in the significant "medicalization" of social service finance that occurred during this period. During the initial burst of government support for social service activities in the 1960s and 1970s, government assistance took the form of discretionary grants and contracts. But when fiscal pressures and ideological shifts put a squeeze on these discretionary social service grant and contract programs, nonprofit social service providers, and advocacy organizations representing various disadvantaged populations, sought an alternative source of revenue to address pressing public needs. In particular, they turned to the still steadily growing entitlement programs in the health field, chiefly Medicare and Medicaid, and rebranded as forms of health care many traditional social service programs, such as care for the developmentally disabled, addiction prevention and recovery services, hospice care, and many more. Indeed, between 1988 and 1992, fifty different amendments were added to the Medicaid program to expand its coverage of both populations and forms

FIGURE 8.8: Sources of Nonprofit Social Service Revenue Growth, 1997–2007

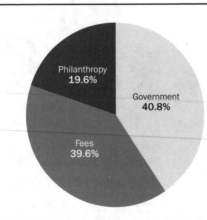

Philanthropy
19.6%

Government
40.8%

Fees
39.6%

Source: See Chapter 8, endnote 17.

of care. In short order, nonprofit social service providers learned how to navigate these new funding streams and to access them on behalf of their clients and patrons.

Also at work in boosting nonprofit social service organization revenue from government during this period of constrained overall government welfare and social service revenue growth, however, was the welfare reform law enacted in 1996.[18] This law set a cap on federal payments to states under the previous Aid to Families with Dependent Children (AFDC) Program and mandated that recipients of such welfare aid—mostly single mothers with young children—transition into jobs within five years. At the same time, the law authorized the states to utilize the resources available through this program not simply to make income-assistance payments to recipients, but also to invest in a variety of supportive services that could help recipients make this transition from welfare to work. When economic conditions fortuitously reduced the welfare rolls, states found themselves flush with resources with which to invest in such supportive services, and many of them turned to nonprofit social service organizations to supply them. As a consequence, without a substantial increase in the amount of resources flowing into welfare spending, the amount of government support made available to nonprofit social service programs expanded substantially thanks to a redefinition of many social services as health services, boosting nonprofit social service organization income from government in the process.

Government funding was not the only driver of nonprofit social service income growth during this recent period. Also notable was the significant rise in philanthropic support. Indeed, private philanthropy was the fastest-growing source of nonprofit social service organization income between 1997 and 2007, rising by 64 percent after adjusting for income, well above the 51 percent increase in overall nonprofit social service organization income. Still, because it started from a relatively small base, philanthropy accounted for only about 20 percent of the nonprofit growth in this field, enough to boost philanthropy from 14 to 17 percent of total nonprofit social service revenue, but not enough to outdistance government or fees.

MARKETIZATION

Finally, a third broad feature of the recent evolution of nonprofit involvement in the social service field has been the further significant penetration of market relationships into this field.[19] This penetration has manifested itself in two principal ways: first, in the growth of fee income as

...e of nonprofit revenue; and second, in the growing competition from ...or-profit providers.

Increased Reliance on Fee Income. The expansion of fee income as a revenue source for nonprofit social service providers occurred most dramatically during the 1980s. This expansion was fueled in part by the significant fiscal constraint imposed on the expansion of government social service funding during the Carter and Reagan administrations, and in part by economic and demographic shifts such as the aging of the population and the massive entry of women into the labor force, which brought middle-class patrons into the market for such social services as day care and elder care. Between 1977 and 1996, while government social service spending declined by 15 percent and private philanthropy grew by a relatively modest 33 percent, nonprofit income from fees and charges jumped by 600 percent after adjusting for inflation. As a consequence, fees went from 13 percent of nonprofit social service revenue in 1977 to 43 percent in 1996.

Philanthropy was the fastest growing source of support to nonprofit social service organizations between 1997 and 2007, but still accounted for only 20 percent of their growth.

This torrid growth of fee income moderated considerably in the more recent 1997–2007 period, in part because the base against which the change was measured had grown so substantially. During this decade, nonprofit social service organization fee income thus expanded by another 41 percent after adjusting for inflation, roughly the same rate as the increase in government support. This was due in important part, however, to an 80 percent increase in the fee income of housing and community development organizations during this period. Among the social assistance organizations, fee income grew by a more modest 30 percent during this period, so that its share of the total revenue of these organizations slipped somewhat, from roughly 48 percent of the total in 1997 to 41 percent in 2007.[20]

For-Profit Competition. The transformation of the market for social services not only helped nonprofit providers expand their fee income, it also helped attract for-profit providers into the social service field. Already by 1977 for-profit firms were well established in the day care field, controlling

57 percent of the establishments and 46 percent of the employees. But during the subsequent 20 years, for-profits expanded their presence in the day care arena and moved into other social service fields as well. Thus, starting with 21 percent of all social service jobs as of 1977, for-profits captured 35 percent of the growth in social service jobs between 1977 and 1997. In some fields, moreover, the transformation of the institutional landscape was even more pronounced. Thus, for-profits captured 69 percent of the new day care jobs and 54 percent of the residential care jobs created between 1977 and 1997, establishing themselves as the major providers of day care and significant providers of residential care.[21]

As reflected in Figure 8.9, this expansion of the for-profit presence in the social service arena has continued in more recent years as well, fueled by the same factors that have allowed nonprofits to grow. Indeed, thanks to their superior access to private investment capital, for-profits were able to add slightly more jobs than nonprofits even though starting from a smaller base (498,000 compared to 471,000 for nonprofits). As a result, while nonprofit social service employment grew by nearly 30 percent between 1997 and 2007, for-profit social service employment grew by 80 percent. Put somewhat differently, with 28 percent of all private social service jobs as of 1997, for-profits captured 51 percent of social service job growth between 1997 and

FIGURE 8.9: For-Profit Share of Social Services Employment in 1997 and Employment Growth, 1997–2007

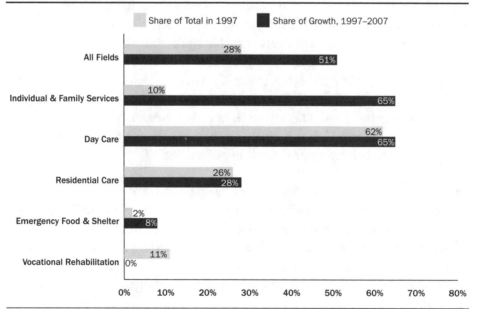

Source: U.S. Census Bureau, *Economic Census*, 1997, 2007.

2007. What is more, for-profits claimed a disproportionate share of job growth compared to their share of employment at the start of the period in every field except for vocational rehabilitation, where nonprofit job growth was also quite limited. Especially striking were the gains that for-profits made in the field of individual and family services, long a field in which nonprofits have held a dominant position.[22] While these changes may reflect in part the emergence of limited-profit "social enterprises" as discussed above, it seems more likely that the shift to consumer-side subsidies of the sort embodied in the Medicaid program has simply attracted more profit-maximizing for-profit businesses into the social services field.

Conclusion

The social services field is thus a true mixed economy, with active involvement on the part of nonprofit, government, and for-profit agencies; and extensive support from government revenues, fee income, and private philanthropy. Traditionally, however, private nonprofit agencies have dominated the *delivery* of social services, and, at least since the 1960s, government sources have dominated the *funding* of them. This partnership has formed the heart of the nation's human service delivery system for the past four and a half decades, and, at the local level, for numerous decades before that.

During the 1980s, however, a significant disruption occurred in this established pattern, as government support dwindled considerably. Social service agencies seem to have weathered this storm, but they did so largely by moving social services increasingly into the market. Growth also occurred in private giving in this field, but the really dynamic element appears to have been the growth of commercial forces. In the process, nonprofit organizations have come to rely far more heavily on fees and service charges of various sorts, and they have had to contend with increasingly vigorous for-profit competition in their traditional fields of action.

In more recent years, the nonprofit role has stabilized considerably, thanks in part to the access these organizations have gained to the more stable funding provided by several government entitlement programs, such as Medicaid and Medicare. What is more, the field has been enlivened by the appearance of a new breed of "social entrepreneurs" who are forming "social enterprises" establishing new combinations of commercial operations and social purposes. All of this has added an element of dynamism to the social services field, transforming it in sometimes confusing but always interesting ways.

ENDNOTES

1. Included here are establishments classified by the U.S. Census of Service Industries as providing: 1) individual and family services (NAICS Code 6241); 2) community food and housing/emergency and other relief services (NAICS Code 6242); 3) vocational rehabilitation services (NAICS Code 6243); 4) child day care services (NAICS Code 6244); 5) residential mental retardation/health and substance abuse facility (NAICS Code 6232); and 6) other residential care facilities (NAICS Code 6239). This definition is somewhat more limited than the one used in Chapter 3 above to depict the financial scale of the nonprofit service and expressive sector. This difference arises from the difference in classification systems used in the two different data systems. The Internal Revenue Service sorts organizations according to the National Taxonomy of Exempt Entities, which uses a broad "human service" category that includes, among other things, recreation and sports organizations and does not have a category for "social services." To bring this classification into better alignment with the North American Industrial Classification System (NAICS), which is the classification used in the Census Bureau's *Economic Census* and in most international economic data systems, and create something closer to the generally understood concept of "social services," we deleted "Recreation and Sports" from the NTEE "Human Services" category of organizations. Even so, the IRS Human Service grouping still includes a broader set of entities than are here embraced within the concept of "social service" organizations. Throughout this chapter, we rely heavily on the *Economic Census* data and hence the definition of this subsector that this source accommodates. Unless otherwise noted, data on nonprofit and for-profit social service organizations and employment reported here are drawn from: U.S. Bureau of the Census, *Economic Census,* 2007, Sector 62: EC0762I1: Health Care and Social Assistance: Industry Series: Preliminary Summary Statistics for the United States: 2007, accessed at: factfinder. census.gov/servlet/IBQTable?_bm=y&-fds_name=EC0700A1&-geo_id=&-_skip=100&-ds_ name=EC0762I1&-_lang=en.

2. Ralph M. Kramer, "Voluntary Agencies and the Personal Social Services," in *The Nonprofit Sector: A Research Handbook,* ed. Walter W. Powell. (New Haven: Yale University Press, 1987), 240–257.

3. The health data reported here are for 2008, the education data for 2007, and the social services data for 2007. No data series comparable to that for education and health spending is available on social services spending. The estimate of social service spending reported here was therefore constructed by adding together government spending on "welfare and social services" and "housing and community services" as reported in the U.S. Bureau of Economic Analysis, National Income and Product Accounts (NIPA), Table 3.16, Government Current Expenditures by Function, subtracting from this the government "welfare" payments reported on NIPA Table 3.12, and then adding to this estimated government funding of social services the philanthropic and fee support of nonprofit social service and housing agencies reported in Chapter 3, and the non-governmental support of for-profit social service agencies reported in the U.S. Census' *Economic Census,* 2007. An alternative estimate of overall spending on social services is available in NIPA Table 2.5.5 on Personal Consumption Expenditures. This estimate puts such spending at a considerably lower $134.1 billion, and this figure includes spending on religion. Some social service spending may be excluded from personal consumption expenditures, however. For the source of the health spending figure cited here, see Chapter 6, endnote 1; for the source of education spending data see Chapter 7, endnote 1.

4. For a discussion of these demographic developments and the implications they have for nonprofit service providers, see: Lester M. Salamon, "The Voluntary Sector and the Future of the Welfare State, *Nonprofit and Voluntary Sector Quarterly* 18:1 (Spring 1989): 16–39; and Chapter 12 below. *See also*: Atul Dighe, "Demographic and Technological Imperatives," in *The State of Nonprofit America*, 2nd ed., ed. Lester M. Salamon (Washington: Brookings Institution Press, 2012).

5. U.S. Census Bureau, *Economic Census* 2007, Sector 62: ECO76211: Health Care and Social Assistance. The Internal Revenue Service reports a considerably smaller 88,878 organizations in NTEE groupings we consider to be closest to "social services" (i.e., Groups I, J, K, L, M, O, and P). Only filers of the 990 Form are included in these IRS figures, however. The *Economic*

Census also excludes some organizations—i.e., agencies that are not registered with the Internal Revenue Service or that do not have at least one paid employee. This likely excludes numerous informal self-help groups and small, church-based service providers. The self-help groups may number as many as 500,000, though no solid data exist. With regard to small faith-based groups, recent research has suggested that 13 percent of the agencies in existence, and 27 percent of the religiously affiliated agencies in existence, do not show up on IRS listings. This would suggest at least 13,000 to 14,000 social service organizations beyond those reported in the available data sources. Kirsten Grønbjerg and Sheila Nelson, "Mapping Small Religious Nonprofit Organizations: An Illinois Profile," *Nonprofit and Voluntary Sector Quarterly*, 27:1 (March 1998): 20.

6. These divisions are naturally somewhat arbitrary because many organizations perform a variety of functions. This is particularly true of the generally large "individual and family service" agencies.

7. Revenue data based on U.S. Census Bureau, *Economic Census*, 2007. Health Care and Social Assistance. See endnote 1 above.

    The estimate of volunteer workers is derived from data available in the Bureau of Labor Statistics' Current Population Survey Volunteer Supplement for 2006, as reported in Kennard T. Wing, Thomas H. Pollack, and Amy Blackwood, *The Nonprofit Almanac: 2008* (Washington, DC: The Urban Institute Press, 2008), 97, 100.

8. Private establishment, employment, and revenue figures here are drawn from the *Economic Census* 2007, available at factfinder.census.gov/servlet/IBQTable?_bm=y&-geo_id=&-ds_name=EC0762I1&-_lang=en. In addition to the 191,288 recorded private social service agencies, most states and local jurisdictions also maintain social welfare agencies. The actual number of separate agencies is thus at least as large as the number of local jurisdictions, though this function is sometimes performed at the county level and sometimes at the city level. Estimating the number of government "establishments" in the social service field is thus exceedingly difficult. Accordingly, only the private agencies are reported here.

    Government employment data were derived from U.S. Census Bureau, *Federal Government Employment and Payroll Data, 2007*, available at: www2.census.gov/govs/apes/07fedfun.pdf; and US Census Bureau, *State and Local Government Employment and Payroll Data, 2007*, available at: www2.census.gov/govs/apes/07stus.txt. Government payments here represent the cost of government direct employment in the social services field. It was computed by subtracting from total social service spending the portion that is accounted for by nonprofit and for-profit private agencies. Additional government funds flow to the private agencies but the attempt here is to show the share of the activity that each sector generates.

9. U.S. Department of Health and Human Services, Public Health Service, *Surgeon General's Workshop on Self-Help and Public Health* (Washington, DC: U.S. Government Printing Office, 1988), 1. The New Jersey Self-Help Clearinghouse, for example, lists 6,750 self-help groups just in the state of New Jersey. See: www.NJgroups.org.

10. Based on data from the National Congregation Survey as reported in Marc Chaves, "Religious Congregations," in *The State of Nonprofit America,* 2nd ed., ed. Lester M. Salamon (Washington: Brookings Institution Press, 2012).

11. Robin Garr, *Reinvesting in America: The Grassroots Movements that Are Feeding the Hungry, Housing the Homeless, and Putting Americans Back to Work* (Reading, MA: Addison-Wesley, 1995); Carmen Sirianni and Lewis Friedland, *Civic Innovation in America: Community Empowerment, Public Policy, and the Movement for Civic Renewal* (Berkeley: University of California Press, 2001).

12. See Grønbjerg and Nelson, endnote 5 above.

13. Dennis R. Young and Lester M. Salamon, "Commercialization, Social Ventures, and For-Profit Competition," in *The State of Nonprofit America,* ed. Lester M. Salamon (Washington, DC: Brookings Institution Press, 2002), 432. Several other terms are in use to depict this phenomenon. Among them are "social-purpose enterprise," "social venture," and "community wealth enterprise."

Several of these terms apply to more general phenomena such as the generation of market-based revenue rather than the more limited definition being used here. For a discussion of the terminological variants in this relatively new arena of combined nonprofit/for-profit action, see: Matthew T. A. Nash, "Social Entrepreneurship and Social Enterprise," in *The Jossey-Bass Handbook of Nonprofit Leadership and Management,* ed. David O. Renz (San Francisco: Jossey-Bass, 2010), 262–298. For an international perspective on this phenomenon, see: Alex Nichols, ed., *Social Entrepreneurship: New Models of Sustainable Social Change* (Oxford, UK: Oxford University Press, 2006); and Marthe Nyssens, ed., *Social Enterprise: At the Crossroads of Market, Public Policies, and Civil Society* (London: Routledge, 2006).

14. For information on the L3C law in Vermont, the first state to adopt such a law, see: www.sec.state.vt.us/corps/dobiz/llc/llc_l3c.htm. Program-related investments were authorized by the Tax Act of 1969 to allow foundations to meet their "payout requirement," i.e., their obligation to distribute 5 percent of the value of their assets each year to support charitable activity, through forms other than outright grants. For further information, see: Christie I. Baxter, *Program-Related Investments: A Technical Manual for Foundations* (New York: John Wiley and Sons, 1997).

    For information on the growth of non-grant forms of social-sector support, see: Lester M. Salamon, *New Frontiers of Philanthropy* (San Francisco: Jossey-Bass, 2012).

15. For detail on the derivation of these revenue estimates, see endnote 18 in Chapter 3. The estimate of nonprofit social service revenue here is derived from Internal Revenue Service data files augmented by information on government voucher payments to social service providers secured from the 2007 Census Bureau *Economic Census.* This estimate is substantially higher than the one reported in the *Economic Census.* This may be due to differences in classification used in these two sources or differences in the cut-off point for reporting—one employee in the case of the *Economic Census* and $25,000 in revenue in the case of the IRS data. Because the IRS data source provides better detail on the sources of revenue we use that source to portray the revenue picture of nonprofit social service organizations here.

    For a useful discussion of recent innovation in the field of low-income housing, see: David Erickson, *The Housing Policy Revolution: Networks and Neighborhoods* (Washington, DC: Urban Institute Press, 2009).

16. GDP figures from U.S. Council of Economic Advisors, *Economic Report of the President, 2009* (Washington, DC: U.S. Government Printing Office, 2009). Data on nonprofit revenues from Internal Revenue Service, Statistics of Income, Microdata File. Data on nonprofit employment from U.S. Census Bureau, *Economic Census* 2007. For detail on the derivation of the revenue estimate, see endnote 18 in Chapter 3.

17. Internal Revenue Service, Statistics of Income, Microdata File, 2007 accessed at: www.irs.gov/taxstats/charitablestats/article/0,,id=97176,00.html. For further detail see Chapter 3, endnote 18.

18. The welfare reform law transformed the Aid to Families with Dependent Children Program into the Temporary Assistance to Needy Families (TANF) Program.

19. For further detail on this phenomenon, see: Lester M. Salamon, "The Marketization of Welfare: Changing Nonprofit and For-Profit Roles in the American Welfare State," *Social Service Review,* 67:1 (March 1993): 17–39; Lester M. Salamon, *Partners in Public Service: Government-Nonprofit Relations in the Modern Welfare State* (Baltimore: Johns Hopkins University Press, 1995), Chapter 14, 220–242.

20. Based on data in Independent Sector, *America's Nonprofit Sector in Brief* (Washington, DC: Independent Sector, 1998); and U.S. Bureau of the Census, *Service Annual Survey 1996* (June 1998). See: Lester M. Salamon, *America's Nonprofit Sector: A Primer,* 2nd ed. (New York: The Foundation Center, 1999), 117. For derivation of 1997–2007 revenue shifts, see Chapter 5, endnote 30 above.

21. Salamon, *America's Nonprofit Sector: A Primer,* 2nd ed.

22. U.S. Bureau of the Census, *Economic Census,* 1997, 2007.

9

Arts, Culture, and Recreation

In addition to the role they play in the delivery of health, education, and welfare services, nonprofit organizations also play a major role in the artistic, cultural, and recreational life of the United States. This role can easily be overlooked, however, because although arts, culture, and recreation organizations make up 22 percent of all nonprofit organizations, most of them are small and the entire subsector accounts for only 3 percent of the nonprofit sector's total revenues.[1] In addition, nonprofits tend to be prominent in only a relatively small portion of the entire arts and recreation field. Yet the importance of the nonprofit sector in this field goes well beyond what these numbers might suggest. Indeed, most of the serious cultural and artistic activity of the nation is organized by nonprofit organizations, as is a significant share of the nation's recreational activities.

Overview: Culture, Entertainment, and Recreation in the United States

To put the role of nonprofit organizations in the cultural and recreational field into context, it is useful to begin with an understanding of the considerable scope of the nation's cultural and recreational life. Americans devoted just over 9 percent of their total consumption expenditures, almost $920 billion, to recreational and cultural activities as of 2008, a figure that has been rising steadily over the past several decades and that is four times more than the amount that is spent on education.[2] Included here are purchases of recreational products such as books, videos, recordings, sporting goods, toys, and televisions, as well as expenses related to various recreational, sports, amusement, and cultural events and activities.

Most of the serious cultural and artistic activity of the nation is organized by nonprofit organizations.

Over 2.5 million people are employed in what the Economic Census identifies as the arts, entertainment, and recreation industry.[3] Of these, the vast majority (88 percent) work in the sports, recreation, and entertainment components of this industry, as shown in Figure 9.1. Only 12 percent—approximately 312,000 people—work in what might reasonably be termed the "arts and culture" component. Included here are roughly 182,000 people who work in the *performing arts*, such as theater, orchestral music, opera, and dance; and another roughly 130,000 who work in various cultural venues, such as museums, art galleries, historic sites, and zoos.

Nonprofit Role in Arts, Culture, and Recreation

OVERVIEW

Nonprofit organizations are involved in both the sports/recreation and the arts and culture segments of this culture and recreation field. Like the other types of providers, moreover, most nonprofit activity is in the sports and recreation segment. But it is in arts and culture where nonprofits play their most distinctive role.

FIGURE 9.1: Employment in Arts versus Recreation Services, 2007

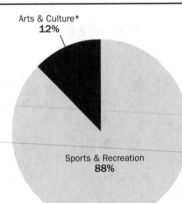

Arts & Culture*
12%

Sports & Recreation
88%

*Arts and culture includes private employment only.
Source: U.S. Bureau of the Census, *Economic Census*, 2007.

More specifically, of the 2.5 million people employed in the arts and recreation field, 23 percent, or just over 564,000 people, are employed in nonprofit organizations. Of the balance, 17 percent are employed by government agencies and 60 percent in for-profit organizations (see Figure 9.2)

As with the rest of the arts and recreation field, most (65 percent) of the 564,000 people employed in nonprofit organizations in this field are engaged in sports and recreation activities rather than arts and cultural ones, as shown in Figure 9.3. Included here are some 3,000 golf courses and country

FIGURE 9.2: Nonprofit versus For-Profit and Government Shares of Arts and Recreation Employment, 2007

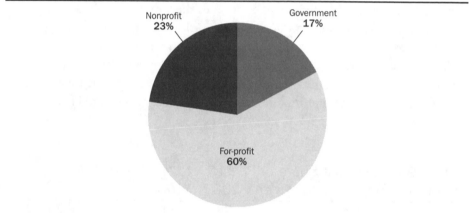

Source: See Chapter 9, endnote 2.

FIGURE 9.3: Employment in Nonprofit Arts and Culture versus Sports and Recreation Organizations, 2007

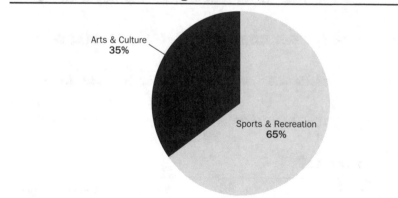

Source: U.S. Bureau of the Census, *Economic Census*, 2007.

clubs, 4,500 fitness and recreational centers, and approximately 3,700 other amusement and recreational facilities employing nearly 375,000 workers.

The remaining 35 percent of the nonprofit culture and recreation employment is in the arts and culture portion of this field. Included here are nearly 10,000 theaters, symphonies, opera companies, chamber music groups, dance groups, museums, art galleries, zoos, and botanical gardens that form the backbone of the nation's cultural life.

NONPROFIT VERSUS FOR-PROFIT AND GOVERNMENT ROLES

For-Profit Dominance in Sports and Recreation. While most nonprofit cultural and recreational organizations are in the sports and recreation field, they are far from the dominant force there. Rather, the for-profit sector plays a far more significant role than does the nonprofit sector in providing sports and recreational services, and the public sector plays a substantial role as well. Thus, of the private employment in sports and recreation, nonprofits account for only 21percent, as shown in Figure 9.4. With government parks and recreation employment included as well, the nonprofit share falls to 17 percent.

FIGURE 9.4: Nonprofit Share of Private Arts and Recreation Establishments and Employment, 2007

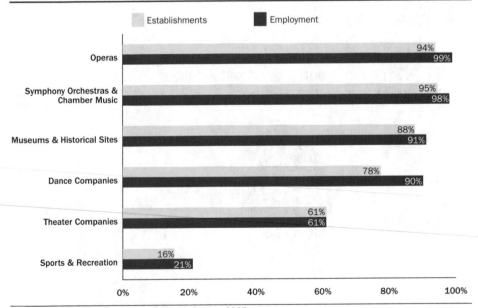

Source: U.S. Bureau of the Census, *Economic Census*, 2007.

These employment numbers can be deceptive, however, because nonprofit organizations mobilize a substantial army of volunteers for sports and recreational activity through Little Leagues, soccer leagues, county fairs, and similar organized community recreation activities. One estimate puts the number of volunteers working for nonprofit cultural and recreational organizations at 2.26 million people as of 2006. Translated into full-time-equivalent workers, this suggests another 280,000 workers mobilized by nonprofit organizations, most of them very likely employed in the recreational and sports component of this field.[4] In addition, another 243,000 people are employed in nonprofit social and fraternal membership clubs, which, though not included in the public-benefit portion of the nonprofit sector of principal concern to us here, nevertheless offer significant recreational activities. With the addition of these two additional components, the nonprofit portion of recreation and sports employment would stand at 33 percent.

Well over 90 percent of the country's symphony orchestras, chamber music groups, and operas are nonprofits.

Nonprofit Dominance in Arts and Culture. While nonprofit organizations play a significant role in sports and recreation, however, they are even more important in relative terms in the arts and culture portion of the arts and recreation field. Thus, as Figure 9.4 also shows:

- Nonprofits are especially prominent in the *performing arts*. Well over 90 percent of the country's symphony orchestras, chamber music groups, and operas are nonprofits, and they employ nearly all of the people working in these fields. Similarly, over 75 percent of all dance companies and over 60 percent of all theater companies are nonprofit, and these institutions employ 90 percent and 61 percent, respectively, of all those working in these two fields. Theater is the one cultural field where for-profits have a substantial presence, but even this can be misleading. For-profit live theatrical companies are prominent mainly in the major cultural centers such as New York. Outside of these centers, however, most theaters are nonprofit organizations. These nonprofit theaters provide a critical proving ground for new plays and approaches and help to ensure the survival of theater outside the major production centers. For-profit firms are dominant in other aspects of the music and entertainment field (for example, rock bands, entertainment groups, and the recording industry), but in the field of live classical music, the nonprofit sector holds virtually unrivaled sway. This situation differs markedly from that in Europe and elsewhere in the world, where government-sponsored symphonies and operas are more prevalent, though governments in many European countries have been moving to transform such institutions into nonprofits.[5]

- Nonprofits also dominate cultural venues, such as museums, zoos, and historical sites. Nearly 90 percent of the private establishments of this sort are nonprofits, and they account for 91 percent of the private employment at such venues. Municipal museums and zoos are also quite common, but many of these are nonprofit in form as well. Even with the true municipal institutions included, however, it seems likely that nonprofits remain by far the dominant form for this type of institution.[6]

In short, much of the cultural and artistic life of the country takes place in and through private, nonprofit organizations. The nonprofit sector has provided a convenient mechanism for organizing activity that enriches the cultural and intellectual life of the country but that may not be able meet a market test.

Revenue Sources

Not only do nonprofit organizations play a major role in the arts, culture, and recreation field, but private philanthropy also plays a larger part in financing this role than it does in any other. At the same time, even here private philanthropy is not the dominant source of support. Thus, as Figure 9.5 shows, private giving accounts for an estimated 39 percent of the income of nonprofit arts and recreation institutions. By comparison, fees, charges, and endowment earnings provide 52 percent of this income and government grants and contracts the remaining 9 percent.[7]

These aggregate data obscure some important variations in the funding base of different components of the overall nonprofit arts and recreation sector, however. In particular, as Figure 9.6 shows, nonprofit sports and recreation organizations have a noticeably different funding structure from their arts and culture cousins, with a considerably greater reliance on fees and earned income (62 percent versus 46 percent) and a correspondingly smaller reliance on private philanthropy (32 percent versus 44 percent). Within the arts and culture segment, moreover, cultural venues such as museums and zoos also differ somewhat in their funding from the performing arts institutions. In particular, the former have greater access to government support and thus rely somewhat less on both fees and philanthropy. Finally, even among the performing arts organizations there are some differences, with orchestras relying more heavily on philanthropy (51 percent) than either theater or dance companies (42 and 44 percent, respectively).

FIGURE 9.5: Revenue Sources of Nonprofit Arts, Sports, & Recreation Organizations, 2007

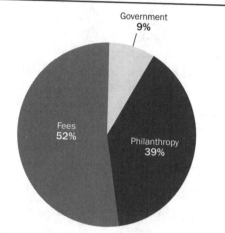

Source: Computed from Internal Revenue Service 990 Tabulations. See Chapter 3, endnote 18.

FIGURE 9.6: Revenues of Nonprofit Arts and Recreation Organizations, 2007, by Subfield and Source

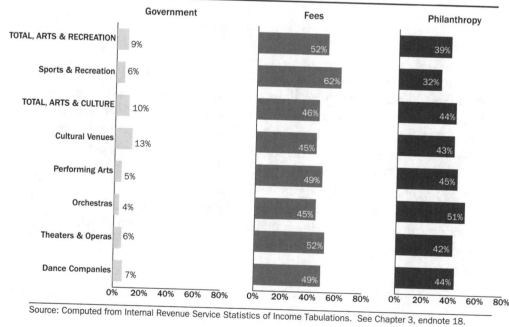

Source: Computed from Internal Revenue Service Statistics of Income Tabulations. See Chapter 3, endnote 18.

These data may overstate somewhat the role that private philanthropy plays in the funding of nonprofit arts and culture institutions, however. One reason for this is that the Internal Revenue Service's giving data include the value of donated artifacts and works of art as well as other capital items such as contributions to building funds or endowment at the full market value of these gifts, even though this support is rarely available for use to support the annual operations of the institutions. Supporting this view, the Census Bureau's *Economic Census* records roughly half as much private giving flowing to nonprofit arts and culture institutions in 2007 as reported in Internal Revenue Service data ($7.6 billion vs. $14.4 billion).[8] One likely explanation for this disparity may be that the Census Bureau takes more care to focus on sources of *annual operating income* as opposed to total gross revenue. Reflecting this, the share of total revenue attributed to private philanthropy in the *Economic Census* is consistently lower than that reported by the Internal Revenue Service for each of the components of the arts and recreation field.[9]

The nonprofit arts and recreation field has been in the midst of quite robust growth over the past several decades.

Recent Trends

OVERVIEW

The nonprofit arts and recreation field has been in the midst of quite robust growth over the past several decades, and that growth has continued, albeit at a slightly slower pace, in the most recent period for which data are available. Thus, as shown in Figure 9.7, the number of arts and recreation establishments increased by a little over a quarter in the ten years between 1997 and 2007, the employment jumped by nearly a third, and inflation-adjusted revenues rose by 35 percent, or roughly in line with the growth of the country's gross domestic product.[10] This compares with a 70 percent growth of establishments, a 90 percent growth of revenues, and a 100 percent spike in employment during the fifteen-year period between 1977 and 2002.[11]

FIGURE 9.7: Recent Trends in Nonprofit and For-Profit Arts and Recreation Organizations, 1997–2007

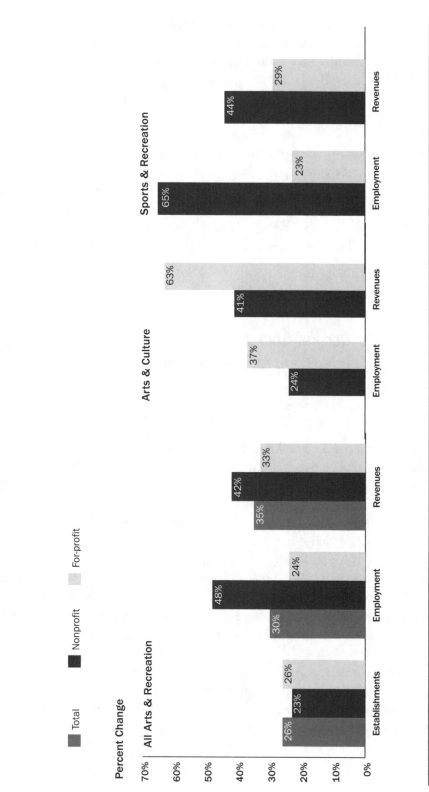

Source: U.S. Census Bureau, *Economic Census*, 1997 and 2007.

Interestingly, as Figure 9.7 also shows, nonprofit employment and revenue grew more robustly than for-profit employment and revenue in this field between 1997 and 2007. Thus, nonprofit arts and recreation employment jumped by nearly 50 percent compared to 24 percent for for-profit firms, and nonprofit revenues increased by 42 percent compared to 33 percent for for-profits.

Unlike the situation earlier, however, this nonprofit edge was confined to the sports and recreation portion of the arts and recreation field rather than the arts and culture one. Thus, nonprofit sports and recreation employment grew three times faster than did for-profit sports and recreation employment (65 percent versus 23 percent), and nonprofit sports and recreation revenues grew at a rate that was 50 percent higher than the for-profit one (44 percent versus 29 percent).

The decade from 1997 to 2007 was a period of real strain for the nonprofit arts sector.

By contrast, in the arts and culture field, these roles were reversed, as for-profit organizations boosted both their employment and revenues faster than did nonprofits during this recent period. Although this was largely due to the growth that for-profits achieved in two fields in which nonprofits have historically not been very active—dinner theaters and independent performers—it was also the case that nonprofits experienced actual employment declines in two fields, opera and orchestras, and rather tepid growth in a third, dance. The only performing arts field in which nonprofits experienced significant employment growth was live theater. And while nonprofit cultural venues gained substantial employment, their for-profit counterparts grew even more robustly (37 percent versus 24 percent).

In short, the decade from 1997 to 2007 was a period of some real strain for the arts component of the nonprofit arts and recreation sector. This suggests that nonprofit cultural and arts institutions were already struggling before the severe recession that began in 2008 made its impact felt.

SOURCES OF NONPROFIT GROWTH

The vulnerability of the nonprofit arts and recreation sector comes into even sharper focus when we examine recent developments in the financing of this set of institutions. To put these developments into context, however, it is useful to examine them against the backdrop of prior trends.

Much like social services, nonprofit arts and culture in the United States received a significant boost in the 1960s from a combination of government and foundation support. In the early part of the period, government support, coupled with foundation initiative, played an important catalytic role in achieving a renaissance of sorts in nonprofit arts. A dramatic expansion of nonprofit theater, for example, grew out of a program initially developed at the Ford Foundation in the early 1960s and subsequently funded in important part by the National Endowment for the Arts (NEA). The goal of this initiative was nothing less than the creation of a nationwide network of high-quality professional theaters that could make live theatrical productions accessible to a broad audience of viewers in communities across the country. "The result," as one recent study reports, "was a remarkable era of institution building, which lasted some 30 years. What had originally been a handful of widely scattered regional theatres became, by the 1994–95 season, a network of hundreds of theatres located throughout the country."[12]

> *During the 1990s, with government support stalled and private giving slowing, nonprofit arts and culture institutions turned extensively to fees and other earned income.*

The NEA and its affiliated state agencies also played a pivotal role in the growth of other types of artistic institutions, both through the direct assistance they provided and through the stimulus they created for local government and private charitable support. As one observer has put it, "The NEA changed the arts environment completely. It was the major catalyst in decentralizing the arts."[13]

However, while government seems to have played a critical role in stimulating the growth of nonprofit arts and cultural institutions in the 1960s and 1970s, that role came under fire during the 1980s as a product of conservative fiscal and social policies. Thus, government support for the arts barely kept pace with inflation between 1982 and 1992. Instead, nonprofit arts organizations turned extensively to private charitable support. Such support accounted for 54 percent of the not inconsiderable growth in nonprofit arts organization income between 1982 and 1992, outpacing even earned income, which accounted for 45 percent of the growth.[14]

During the 1990s, a somewhat different dynamic seems to have occurred. With government support still stalled and the growth of private giving slowing considerably, nonprofit arts and culture institutions turned extensively to fees and other earned income. Close to half of all the growth in nonprofit arts organization income came from this source between 1992 and 1996. For some components of the arts and culture subsector, moreover, the share was considerably higher than this. Thus, for example, 70 percent of the growth in income of a cross-section of nonprofit theaters between 1991 and 1995 came from earned income. By contrast, government revenue actually declined and private giving contributed 30 percent of the growth.[15] Behind these numbers lie not only increases in ticket prices for nonprofit cultural events, but also a vast array of other semi-commercial ventures, from bookings of Broadway plays to the creation of for-profit companies engaged in real estate development and marketing of museum reproductions.[16]

FIGURE 9.8: Sources of Nonprofit Arts and Recreation Organization Revenue Growth, 1997–2007, by Source

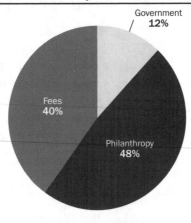

Government
12%

Fees
40%

Philanthropy
48%

Total = $10.5 billion

Source: Internal Revenue Service Statistics of Income Tabulations. See Chapter 3, endnote 18.

During the most recent period, from 1997 to 2007, this growth of reliance on fees and charges by nonprofit cultural and recreation institutions seems to have encountered some resistance. Thus, while overall nonprofit cultural and recreation organization income increased by 40 percent in real terms during this period, fee income increased only 28 percent. This forced organizations to rely more heavily on government and private giving, the former of which grew by a substantial 62 percent and the latter by 55 percent. Because government is a relatively small provider of support to nonprofit arts and cultural organizations, however, it was really private giving that had to shoulder the growth. Thus, as shown in Figure 9.8, philanthropy accounted for 48 percent of nonprofit arts and recreation organization growth between 1997 and 2007, compared to 40 percent for fees and 12 percent for government.[17]

This reliance on private giving to fuel growth was considerably more apparent among the arts and culture organizations than the sports and recreation ones, however. Thus, as Table 9.1 shows, sports and recreation organizations financed 53 percent of their growth from fees and charges, compared to only 29 percent among the arts and culture organizations. What is more, the performing arts organizations had even less opportunity to bolster their income from expanded fees as resistance apparently set in among patrons to expanded ticket prices. As a result, they had to rely on private giving for over 70 percent of their revenue, and their growth lagged behind their for-profit counterparts as a consequence. Perhaps most significantly, this situation very likely set them up for special difficulties once the recession hit in 2008 and beyond.

TABLE 9.1 Sources of Nonprofit Culture and Recreation Organization Growth, 1977–2007, by Type of Organization

Type of Institution	Share of Revenue Growth			Total
	Government	Philanthropy	Fees	
Performing arts	4.6%	71.1%	24.3%	100%
Cultural venues	16.3%	52.9%	30.8%	100%
All arts	**12.3%**	**59.4%**	**28.6%**	**100%**
Sports & recreation	10.7%	36.4%	52.9%	100%
Total	**11.5%**	**48.4%**	**40.1%**	**100%**

Source: Internal Revenue Service Statistics of Income Tabulations. See Chapter 3, endnote 18.

Conclusions

Nonprofit organizations play a critical role in the recreational and cultural life of the United States. Many of the major recreational institutions of local communities—swimming clubs, tennis clubs, Little Leagues, soccer leagues, country clubs—are nonprofit in form. Equally important, nonprofit organizations form the backbone of the nation's cultural life, producing most of the live theater, symphonic music, and opera, and providing venues for art and for cultural artifacts.

The economic recession that began in 2008 hit nonprofit cultural institutions especially hard, since it put a serious freeze on private charitable resources.

The expansion of these nonprofit cultural institutions benefited greatly from an important partnership that emerged in the 1960s and 1970s between government and private philanthropy. Beginning in the 1980s, however, this partnership came under serious strain when government support was significantly reduced. Despite this, nonprofit arts and cultural institutions have continued to expand. In part this has been due to the generosity of private benefactors. But in somewhat greater part, it has been due to the willingness of patrons to pay for the services they receive and the ability of arts institutions to find other, semi-commercial sources of support.

More recently, however, some resistance has surfaced to further expansion of nonprofit arts organizations' fee income. With government support also constrained, the arts world has been thrown back more heavily onto private philanthropy for financial sustenance. As a consequence, the philanthropy share of performing arts income grew from 38 percent of total income in 1997 to 45 percent in 2007. The economic recession that began in 2008 has hit nonprofit cultural institutions especially hard, therefore, since the recession put a serious freeze on private charitable resources. It remains to be seen, therefore, how the nonprofit arts and cultural world regains its financial footing in the wake of this economic challenge.

ENDNOTES

1. Revenue data from the Internal Revenue Service, *Statistics of Income*, Form 990 microdata files.

2. U.S. Bureau of Economic Analysis, National Income and Product Accounts, Table 2.5.5, "Personal Consumption Expenditures by Function," revision of August 2010, accessed at www. bea.gov/national/nipaweb/SelectTable.asp?Selected=N. Not all the establishments receiving from personal consumption expenditures for recreation are in the arts, recreation, and entertainment industry, however. Some are in book and video production, others in the production of sports and recreational vehicles, and still others in pet supplies and other products related to recreation. The education figure cited here differs from the total education expenditure figure cited in Chapters 7 and 8 above because it covers only "personal consumption expenditures," i.e., expenditures by households as opposed to government expenditures.

3. Data here cover nonprofit, for-profit, and government employment in a wide array of recreation and sports fields as well as performing arts and artistic venues. Data on nonprofit and for-profit employment are from U.S. Census Bureau, *Economic Census* 2007, Sector 71: EC077111: Arts, Entertainment, and Recreation: Industry Series. Accessed at factfinder.census.gov/servlet/ IBQTable?_bm=y&-geo_id=&-ds_name=EC077111&-_lang=en. Data on state and local government employment are for "Parks and Recreation" and were obtained from U.S. Census Bureau, *Census of Government 2007*, available at: harvester.census.gov/datadissem/Results.aspx. Federal employment data are for "Parks and Recreation" and were obtained from U.S. Census Bureau, Federal Government Employment and Payroll, 2007, accessed at: ftp2.census.gov/govs/ apes/07fedfun.pdf. All government employment is assigned to the Sports and Recreation portion of the arts and recreation field. No data are available on public museum employment. In addition to the arts, culture, and recreation activity carried out by organizations specifically identifiable as primarily engaged in these activities, numerous other organizations play important roles in arts, culture, and recreation as a secondary activity. Included here, for example, are theaters, museums, and sports programs affiliated with universities, church choirs that perform in other venues, and innumerable informal chamber groups, book clubs, sports teams, and related community recreational activities.

4. Volunteer data based on Bureau of Labor Statistics data as reported in Kennard T. Wing, Thomas H. Pollack, and Amy Blackwood, *The Nonprofit Almanac: 2008* (Washington, DC: The Urban Institute Press, 2008), Table 3.13.

5. As just one example of this phenomenon, Italy's famous La Scala Opera Company, formerly a public company, was recently transformed into a foundation.

6. Unfortunately, solid data on the number of government museums and galleries are not available. One estimate puts the share of art galleries that are public agencies at 12 percent, with an additional 14 percent affiliated with public universities. Among history museums and science museums, the public share is estimated to range from 40 to 60 percent. See: Paul DiMaggio, "Nonprofit Organizations in the Production and Distribution of Culture," in *The Nonprofit Sector: A Research Handbook,* ed. Walter Powell (New Haven: Yale University Press, 1987), 198. In addition, as noted earlier, a number of museums operate as parts of universities.

7. Revenue estimates were computed from Internal Revenue Service, Statistics of Income microdata file tabulations of Form 990 returns. See Chapter 3, note 18. Aggregate estimates here differ slightly from those reported in Chapter 3 above due to our attempt to align the coverage of types of entities here with those covered by the *Economic Census*, which uses a different classification system than that used in the Internal Revenue Service data. The data reported here also differ somewhat from that reported in the *Economic Census* due to differences in coverage and estimating techniques. For example, as noted in the text, we suspect that the *Economic Census* covers only "annual operating income," whereas the IRS includes total income whether restricted to annual operations or channeled into endowment.

8. Economic Census data here from U.S. Bureau of the Census, *Economic Census* 2007, Sector 71: Arts, Entertainment, and Recreation Industry Series: Product Lines by Kind of Business.

9. Thus, for orchestras, the IRS data report 45 percent of nonprofit income from philanthropy as of 2007 whereas the *Economic Census* reports 40 percent. For theater and operas, the respective figures are 42 percent and 35 percent; for dance, they are 44 percent and 38 percent; and for museums and other venues, they are 43 percent and 31 percent.

10. The data here are drawn from U.S. Bureau of the Census, *Economic Census,* 1997 and 2007, Arts and Recreation, Geographic Area Series, Summary Statistics. *Economic Census* data on revenues are used here to allow comparison with for-profit firms. As shown below, IRS estimates of nonprofit revenue growth are somewhat higher than *Economic Census* estimates.

11. Based on data from the *Economic Census*, 1997 and 2002, as reported in Lester M. Salamon, *America's Nonprofit Sector*, 2nd ed. (New York: The Foundation Center, 1999), 127.

12. Steven Samuels and Alisha Tonsic, *Theater Facts 1995* (New York: Theater Communications Group, 1996), 2.

13. John Urice, "The Future of the State Arts Agency Movement in the 1990s: Decline and Effect," *The Journal of Arts Management, Law, and Society* 22:1 (Spring 1992), cited in Nina Kressner Cobb, *Looking Ahead: Private Sector Giving to the Arts and the Humanities* (Washington, DC: President's Committee on the Arts and the Humanities, n.d. [1997]), 17.

14. As noted earlier, however, these data may overstate the value of private giving by including the value of contributed works of art. Calculating private giving as a share of total operating support can therefore be misleading.

15. Samuels and Tonsic, *Theater Facts* 1995, 9–10.

16. See, for example: Chris Jones, "Monster or Mainstay?" *American Theatre* (March 1996).

17. Based on IRS Statistics of Income Special Tabulations of Form 990 Returns. See endnote 7, this chapter.

10

Advocacy, Legal Services, and International Aid

Important as the nonprofit sector is in the provision of various services—from health and education to arts and culture—it also plays other, possibly even more important, roles as well.

This chapter examines two of the most fundamental of these other roles: first, the nonprofit role in *civic and policy advocacy*, the representation of views or interests, particularly public interests, in the shaping of public policy; and second, the nonprofit role in *international assistance*, the effort to relieve suffering and promote economic growth in less developed countries. In both, the nonprofit sector makes unique, and quite substantial, contributions.

Nonprofit Advocacy Activity

Advocacy, the representation of interests and concerns, usually in the political process, is one of the most distinctive functions of the nonprofit sector. Through their involvement in this function, nonprofit organizations embody one of the most cherished values in American life: the right of free expression and its corollary, the right to associate together to give effective voice to common concerns.

This right has received particular attention over the past four or five decades as part of a general movement toward empowerment of the poor, of consumers, of women, of racial and ethnic minorities, and of numerous other segments of the population. Indeed, as one long-time student of the nonprofit sector has argued, this advocacy function may be the most important one the sector performs, and certainly the one "for which society is most dependent on it."[1] This is so for the obvious reason that effective action on pressing public problems requires sustained effort, and for this, uncoordinated individual activity is not sufficient: organization is needed. Future Supreme Court Justice Lewis Powell understood this point well in a famous memo he wrote in 1971 urging business leaders to organize themselves more effectively to counter pressures from consumers and environmental activists. Noted Powell: "Strength lies in organization, in careful long-range planning and implementation, in consistency of action over an indefinite period, in the scale of financing available only through joint effort, and in the political power available only through united action and national organizations."[2]

Through their involvement in advocacy, nonprofit organizations embody one of the most cherished values in American life: the right of free expression.

PUBLIC-INTEREST ADVOCACY

Interestingly, in some respects, nonprofit organizations absorbed this lesson earlier than did the business community, at least at the national level. Indeed, a whole class of public-interest advocacy organizations emerged in the 1960s and 1970s specializing in identifying, analyzing, and formulating potential solutions to public, or community, problems. Beyond this, however, numerous public-benefit service agencies (for example, social service providers) include advocacy as a part of their activity, or belong to regional or national associations that advocate on behalf of the clients that the agencies serve. Finally, at the community level, there are thousands of civic organizations through which individuals engage in community life.

Types of Advocacy Activity. Nonprofit organizations have not been completely free to exercise their responsibilities in the civic arena, however. To the contrary, a variety of legal constraints limit certain forms of nonprofit civic engagement. In fact, seven different bodies of law affect nonprofit involvement in policy activity and each uses slightly different terminology.[3] To understand the nonprofit role in the policy arena, therefore, it is necessary to begin by distinguishing three types of advocacy-related activity and the ways they are treated under U.S. law.

•   *Political campaign activity.* The first basic type of advocacy activity is "political campaign activity." Political campaign activity is involvement in a political campaign to support or oppose a candidate for public office. Nonprofit charitable organizations [501(c)(3) organizations] are absolutely prohibited from engaging in such campaign activity.[4] What is more, private foundations grants that are used for activities to influence the outcome of a specific public election are strongly discouraged by means of a tax, which is raised to 100 percent if the expenditure is not corrected within a year.[5]

•   *Lobbying.* A second type of advocacy activity involves efforts to influence the passage or defeat of particular pieces of legislation. This type of advocacy is called "lobbying" and it is subject to a limitation. Nonprofit public-benefit organizations—that is, 501(c)(3) organizations—are permitted to engage in such lobbying activity, but only to the extent of devoting an "insubstantial part" of their activities to it. Since 1976, such organizations have had two options for determining what constitutes an "insubstantial part" of their activities for this purpose: first, they can rely on a common-sense notion of what is "substantial," taking account of the circumstances of the organization and the nature of the situation; or second, they can "elect" to come under a set of specific mathematical guidelines about the share of their expenditures they can devote to lobbying (that is, 20 percent of the first $500,000 of expenditures and a declining percentage of amounts over that, up to a total of $1 million).[6] Whichever method is used, charities can exclude from "lobbying costs" any amounts spent on generating or disseminating nonpartisan research, responding to legislative requests for information, protecting the organization itself, communicating with the members of the organization about a piece of legislation (so long as no request is made to the member to communicate with the legislature about the legislation), and routinely communicating with government officials. In short, a wide range of activity is still permitted without running afoul of the limitations on nonprofit lobbying. Finally, charities that wish to engage in lobbying beyond the limits set in the law can choose to surrender their 501(c)(3) status and register as 501(c)(4) organizations, or set up 501(c)(4) subsidiaries. Such organizations have no restrictions on their lobbying, but the trade-off is that they are not eligible to receive tax-deductible contributions. In addition, the Lobbying Disclosure Act of 1995 prohibits even 501(c)(4) organizations from engaging in lobbying if they receive any government grants, loans, or awards. And the lobbying restrictions on foundations are equally, or more, severe, subjecting *all* expenditures in support of attempts to influence legislation to a tax, rather than just an amount above a certain threshold, as is the case for other nonprofit organizations. Given the prohibition on lobbying even by 501(c)(4) organizations if they receive government support, this further prohibition on foundation support even for permissible nonprofit lobbying exerts a further serious restriction on the ability of nonprofits to support their involvement in policy activity.

Nonprofit, public-benefit, 501(c)(3) organizations are permitted to engage in lobbying activity, but only to the extent of devoting an "insubstantial part" of their activities to it.

• *Issue Advocacy.* The final type of nonprofit policy-related activity is basic "issue advocacy." Issue advocacy consists of research, education, and dissemination activity related to identifying problems or potential solutions to them and bringing them to the attention of the public or policymakers. Nonprofit public-benefit organizations—that is, those eligible to receive tax-deductible contributions—are permitted to engage in such issue advocacy basically without limit so long as the activity does not cross the line into an attempt to influence the passage or defeat of a *specific piece of legislation*, and even then such activity is permitted so long as it does not constitute a "substantial part" of the organization's activity, as discussed above.

Here as well, however, attempts have been made to limit the scope of permissible activity. Thus, Office of Management and Budget Circular A-122 on nonprofit cost accounting promulgated by the Reagan Administration in 1984 prohibited nonprofits from using federal grant dollars to support "political advocacy," a concept quite a bit broader than the narrower concept of lobbying. A subsequent OMB Circular (A-87) in 1990 then tightened the process nonprofits must use to ensure that this prohibition is enforced. What is more, the 1995 Lobbying Disclosure Act required organizations that employ even one person who devotes 20 percent or more of his or her time to lobbying to register with the Secretary of the Senate and the Clerk of the House of Representatives regardless of whether the organization as a whole devotes that much of its revenues to lobbying.

Extent of Nonprofit Advocacy. Despite this rather restrictive legal environment for nonprofit advocacy, nonprofits have hardly surrendered this crucial function. To the contrary, they pursue it in a variety of ways.

The nonprofit sector has been the principal vehicle for most of the major social movements in American life over the past century.

- *Nonprofit role in recent social movement activity.* The nonprofit sector has been the principal vehicle for most of the major social movements that have animated and energized American life over the past century or more—the women's suffrage movement, the civil rights movement, the environmental movement, the consumer movement, the women's rights movement, the abortion rights movement, the anti–abortion rights movement, the gay rights movement, the conservative movement, and many more. To the extent that such movements have taken organizational expression, it is through nonprofit organizations that they have been able to function. The sector has thus provided a convenient safety valve for public concerns and a mechanism for mobilizing citizen action and attention on matters of public importance.

- *Nonprofit advocacy organizations.* More generally, as the legal complications confronting nonprofit lobbying and advocacy have grown more complex, a sizable cadre of specialized nonprofit advocacy organizations has emerged that can cope with the resulting complexities. According to the most recent *Economic Census*, there were nearly 17,000 such organizations in existence as of 2007. Included here, as shown in Table 10.1, were some 2,800 human rights organizations, 6,200 environmental organizations, 6,250 other social advocacy groups, and 1,500 civic groups estimated to be engaged in community advocacy activities.[7] As reflected in Table 10.2, many of these organizations are household names, such as the American Civil Liberties Union, the American Association of Retired Persons, and the National Rifle Association, but others are known mainly to those "within the beltway" or in statehouses across the country. Taken together, these organizations employed an estimated 148,000 people as of 2007 and boasted revenues of $21.8 billion. As Table 10.1 shows, the human rights organizations tend to be larger on average and therefore account for a larger share of the revenues than of the organizations (29.2 percent versus 16.9 percent) while the "other social advocacy groups" account for a smaller share of the revenues than of the organizations (31.3 percent versus 37.2 percent).

• Roughly half of the income of these nonprofit advocacy organizations comes from private giving, as shown in Figure 10.1. The other half is split between fees (29 percent) and government (21 percent).

TABLE 10.1: Nonprofit Advocacy Organizations, 2007

Type of Organization	Establishments		Revenue		Employment	
	Number	% of total	Amt ($billions)	% of total	Number	% of total
Human rights	2,839	16.9%	$6.4	29.2%	32,040	21.7%
Environment	6,195	36.9%	7.8	36.0%	55,275	37.4%
Other social advocacy	6,254	37.2%	6.8	31.3%	47,482	32.2%
Civic	1,504	9.0%	0.8	3.5%	12,817	8.7%
Total	16,792	100.0%	21.8	100.0%	147,614	100.0%

Source: U.S. Bureau of the Census, *Economic Census*, 2007. See Chapter 10, endnote 7.

FIGURE 10.1: Sources of Revenue of Nonprofit Advocacy Organizations, 2007

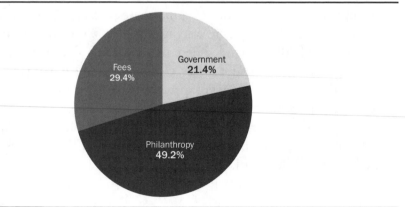

Source: U.S. Bureau of the Census, *Economic Census*, 2007.

TABLE 10.2: Sample Nonprofit Advocacy Organizations

American Association of Retired Persons (AARP)

American Cancer Society

American Civil Liberties Union Inc.

American Heart Association

Center on Budget and Policy Priorities

Children's Defense Fund

Horizons for Homeless Children Inc.

Humane Society of the United States

National Association for the Advancement of Colored People (NAACP)

National Council of La Raza

National Rifle Association of America

National Urban League

National Wildlife Association

Nature Conservancy

Source: Form 990 data files, 2009

Some notable differences exist, however, in the funding base of different types of nonprofit advocacy organizations. In particular, the human rights and environmental organizations tend to rely less on government and more on philanthropy than the overall figure suggests, though even among these organizations government accounts for about 13 percent of the revenue on average (see Table 10.3). Among the more than 6,000 other social advocacy organizations, however, government support accounts on average for a far more robust 40 percent of the revenue, more than any other source. This suggests that receipt of government funding does not impede organizational involvement in advocacy work and may, indeed, help spur it.[8]

TABLE 10.3: Sources of Revenue of Nonprofit Advocacy Organizations, 2007

| Type of Organization | Sources of Revenue | | | |
	Philanthropy	Fees	Government	Total
Human rights	56.0%	30.8%	13.2%	100%
Environment	55.9%	31.1%	13.0%	100%
Other social advocacy	38.5%	21.2%	40.3%	100%
Civic	19.9%	73.4%	6.8%	100%
Total	**49.2%**	**29.4%**	**21.4%**	**100%**

Source: U.S. Bureau of the Census, *Economic Census,* 2007.

FIGURE 10.2: Growth in Nonprofit Advocacy Organizations, 1997–2007

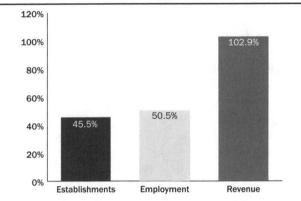

Source: U.S. Bureau of the Census, *Economic Census*, 1997 and 2007.

Nonprofit advocacy organizations grew extensively in the United States during the 1960s and early 1970s as a by-product of the "rights revolution" that took place during this period.[9] But that growth seems to have continued in more recent years as well. Thus, between 1997 and 2007, the number of nonprofit advocacy organizations grew by nearly 46 percent, the number of people they employed grew by more than 50 percent, and their revenues, after adjusting for inflation, surged by more than 100 percent (See Figure 10.2).[10]

Growth between 1997 and 2007 was especially strong among environmental organizations, which increased their numbers by nearly 75 percent, their employment by close to 100 percent, and their revenues by 150 percent. Indeed, roughly half of the new nonprofit advocacy organizations formed between 1997 and 2007 were in the environmental area, and these organizations accounted for 42 percent of the growth in advocacy organization revenue. By contrast, other social advocacy and advocacy-oriented civic organizations grew more slowly in numbers, revenues, and especially employment (see Table 10.4).

TABLE 10.4: Changes in Nonprofit Advocacy Organizations, 1997–2007

Type of Organization	% Change in		
	Establishments	Employment	Revenue
Human rights	57.2%	76.9%	126.6%
Environment	73.6%	98.1%	152.4%
Other social advocacy	31.8%	21.6%	63.9%
Civic	6.0%	-1.9%	15.6%
All	**45.5%**	**50.5%**	**102.9%**

Source: U.S. Bureau of the Census, *Economic Census*, 1997 and 2007. See Chapter 10, endnote 7.

- *Advocacy activity by service-providing nonprofits.* Beyond the dedicated lobbying organizations, a considerable amount of public-benefit advocacy takes place through regular 501(c)(3) service and expressive organizations. As noted, such organizations are permitted to engage in issue advocacy essentially without limit, though not with public funds, and can engage as well in lobbying so long as it is not a "substantial part" of the organizations' activities. Recent research shows that well over 70 percent of nonprofit 501(c)(3) organizations have taken some part in some type of public policy activity, such as encouraging members to write to a policymaker on an issue of concern.[11] At the same time, the degree of involvement in terms of both its nature and its frequency is rather limited. Thus, fewer than one-third of respondents to a Johns Hopkins Nonprofit Listening Post survey of human service, community development, and arts-organization executives reported even distributing information materials or responding to official requests for information three or more times in the year prior to the survey, and barely 10 percent reported testifying at hearings or writing an op-ed or letter to the editor on a policy issue this often.

> **Many civic organizations are informal neighborhood clubs that serve social as well as civic functions, but many are formally incorporated nonprofits.**

One major reason for the relatively limited engagement in advocacy and lobbying by mainline nonprofit organizations is the limited financial support available for this function. As noted earlier, existing laws prohibit the use of government funding for "political advocacy," a rather ambiguous term, and foundation expenditures in support of lobbying are subject to a tax. With public and foundation funding for lobbying and some forms of advocacy thus constrained, organizations must use precious other charitable dollars to sustain this crucial advocacy role. It is thus not surprising that only about 14 percent of the organizations surveyed by the Johns Hopkins Nonprofit Listening Post Project reported devoting more than 2 percent of their budgets to advocacy.[12]

- *Civic associations.* In addition to the national or state-oriented advocacy activity, other advocacy activity takes place through nonprofit civic organizations. Many of these organizations are informal neighborhood clubs that serve social as well as civic functions. But many are formally incorporated nonprofit organizations functioning to help develop housing and jobs in local areas. Many of these latter organizations were stimulated by the federal antipoverty program of the mid-1960s, which fostered the creation of Community Action Agencies involving the participation of the poor; and by the federal Community Development Block Grant Program, which has encouraged and, to some extent, funded the formation of neighborhood organizations to help oversee the process of community development in inner-city neighborhoods.

One of the more interesting features of nonprofit public-interest policy advocacy during the past four decades has been the use of the legal system to promote policy changes.

These organizations often provide a mechanism for neighborhood involvement in local decision making. The Planning Department of the City of Baltimore, Maryland, for example, maintains a register of over 770 local neighborhood or community organizations that are regularly consulted on property development and other issues in their areas. This represents a 28 percent increase in the number of such organizations between the mid-1990s and 2010.[13] More generally, the Census Bureau identified close to 26,000 civic and social organizations exclusive of scout organizations as of 2007, employing 188,000 workers and bringing in revenues of almost $11.6 billion. Although roughly 9,000 of these are service clubs that may have limited advocacy roles, they nevertheless provide some degree of engagement in local public affairs.[14]

LEGAL SERVICE ORGANIZATIONS

One of the more interesting features of nonprofit public-interest policy advocacy during the past four decades has been the use of the legal system to promote policy changes. At the heart of this development has been an array of specialized nonprofit, public-interest legal organizations in such fields as environmental protection, civil rights, consumer rights, and the like. Many of these organizations were specially created to pursue public-interest policy change through legal action. Others grew out of the efforts sparked by the federal antipoverty program of the 1960s to make legal services available to the poor and to use the law to alter government policies hostile to the poor.

Thanks to a Supreme Court ruling in 1966, which changed the definition of "standing" in certain legal cases, it became possible for these public-interest legal organizations to bring cases not only on behalf of particular injured individuals, but also on behalf of entire classes of similarly situated persons. This made it possible to claim sufficient damages to warrant the costs of a case, even though the damages sustained by any individual member of the affected group may have been relatively small.

Arrayed against the nearly 17,000 nonprofit public-interest advocacy organizations are close to 72,000 nonprofit business and professional associations.

Many of the nonprofit advocacy organizations pursuing legal changes are doubtless classified by the Census Bureau as environmental, or civil rights, or housing organizations. But as of the early 1990s there were also 1,725 nonprofit legal aid organizations in existence with some 21,300 employees. By the mid-1990s, these organizations had revenues of some $1.3 billion. This represented an increase of nearly 60 percent in the number of agencies, and over 70 percent in their employment and revenues, compared to 1977.[15] This growth has continued in more recent years as well. By 2007, as a consequence, there were 2,314 such legal aid nonprofits employing over 26,000 people. This constitutes a 34 percent increase in establishments and a 23 percent increase in employment from the early 1990s. In addition, the revenues of these nonprofit legal aid organizations have grown by 52 percent since 1996, yielding revenues of $2.7 billion in 2007.[16]

How many of these organizations are principally engaged in policy advocacy and class-action law as opposed to more traditional legal services (for example, divorces, wills, property settlements) for indigent clients is likely far less today than it was during the 1960s and early 1970s, however. Because of the controversies these early change-oriented legal service agencies provoked by bringing class-action lawsuits against restrictive government laws aimed at the poor, major efforts were launched by the Nixon administration in the early 1970s to restrict the advocacy work of the federally funded legal service organizations and focus their efforts more narrowly on more traditional legal services for individual clients. Efforts to terminate the funding of these services during the Reagan administration further hampered their efforts. What is more, the nonprofit legal service and legal advocacy organizations are a pale reflection of the almost 190,000 for-profit legal firms employing close to 1.2 million employees identified in Census records as of 2007.[17] Nevertheless, this range of nonprofit organizations, though stripped of much of its advocacy role, has survived several onslaughts and provides an important public-interest dimension to legal representation in the country.

PRIVATE-INTEREST ADVOCACY

If nonprofit advocacy has been overshadowed in the legal arena, it has confronted similar, or more severe, challenges elsewhere, in what two writers have recently termed the politics of "organized combat."[18] In some sense arrayed against the nearly 17,000 nonprofit public-interest advocacy organizations are close to 72,000 nonprofit business and professional associations registered with the Internal Revenue Service as of 2009. The 24,245 of these that filed information returns with the Internal Revenue Service reported revenues of $38.7 billion as of 2007, nearly twice as much as the nonprofit public-interest organizations examined earlier.[19] Most of these organizations devote at least a part of their efforts toward the representation and promotion of the interests and views of their business or professions in the political process. They do this by contributing to political campaigns, conducting research on issues affecting their members, testifying before Congress and state legislatures, and presenting the views of their constituencies to political leaders, the press, and the general public in dozens of different ways. This is in addition, of course, to the personnel employed by corporations directly and the legal firms on retainer to represent corporations in the political process.

As the scope of government involvement in national life has grown, so too has the scope and density of this private-interest representation, particularly in the nation's capital. Indeed, after suffering a series of defeats at the hands of the burgeoning nonprofit consumer, environmental, and civil rights surge of the 1960s and early 1970s,[20] business interests responded with a substantial mobilization. Thus, the number of corporations with public affairs offices in Washington quintupled between 1968 and 1978, and the number of corporate political action committees (PACs) went from fewer than 300 in the mid-1970s to 1,200 by the mid-1980s.[21] Nor did the business sector restrict its activity to the formation and growth of 501(c)(6) business associations. Increasingly, businesses joined together to form pseudo-grassroots 501(c)(3) and 501(c)(4) organizations. Some portion of the growth of nonprofit advocacy organizations cited earlier thus likely represents the growth of organizations essentially sponsored by business coalitions.

Despite the onslaught of civil rights, consumer, and environmental advocacy in the 1960s and 1970s, therefore, business dominance of the Washington interest-group scene was more pervasive by the early 1980s than it had been two decades earlier. Thus, although the overall number of interests represented in Washington increased greatly, the number representing business interests increased even faster so that the business proportion of the total swelled from 57 percent to 72 percent between 1960 and 1980, while that for citizens' groups declined from 9 percent to 5 percent and the proportion for labor decreased from 11 percent to 2 percent.[22] Data on lobbyist registrations made available thanks to the 1995 Lobbying Disclosure Act tell a similar story. As of 1996, as shown in Table 10.5, business interests constituted 59 percent of registered lobbyists in Washington, 64 percent of reports filed, and 62 percent of total issues mentioned.[23] By contrast, nonprofits and citizen groups could claim only 9 percent of registered lobbyists, 8 percent of reports filed, and 10 percent of issues mentioned. And, as noted earlier, some of these supposedly public-interest, nonprofit lobbying groups undoubtedly really represented various industries.[24] Labor, meanwhile, has shrunk to only 1 percent of lobbyists, 2 percent of reports filed, and 3 percent of issues mentioned as of 1996.

TABLE 10.5: The Washington Lobbying Corps, 1996

	Registrations n=5917	% of Total Reports n=19,962	Issues n=49,518
Business	59%	64%	62%
Professional	6%	6%	7%
Unions	1%	2%	3%
Nonprofits and citizen groups	9%	8%	10%
Government organizations	12%	10%	8%
Other	13%	10%	10%
Total	**100%**	**100%**	**100%**

Source: Frank R. Baumgartner and Beth L. Leech, "Interest Niches and Policy Bandwagons," *Journal of Politics* 63, November 2001, p. 1196.

Although the 2007 *Economic Census* suggests some consolidation in the number and economic scale of business and professional associations between 1997 and 2007,[25] there is little evidence of this on the ground in the centers of political power. Thus, for example, the online version of the Washington, DC, telephone directory now takes over 30 pages to list the 2,523 organizations with the word "association" in their titles, ranging from such stalwarts as the American Bar Association to less well-known associations such as the National Paint and Coatings Association and the

National Confectioners Association (see Table 10.6). Indeed, few facets of national economic or professional life are not represented by at least one, and usually more than one, business or professional association, and increasing numbers of these are establishing headquarters in the nation's capital and joining in the effort to influence public policy.

TABLE 10.6: Illustrative Washington-Based Nonprofit Business and Professional Associations

National Association of Broadcasters
National Association of Estate Agents
National Association of Homebuilders
National Association of Manufacturers
National Association of Mutual Insurance Companies
National Association of Waterfront Employers
National Automobile Dealers Association
National Bankers Association
National Cable and Telecommunications Association
National Candle Association
National Confectioners Association
National Funeral Directors Association
National Grocers Association
National Insulation Association
National Kitchen and Bath Association
National Mining Association
National Paint and Coatings Association
National Petrochemicals and Refiners Association
National Textile Association
National Wood Window and Door Association

Source: Washington Metropolitan Area White Pages, Online Edition

Nonprofit Foreign Assistance

Nonprofit organizations also play an important role in international activities. Internal Revenue Service sources identify at least 4,705 organizations actively engaged in such international work. Most of these are involved in international relief or development work, but others are engaged in promoting peace and understanding among nations, channeling private philanthropic resources to favored institutions overseas (so-called "friend of" organizations), or improving knowledge of other countries.

INTERNATIONAL ASSISTANCE ORGANIZATIONS

Perhaps the most visible portion of this international nonprofit activity is that involving international relief and development.

Scale. As of 2007, there were 563 U.S. private, voluntary organizations (PVOs) involved in international relief and development assistance registered with the U.S. Agency for International Development (USAID).[26] These organizations had revenues that year totalling $26.0 billion.[27] By comparison, total U.S. government development and humanitarian assistance that year amounted to only $15.5 billion.[28]

Revenue Sources. As shown in Figure 10.3, 57 percent of the income of these 563 international assistance agencies came from private giving as of 2007. Another 25 percent came from governmental sources, of which 15 percent was U.S. government sources and 10 percent other governments or international organizations. The remaining 18 percent of the income of these organizations came from fees and charges.[29]

Government support is considerably more important than these averages suggest, however, among the largest private voluntary relief and development agencies. A number of these agencies are quite enormous operations, with annual incomes in excess of $200 million. And for many of them, the same pattern of government-nonprofit cooperation evident in other fields

FIGURE 10.3: Sources of Nonprofit Foreign Assistance Agency Revenue, 2007

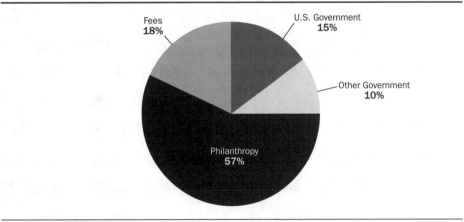

Source: USAID, *2009 Volag Report of Voluntary Agencies.*

operates in this field as well. Thus, as Figure 10.4 shows, Catholic Relief Services, a $530 million organization, received 63 percent of its revenue from government sources in 2007; the Academy for Educational Development (AED) received 89 percent of its $405 million budget from government; and Save the Children Federation received 49 percent of its $371 million from government. Clearly, governments both in the United States and elsewhere rely heavily on these nonprofit relief and development organizations to carry out humanitarian assistance and development activities in overseas locations.[30]

Recent Trends. This pattern of government support, though substantial, is nevertheless much more restricted than was the case in the past. Indeed, like many other parts of the nonprofit sector, the nonprofit foreign assistance community has been affected by a number of dramatic changes in recent years. Foremost among these changes have been the following:[31]

- *A substantial growth in the numbers of agencies in the field.* The number of PVOs registered with USAID more than doubled between 1980 and 1996, increasing from 156 to 424. From 1997 to 2007, another 139 PVOs registered with USAID, boosting the total by one-third in only 10 years. This reflects the growing globalization of the world economy and

FIGURE 10.4: Sources of Income of Nonprofit Foreign Aid Organizations: Total and Selected Agencies, 2007 ($ millions)

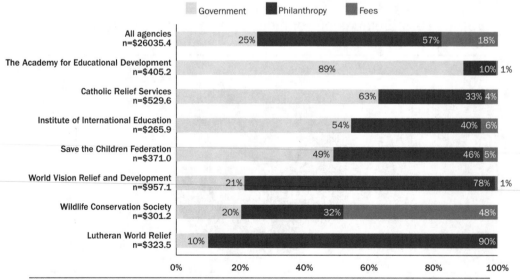

Source: USAID, *2009 Volag Report of Voluntary Agencies.*

the increased incidence of multiple, complex, international humanitarian crises, many of them increasingly man-made.

- *A significant broadening of the function of these agencies from relief to development.*[32] One reflection of this is the fact that the share of government support to these agencies that took the form of Public Law 480 surplus food distribution and other in-kind assistance declined from 59 percent in 1980 to only 15 percent in 1996, and declined further to just 7 percent in 2007. By contrast, the share of government assistance to these agencies that took the form of direct grants and contracts increased from 41 percent in 1980 to 93 percent in 2007.

- *A significant decline in the U.S. government share of support.* Despite a long-standing partnership between government and private voluntary organizations in the provision of overseas relief, U.S. PVOs have had to contend with a significant reduction in the growth of U.S. development assistance over the past nearly thirty years. Thus, for example, although the number of agencies registered with USAID more than doubled between 1980 and 1996, the real value of government support to these agencies increased by only 10 percent. As a share of total support, therefore, U.S.

FIGURE 10.5: Growth of U.S. Nonprofit Foreign Assistance Agency Activity, 1997–2007, by Source, Inflation Adjusted

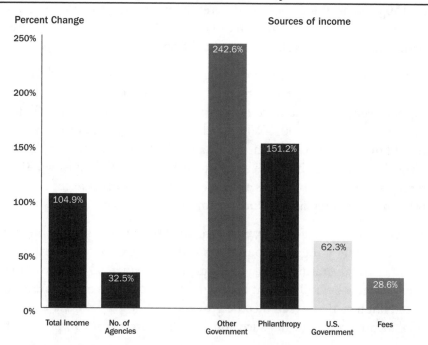

Source: USAID, *2009 Volag Report of Voluntary Agencies*; 1999 Volag unpublished data provided by USAID Office of Development Partners.

government support fell from 41 percent in 1980 to 21 percent in 1996. The late 1990s and 2000s saw a renewed commitment to international development on the part of the U.S. government. As Figure 10.5 shows, U.S. government support to PVOs increased by 62 percent in real terms from 1997 to 2007. However, overall PVO revenue increased by 105 percent during this period. As a result, the U.S. government share of PVO revenue continued to decline, dropping from 19 percent in 1997 to 15 percent in 2007.

- *Substantial growth in support from other governments and international organizations.* Where, then, did most of the growth come from? Part of the answer, as Figure 10.5 shows, is other governments and international organizations. Such support more than doubled between 1997 and 2007 as multilateral assistance partly displaced bilateral aid. With 6 percent of PVO income as of 1997, other governments and international organizations accounted for 14 percent of the growth of U.S. PVO income between 1997 and 2007.

- *Moving from modest to robust growth in private charitable support.* The real engine of PVO growth over the past several decades, however, has been private giving. Between 1980 and 1996, for example, private giving to U.S. PVOs grew by 128 percent, offsetting the limited growth in government support during this period. This growth then accelerated in the more recent 1997–2007 period, boosting private giving to U.S. PVOs by 150 percent. Put somewhat differently, private giving accounted for 67 percent of the overall growth of U.S. PVO income during this recent period and boosted its share of the total from 47 percent to 57 percent.

Much of this growth in private giving took the form of donated supplies and services, however, rather than actual contributions. Thus, in-kind support went from one-third of all private contributions as of 1997 to more than half as of 2007. While such clothing, supplies, drugs, and related material are vitally important and highly useful, they are more difficult to manage than cash support. In a sense, as Public Law 480 direct food assistance has shrunk as a share of PVO governmental support it has been more than replaced by private, in-kind assistance.[33]

- *Slowing growth in private earnings.* The final source of revenue of nonprofit private voluntary organizations is fees and charges from transporting materiel and operating service facilities. The commercial income of these agencies grew by 450 percent between 1980 and 1996, contributing $1.8 billion to the overall income growth and boosting the share of total income coming from such commercial sources from 10 percent in

1980 to 26 percent in 1996. More recent growth has been more tepid, however. Thus, as shown in Figure 10.5, while overall PVO income increased by 105 percent between 1997 and 2007 after adjusting for inflation, commercial income increased by a much smaller 29 percent. As a consequence, such income fell from 28 percent of total PVO income in 1997 to 18 percent in 2007.

Conclusion

Beyond their significant domestic service roles, American nonprofit organizations thus play other vital functions in American life. For one thing, they provide critical vehicles for advocacy and civic action, ensuring a free and open "civil society" in which different groupings of individuals can make their views known in the policy process at both the national and local levels. Nonprofit organizations are in this sense "empowering" institutions, providing a mechanism for joint action on behalf of even the least well-represented groups or views and helping to level the playing field for disadvantaged persons in the legal sphere as well.

In addition, nonprofit organizations are active in the international arena, extending the reach of traditional government-to-government relief and development aid and mobilizing considerable quantities of private resources as well. This role has grown extensively in recent years as the number and seriousness of complex humanitarian crises has escalated.

To be sure, in none of these spheres has the nonprofit sector been free to operate without constraints or, in the case of advocacy, without formidable competition. Yet, in each of them it is making its own distinctive and important contributions.

ENDNOTES

1. Brian O'Connell, *People Power: Service, Advocacy, Empowerment* (New York: The Foundation Center, 1994), 49.

2. Quoted in Jacob S. Hacker and Paul Pierson, *Winner-Take-All Politics: How Washington Made the Rich Richer—and Turned its Back on the Middle Class* (New York: Simon and Schuster, 2010), 117.

3. Bruce R. Hopkins, *The Law of Tax-Exempt Organizations*, 9th ed. (New York: John Wiley and Sons, 2007), 638.

4. A slight variation on political campaign activity is permissible, however. This is activity designed to influence the *nomination* or *appointment* of any individual to public office and not just the election. All tax-exempt organizations, including charitable ones, are permitted to engage in such "political activity." However, they must pay taxes on any income so used at the highest corporate tax rate. Hopkins, *The Law of Tax-Exempt Organizations* (2007), 677–717.

5. Included here are various amendments to the Internal Revenue Code, legislation on the registration of lobbyists, and various Office of Management and Budget circulars pertaining to permissible uses of federal financial support. See: Hopkins, *The Law of Tax-Exempt Organizations* (2007), 382–384.

6. In addition to the basic limitation on lobbying expenditures as a share of total organizational expenditures, organizations that elect to follow the more specific rules are also prohibited from devoting more than 25 percent of their allowable lobbying expenditures to grassroots lobbying, i.e., influencing the general public on legislative matters. The penalty for exceeding these limitations on lobbying is an excise tax of 25 percent of the excess lobbying expenditures. For further detail, see: Hopkins, *The Law of Tax-Exempt Organizations* (2007), 637–677.

7. Included here are organizations in NAICS codes 813311, 813312, 813319, and 813410. In the case of the latter, which covers civic and social organizations, only 5 percent of the total organizations are included based on survey results suggesting that only 5 percent of civic and social organizations engage in what could broadly be considered advocacy activities. The 17,000 estimate is likely an understatement because the economic census includes only organizations with at least one paid staff. However, the figure is consistent with an estimate derived from Internal Revenue Service data on advocacy organizations. That estimate was compiled by pulling all organizations in NTEE Group R (Civil Rights and Advocacy), all organizations in Groups S20-22 (which cover neighborhood associations), all organizations in Groups S80-82 (which cover service organizations), and all organizations in other categories coded as engaged in "alliances and advocacy" (activity code 01) or research institutes and policy analysis (activity code 05). This yielded an estimate of 22,090 organizations, but 11,243 of these were service clubs and social clubs, only a fraction of which likely engage in advocacy activities. Of the 22,090 "advocacy" organizations identified through Internal Revenue Service sources, 55 percent are 501(c)(3) organizations and 45 percent are 501(c)(4)s. However, the vast majority of the 501(c)(4)s are service and social clubs. Excluding them leaves a relatively small cadre of 1,611 clearly identified 501(c)(4) advocacy or lobbying organizations. Because of ambiguities in the IRS data, we have relied principally on the Economic Census data to depict this component of the nonprofit sector here. The source for the Economic Census data is: U.S. Bureau of the Census, *Economic Census 2007*, Sector 81: EC0781I1: Other Services (Except Public Administration): Industry Series: Preliminary Summary Statistics for the United States: 2007, accessed at: factfinder.census.gov/servlet/IBQTable?_bm=y&-geo_id=&-ds_name=EC0781I1&-_lang=en. The source for the IRS data is: Internal Revenue Service, *Statistics of Income*, Microdata File, downloaded from: www.irs.gov/taxstats/charitablestats/article/0,,id=97176,00.html. Unless otherwise noted, all data on nonprofit advocacy organizations in this chapter derive from the *Economic Census* 2007 and its 1997 counterpart and cover the organizations noted above.

8. This is consistent with research findings reporting a positive correlation between government support and nonprofit involvement in advocacy activity. See, for example, Lester M. Salamon and Stephanie L. Geller, "Nonprofit America: A Force for Democracy?" *Communiqué No. 9* (Baltimore, MD: Johns Hopkins Center for Civil Society Studies, 2008).

9. See, for example, Cass Sunstein, *After the Rights Revolution: Reconceiving the Regulatory State* (Cambridge: Harvard University Press, 1990).

10. U.S. Bureau of the Census, *Economic Census,* 1997 and 2007, Sector 81.

11. Gary D. Bass, David F. Arons, Kay Guinane, and Mathew F. Carter, with Susan Rees, *Seen but Not Heard: Strengthening Nonprofit Advocacy* (Washington, DC: The Aspen Institute, 2007), 17; Salamon and Geller, "Nonprofit America: A Force for Democracy?" 3.

12. Salamon and Geller, "Nonprofit America: A Force for Democracy?" 6.

13. 1991 data from Baltimore City Department of Planning, *Baltimore City's Community Association Directory* (1991); 2010 data from online *Community Association Directory*, available at cityservices.baltimorecity.gov/cad/, accessed July, 2010.

14. Source: *Economic Census* 2007, Sector 81: EC078111: Other Services (Except Public Administration): Industry Series: Preliminary Summary Statistics for the United States: 2007. These figures correspond roughly with the 18,930 organizations that Internal Revenue Service data report in Group S, Community Improvement. These organizations showed total revenue in 2007 of $11.7 billion according to IRS Statistics of Income data cited in endnote 7 above.

15. Lester M. Salamon, *America's Nonprofit Sector: A Primer*, 2nd ed. (New York: Foundation Center, 1999), 142.

16. 2007 data from *Economic Census* 2007, Sector 54: EC075411: Professional, Scientific, and Technical Services: Industry Series: Preliminary Summary Statistics for the United States: 2007.

17. Ibid.

18. Hacker and Pierson, *Winner-Take-All Politics*, 102.

19. The numbers of business and professional associations is drawn from the Internal Revenue Service, Exempt Organization Master File. Business and professional associations refer to those registered with the IRS under section 501(c)(6) of the Internal Revenue Code. Data on the revenue of these organizations is drawn from Internal Revenue Service Statistics of Income, "Table 3: form 990 returns of 501(c)(3)-(9) Organizations: Balance Sheet and Income Statement Items, By Code Section, Tax Year 2007."

20. See, for example: Jeffrey M. Berry, *Lobbying for the People: The Political Behavior of Public Interest Groups* (Princeton: Princeton University Press, 1977); and Jeffrey M. Berry, "Citizen Groups and the Changing Nature of Interest Groups in America," *Annals of the American Academy of Political Science* 528 (July 1993): 30–41.

21. David Vogel, *Fluctuating Fortunes: The Political Power of Business in America* (New York: Basic Books, 1989); Hacker and Pierson, *Winner-Take-All Politics*, 118–124.

22. Kay Lehman Schlozman and John T. Tierney, *Organized Interests and American Democracy* (New York: Harper and Row, 1986), 77–78

23. Frank R. Baumgartner and Beth L. Leech, "Interest Niches and Policy Bandwagons," *Journal of Politics* 63 (November 2001): 1196.

24. One recent example of this phenomenon is "Americans for Prosperity," a Virginia-based nonprofit group financed in part by Charles G. and David H. Koch, owners of Koch Industries, a major energy and consumer products conglomerate. This group has played a prominent role in promoting the Tea Party and encouraging efforts to rein in public employee unions around the country, including a highly contentious showdown in Wisconsin in 2011. Americans for Prosperity boasts a budget of $40 million as of 2010, up from $7 million three years earlier. See: Eric Lipton, "Billionaire Brothers' Money Plays Role in Wisconsin Budget Dispute," *New York Times*, February 22, 2011, A16.

25. According to the *Economic Census* 2007, the number of business and professional associations declined by 2.5 percent between 1997 and 2007, from 24,167 to 23,570. Employment at these organizations continued to grow during this period, though only by 5.4 percent, while revenues increased an inflation-adjusted 20.8 percent. Sources: *Economic Census* 2007, Sector 81: EC078111: Other Services (Except Public Administration): Industry Series: Preliminary Summary Statistics for the United States: 2007; *Economic Census* 1997, Sector 81: Other Services (except Public Administration): Geographic Area Series: 1997.

26. U.S. Agency for International Development, *2009 Volag Report of Voluntary Agencies* (Washington, DC: U.S. Agency for International Development, 2009).

27. *2009 Volag Report*. Internal Revenue Service data record 4,018 international development organizations with expenditures of $17.4 billion. Because of potential classification problems with the IRS data, we use the data assembled by the U.S. Agency for International Development directly from U.S. foreign assistance organizations instead.

28. U.S. Office of Management and Budget, *Budget of the United States Government, Fiscal Year 2012* (Washington: U.S. Government Printing Office, 2011), accessed at www.whitehouse.gov/omb/budget/Historicals. As noted below, some portion of this U.S. government funding goes to and through the private voluntary organizations.

29. Computed from data in USAID, *2009 Volag Report of Voluntary Agencies*, 158–159.

30. For an excellent discussion of the role of nonprofit relief and development organizations, see: Abby Stoddard, "International Assistance," in *The State of Nonprofit America*, 2nd ed., ed. Lester M. Salamon (Washington: Brookings Institution Press, 2012).

31. Changes from 1980 to 1996 are based on data from U.S. Agency for International Development, *Voluntary Foreign Aid Programs*, 1981 and 1998 editions. Changes from 1997 to 2007 are based on the *2009 Volag Report on Voluntary Agencies*, and *1999 Volag* unpublished data provided by USAID Office of Development Partners.

32. 1980 and 1996 data are from U.S. Agency for International Development. Advisory Committee on Voluntary Foreign Aid, *An Assessment of the State of the USAID/PVO Partnership* (Washington, DC: Advisory Committee on Voluntary Foreign Aid, June 1997), 3; 1997 data from *1999 Volag* unpublished data provided by USAID Office of Development Partners; 2007 data from USAID, *2009 Volag Report of Voluntary Agencies*.

33. Public Law 480, also known as Food for Peace (and commonly abbreviated PL 480), is a funding mechanism by which U.S. food can be used for overseas aid. The program was enacted in 1954 through the Agricultural Trade Development Assistance Act.

11

Religion

Not only do nonprofit organizations provide a major mechanism for the pursuit of civic and secular concerns; they are also the principal vehicle for the pursuit of spiritual ones. The practice of religion is one of the purposes explicitly identified in the Internal Revenue Code as entitling organizations to exemption from income taxation, and virtually all churches and related religious institutions in the country are nonprofit in form. Indeed, religious institutions are near the epicenter of American philanthropy: they absorb over one-third of all private charitable contributions and close to 40 percent of all volunteer hours, in both cases more than any other type of organization.[1] In turn, they provide useful support, financial and otherwise, to other components of the nonprofit world. Although they differ in purpose from the other nonprofit organizations we have examined thus far in that they are primarily "member-serving" as opposed to "public-serving" organizations, no account of the U.S. nonprofit sector would be complete without some attention to them.

Previous chapters have already treated some aspects of religion's place in the American nonprofit scene. Many of the hospitals, educational institutions, and social service agencies examined earlier have some affiliation with religious institutions, though most of them nevertheless operate as separate institutions. In this chapter, by contrast, we focus on the religious community proper, that is, on the congregations or places of religious worship such as churches, mosques, synagogues, temples, and related institutions through which the practice of religion is carried out.

To do so, we begin by examining the special position that religious organizations occupy in American law and the difficult definitional issues this poses. We then look at the scale of the religious-organization universe and the financial base on which it rests. Against this backdrop we turn to the non-religious functions that many of these institutions also perform. A final section examines some of the key trends facing America's religious institutions at the present time.

Religious institutions enjoy a privileged position in American law, even compared to other types of nonprofit organizations.

The Special Position of Religion

Religious institutions enjoy a privileged position in American law, even compared to other types of nonprofit organizations. This position derives from the First Amendment to the U.S. Constitution, which forbids Congress from passing any law that might have the effect of "establishing" or advancing one or more religions or impeding their "free exercise." One consequence of this provision is that religious organizations are exempt from the general requirement on other charitable organizations to secure official recognition of their tax-exempt status from the Internal Revenue Service in order to receive tax-deductible gifts. Rather, religious organizations are automatically presumed to be exempt from taxation and eligible to receive tax-deductible gifts, whether or not they officially secure recognition of this exemption. As a consequence, only a fraction of the churches and other religious organizations believed to exist in the nation are formally recorded on Internal Revenue Service records. In addition, religious organizations are exempt from the requirement to file an annual information return (Form 990) detailing their receipts and expenditures, as is required of all other nonprofit charitable organizations with revenues of $25,000 or more.[2]

Because of the First Amendment's proscriptions, moreover, neither Congress nor the courts have been eager to spell out what constitutes a "religion" for these purposes, with the result that considerable ambiguity exists. In one celebrated case, a court did deny a claim for tax exemption made by a self-proclaimed religious order, the Neo-American Church, which identified as its chief religious precept the obligation of adherents to imbibe psychedelic substances such as LSD and marijuana that were said to constitute "the true Host of the Church."[3] More generally, the courts have sidestepped the question of what constitutes a "religion" and have only denied exempt status where it becomes clear that the chief purpose of an organization, whether religious or other, is tax evasion and the financial enrichment of the founder.[4]

Not only is there no clear definition of what constitutes a religion for purposes of tax-exempt status, but also there is no clear definition of what constitutes a "church" or other place of religious worship. This has become increasingly problematic, however, because of the rise of so-called "personal churches" in which the personal finances of the religious leader and those of the "church" or religious organization become thoroughly intermixed. To avoid fraud, therefore, the Internal Revenue Service has developed a set of minimum attributes to qualify an entity as a "church" or other religious congregation, such as the existence of a congregation or body of believers who assemble regularly to worship, a set of beliefs, and the actual conduct of some form of organized religious worship.[5]

Religious congregations represent over 20 percent of all identifiable nonprofit organizations in the country, and over one-quarter of public-serving organizations.

The Scale of America's Religious Subsector

NUMBER OF CONGREGATIONS

Given the special position of religious congregations in American law and the resulting exemption of congregations from the reporting requirements that apply to other nonprofit organizations, gaining a clear view of the scope of the congregational universe poses even greater challenges than does establishing the contours of other components of the nonprofit sector. Nevertheless, a number of recent sources make it possible to generate at least a first approximation of some of the major dimensions of America's religious institutions. What such an approximation makes clear is that religious institutions are a substantial presence on the American nonprofit scene. As shown in Table 11.1, at the present time close to 430,000 religious congregations exist in the United States.[6]

This represents over 20 percent of all identifiable nonprofit organizations in the country, and over one-quarter of the public-serving, or charitable, type of organizations.

TABLE 11.1: U.S. Religious Congregations, Circa 2008

Indicator	Amount
Denominations	≈200
Places of worship	428,975
Members (millions)	196.6
Revenues (billions, 2007)	$119.2
Employment (thousands)	179.4
Volunteers (thousands, FTE)	1800.0

Source: See Chapter 11, endnotes 6, 8, 11, 13.

As reflected in Table 11.2, the vast majority of these churches, representing 74 percent of the total, are Protestant in denomination. Unaffiliated churches are the second-largest in number, with 19 percent. The remaining religions combined account for approximately 7 percent of all congregations, of which Roman Catholic churches comprise 4 percent.

TABLE 11.2: U.S. Religious Congregations and Members by Major Denomination, Circa 2008*

Denomination	Congregations Number	Congregations Percent**	Members (millions) Number	Members (millions) Percent**
Protestant	318,588	74.3%	92.6	47.1%
Roman Catholic	18,674	4.4%	68.1	34.6%
Jewish	3,727	0.9%	6.1	3.1%
Orthodox/Other Catholic	1,451	0.3%	2.6	1.3%
Buddhist/Hindu/Other Eastern	3,821	0.9%	n.a.	n.a.
Muslim	1,209	0.3%	1.6	0.8%
Unaffiliated	81,505	19.0%	25.6	13.0%
Total	**428,975**	**100.0%**	**196.6**	**100.0%**

*Reporting year varies by denomination.
**Figures may not total 100 percent due to rounding.
Source: See Chapter 11, endnotes 6 and 8.

This picture does not begin to convey the vast assortment of different sects and denominations that characterize the American religious scene, however. Indeed, the latest edition of the *Yearbook of American and Canadian Churches* lists nearly 200 different Christian denominations alone in the United States, ranging from the Advent Christian Church, with 294 churches and 23,629 members, to the Wisconsin Evangelical Lutheran Synod, with

1,286 churches and 390,213 members.[7] Even this fails to capture the enormous diversity of American religious congregations because it covers only Christian faiths and thus leaves out the diverse array of Jewish, Muslim, Buddhist, Hindu, and other faiths that occupy the American religious landscape.

NUMBER OF MEMBERS

Close to 200 million Americans are members of these congregations. This means that two-thirds of the population is officially considered to be affiliated with a religious congregation in some form.[8]

Of these, as Table 11.2 shows, the majority are Protestants, as is the case with the majority of churches. However, the Protestant dominance is not nearly as large in terms of members as it is in terms of numbers of institutions, since many of the Protestant churches are quite small. Thus, while accounting for 74 percent of the congregations, Protestant churches engage a much smaller 47 percent of the religious congregation members. By contrast, with just over 4 percent of the congregations, the Catholic Church accounts for 35 percent of the religious congregants. Another 13 percent of congregation members belong to unaffiliated congregations and the remaining 5 percent to other religions, including Judaism, Orthodox or other Catholic denominations, eastern churches, Islam, and others.[9]

Despite the plethora of religious denominations, nearly half of all congregants belong to one of only three large denominations—the Roman Catholic Church, the Southern Baptist Convention, and the United Methodist Church—with the Catholic Church alone, as noted above, representing nearly 35 percent. Similarly, even within particular denominations there are important differences in the sizes of congregations. Thus, according to the recent National Congregations Study, while most congregations are small, with 75 or fewer regular participants, the largest 10 percent of all congregations account for more than half of all congregants.[10] Although there is considerable religious diversity, therefore, a relative handful of denominations and congregations dominate the religious landscape.

REVENUES

Although the importance of religious organizations is best measured in other terms, these organizations also turn out to be important in purely economic terms. As reported in Table 11.1, religious organizations had revenues in excess of $119 billion in 2008. This is three times the scale of the nonprofit arts and culture sector and two-thirds as large as the revenues of nonprofit social service agencies.[11]

As noted in Figure 11.1, the vast majority (85 percent) of this revenue comes from private giving. Indeed, as Figure 11.2 shows, religious institutions absorb about one-third of all charitable contributions in the United States, making them the largest recipients of charitable dollars of any type of nonprofit institution. The balance of the support comes from fees (mostly from rentals of congregation facilities), endowment earnings, and miscellaneous sources.[12]

FIGURE 11.1: Sources of Religious Congregation Revenue, 2007

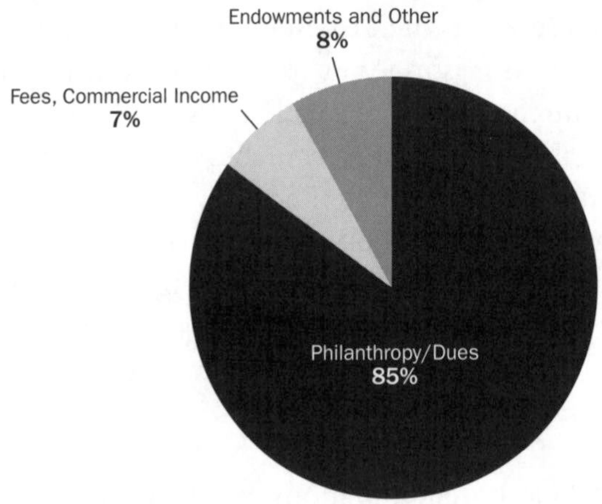

Endowments and Other
8%

Fees, Commercial Income
7%

Philanthropy/Dues
85%

Source: See Chapter 11, endnote 11.

FIGURE 11.2: Religion's Share of Giving and Volunteering, 2007

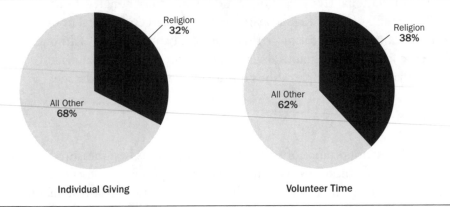

Religion
32%

All Other
68%

Individual Giving

Religion
38%

All Other
62%

Volunteer Time

Source: *Giving USA 2009*, p. 212. United States Census Bureau, *Current Population Survey*, September Supplement, 2007.

EMPLOYMENT

Religious organizations are also employers, though their paid workforce pales in comparison to their volunteer workforce. Close to 180,000 people were employed by religious congregations in the United States as of 2006, almost as many as work for nonprofit arts and culture institutions. In addition, these organizations attracted volunteer effort that was the equivalent of 1.8 million additional full-time workers. As reflected in Figure 11.2, religious congregations thus absorb 38 percent of the volunteer activity in the country, substantially more than any other component of the nonprofit sector.[13]

Religious institutions are the largest recipients of charitable dollars of any type of nonprofit institution.

Religion's Contribution to Other Fields

Most of the revenues flowing to religious congregations go to support religious worship and religious education. However, religious institutions also channel financial resources and volunteer effort to other uses, including various human service activities. According to the *Yearbook of American and Canadian Churches*, American churches devoted 15 percent of their revenues to "benevolences" as of 2008, but "benevolences" here refers not just to various non-religious human services such as soup kitchens and homeless shelters, but also to the support of religious institutions outside of the local congregation, such as seminaries, religious schools, and the parent denominational bodies.[14] On the other hand, some of the revenue that congregations spend on their operations likely benefits people other than the congregants themselves, as when congregation facilities are used for community meetings or soup kitchens. Gaining a clear picture of the extent of congregational resources going for social and community purposes is thus quite difficult, with estimates ranging from 10 to 23 percent of congregational revenue.[15] This means, however, that anywhere from 77 to 90 percent of congregational resources goes for the operational needs of the congregations.

Financial resources are not the only ones that religious congregations contribute to societal problem solving, however. Also important is the time that clergy, other paid staff, and volunteers mobilized by religious congregations devote to a variety of service activities. As it turns out, 82 percent of congregations surveyed as part of the 2006–07 National Congregations Study reported involvement in some type of social service activity. More specifically:

- 42 percent of surveyed congregations reported having engaged in feeding people;

- 20 percent participated in home building, repair, or maintenance projects;

- 16 percent distributed clothing; and

- 12 percent provided some type of service for the homeless.[16]

The actual extent of congregational engagement in such social service activities is fairly limited, however. Only 11 percent of the congregations surveyed in the National Congregations Study had a staff person devoting at least a quarter of his or her time to social service work. Even volunteer participation is limited, with the median congregation involving only 13 volunteers in such efforts over the course of a year. What is more, clergy involvement in community and civic affairs, including social service activities, is also quite limited, taking up on average only 1 to 2 hours per week. In short, while congregations are adept at mobilizing "small groups of volunteers to carry out well-defined, limited tasks on a periodic basis," they can hardly be counted on to solve social problems such as poverty, drug addiction, or hunger.[17] Perhaps their most important social function is helping members with tasks that might otherwise have to be performed by other agencies.

Recent Trends

The American religious community has undergone immense changes in recent years as the nature and composition of the U.S. population and the character of U.S. life have changed.

SLOW GROWTH OF ORGANIZATIONAL REVENUES

In the first place, despite the recent emergence of "mega-churches," the overall growth of religious organization revenue has lagged behind that of other types of nonprofit organizations, and of the economy as a whole.

Thus, between 1977 and 1996, the inflation-adjusted value of congregation revenues grew by only 43 percent, well behind the 61 percent growth rate registered by the U.S. economy as a whole and only half as large as the 96 percent growth rate of the nonprofit sector as a whole.[18]

This pattern has persisted more recently, moreover. Thus, as shown in Figure 11.3, congregational revenue, after adjusting for inflation, increased only 18 percent between 1997 and 2007, just about half as great as the rate of increase of the U.S. economy and roughly one-third the rate of growth of the overall nonprofit sector.[19]

LIMITED GROWTH IN PRIVATE GIVING

Underlying this relatively limited growth in religious congregation revenue, of course, has been the relatively limited growth of private charitable giving, long the major source of congregation revenue. According to one study of a sample of Protestant denominations, per-member giving to churches grew by only 18 percent between 1968 and 1991, after adjusting for inflation, a rate of increase well under 1 percent per year.[20]

FIGURE 11.3: Trends in Revenue of Religious Congregations Compared to All Nonprofits, All Giving, and U.S. GDP, 1997–2007

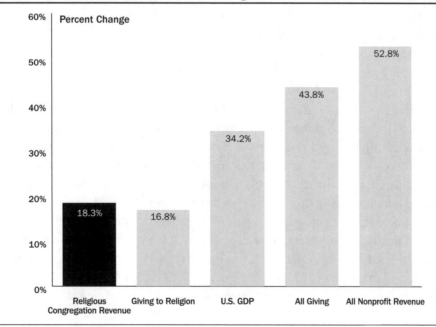

Source: See Chapter 11, endnote 19.

Even more troubling, while the absolute value of contributions to churches increased slightly, church giving as a share of personal income declined. In 1968, per-member giving as *a share of personal income* was 3.09 percent. By 1991 it had fallen to 2.54 percent, a drop of nearly 20 percent. What is more, the decline was particularly marked for giving to benevolences as opposed to giving to congregational finances (down 32 percent versus 14 percent for overall contributions).

As reflected in Figure 11.3, this pattern has continued into more recent years, putting a further squeeze on congregational finances. Thus, while overall charitable giving increased by 44 percent between 1997 and 2007, the value of giving to religion increased only 17 percent. In the process, religion's share of charitable giving sank from over 50 percent as late as 1988 to 32 percent as of 2007.[21]

MEMBERSHIP SHIFTS

Behind the financial challenges facing American congregations are a variety of profound shifts in the membership base of American congregations, shifts that have been underway for some time. According to one study of church membership, while the number of adherents to eighty Christian denominations increased by approximately 12 percent between 1980 and 1990, roughly in line with overall population growth, thirty-one of the eighty denominations reported actual declines in membership over this period and another sixteen reported growth rates below the growth rate of the population. Well over half of the denominations thus lost ground relative to the size of the population during this period.[22] What is more, the pattern of gains and losses was not distributed randomly across the denominations. Rather, the mainline churches generally lost members while the less established churches, many of them with a strong evangelical flavor, experienced often substantial growth. Thus, of fourteen denominations in this study of membership change that are affiliated with the National Council of the Churches of Christ, a mainline body, eleven, or almost 80 percent, reported actual membership declines between 1980 and 1990, and one other reported growth that lagged behind the growth rate of the general population. Included here, moreover, were such major denominations as the Episcopal Church (-13.4 percent), the Presbyterian Church (-11.5 percent), the United Church of Christ (-4.9 percent), the United Methodist Church (-4.0 percent), and the American Baptist Churches (-2.5 percent).

More recent data make clear that many of these trends have continued. Thus, between 1990 and 2008, church membership among Christian churches grew by only 4.5 percent while the adult population grew by 30 percent.[23] Several dynamics lay behind this outcome. For one thing, the number of Americans claiming some religious identification, though still quite high, has declined noticeably, from 86 percent of the adult population in 1990 to 76 percent in 2008, while the share reporting no religious identification nearly doubled as a share of the population, from 8 percent in 1990 to 15 percent in 2008. Put somewhat differently, the absolute number of non-identifiers increased by more than 100 percent, as shown in Figure 11.4.[24]

At the same time, the absolute decline in mainline Protestant identifiers continued. Overall, the number of mainline Protestant identifiers declined by 13 percent between 1990 and 2008 even as the overall adult population of the country increased by 30 percent. Mainline Protestant identifiers thus went from 18 percent of the population in 1990 to 12 percent in 2008.[25] Reflecting this, by 2008 these mainline Protestant denominations accounted for only 12 percent of all Christian congregants.

FIGURE 11.4: Recent Trends in Religious Identification of U.S. Adults, 1990–2008

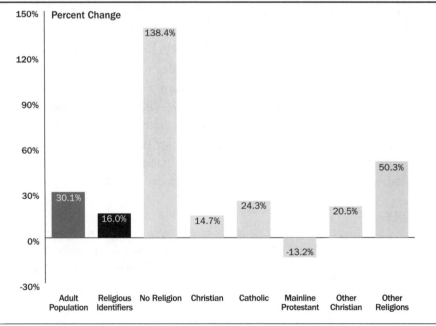

Source: See Chapter 11, endnote 24.

Offsetting these declines, however, were some significant expansions, no doubt due in important part to the surge of 32.5 million immigrants into the country between 1961 and 2008 following passage of the Immigration and Nationality Act of 1965. One reflection of this has been the growth of non-Christian religious identifiers—Muslims, Buddhists, and Hindus, among others—which increased by 50 percent between 1990 and 2008, though still constituting fewer than 5 percent of all adults. Even more striking, however, has been the expansion of adherents to the Catholic Church, which increased by 11 million people, or by 24 percent, between 1990 and 2008, reversing earlier losses and boosting the Catholic Church to 42 percent of all Christian congregants. Finally, the number of people identifying with other Christian denominations, including both new immigrant churches with a Christian identity and the fast-growing Pentecostal denominations, increased by 16 million people, or over 20 percent.

Conclusion

In short, the nonprofit sector includes not only institutions that deliver services and advocate on behalf of public issues. It also houses the institutions that look after the spiritual health of the nation. These institutions have long played a vital role in sustaining a tradition of voluntary giving and voluntary action, and they retain that role today.

At the same time, like so many other components of the American nonprofit scene, the religious institutions face important challenges. A significant secularization has affected major areas of American life, leading to a weakening of the historic bonds to established religious institutions. This is manifested in declining memberships and declining shares of personal income devoted to religious giving. At the same time, immigration is fueling the growth of some denominations while new religious bodies are emerging, many of them more traditional in their approaches and more evangelical in their style. How these various impulses will play out in the future evolution of American congregations is difficult to predict at this time. But it seems clear that some significant institutional adjustments lie ahead.

ENDNOTES

1. Data on charitable contributions to religious organizations from *Giving USA 2009* (Bloomington, IN: Giving USA Foundation, 2009). Data on volunteering from U.S. Bureau of Labor Statistics, "Volunteering in the United States—2010" (January 26, 2011), accessed at: www.bls.gov/news.release/pdf/volun.pdf.

2. Only 18,600 religious organizations out of the estimated 430,000 congregations in the United States thus filed the 990 Form with the Internal Revenue Service in 2005. Kennard T. Wing, Thomas H. Pollack, and Amy Blackwood, *The Nonprofit Almanac: 2008* (Washington, DC: The Urban Institute Press, 2008), Table 5.6, 151.

3. Bruce R. Hopkins, *The Law of Tax-Exempt Organizations*, 6th ed. (New York: John Wiley and Sons, 1992), 223–224.

4. For a discussion of the dilemma of defining "churches" for tax-exemption purposes, see: Bruce R. Hopkins, *The Law of Tax-Exempt Organizations*, 9th ed. (New York: John Wiley and Sons, 2007), 309–315, and Chapter 2 above.

5. Hopkins, *Law of Tax-Exempt Organizations*, 9th ed. (2007), 320.

6. Because religious congregations are not required to secure tax-exempt status or to file the information forms required of other charitable organizations, data on the scale of the religious congregation universe is highly imperfect. The estimate here, therefore, is based on a number of sources. Data on the number of Christian denominational churches, including Protestant, Roman Catholic, and Orthodox faiths, was derived from Eileen W. Lindner, ed., *Yearbook of American and Canadian Churches 2010*, 78th Issue, prepared for the National Council of the Churches of Christ (Nashville: Abingdon Press, 2010). These data derive from surveys of denominational bodies and generally cover the year 2008, though data on some denominations cover earlier years. Data on Jewish synagogues, Muslim mosques, and Buddhist, Hindu, and other eastern religions (e.g., Baha'i, Jain, Zoroastrian) were derived from the Association of Religion Data Archives (ARDA), accessed at: www.thearda.com/mapsReports/reports/US_2000.asp. This source presents congregational and membership data only through 2000. The estimate of unaffiliated congregations was derived from the National Congregations Study, 2006–7, as reported in Mark Chaves, "Religious Congregations," in *The State of Nonprofit America*, 2nd ed., ed. Lester M. Salamon (Washington, DC: Brookings Institution Press, 2012).

7. Lindner, *Yearbook of American and Canadian Churches 2010*, 361–71.

8. Great care must be taken in interpreting these figures because the data are based on self-reporting by religious bodies and the different bodies use different definitions of membership. Thus, for example, Roman Catholics count all baptized individuals, including infants, whereas some Protestant bodies include only those persons who have been formally received into the church, which generally occurs later in life, thereby excluding many millions of young children. Data on the number of Jewish congregants include all individuals in households in which one or more Jews reside and therefore include non-Jews living in such households as a result of intermarriage. Similarly, except in the case of Muslims, the numbers reported here do not represent the number of people who *identify* themselves as adherents to particular religions, which may be larger or smaller than the numbers reported by the religious bodies as constituting their "membership." See: Lindner, *Yearbook of American and Canadian Churches 2010*, 355. For sources of data on membership of various denominations, see endnote 6 above. Membership data are not available on the Buddhist, Hindu, and other eastern religious congregations.

9. For sources of data on membership, see endnote 6 above.

10. Mark Chaves, Shawna Anderson, and Jason Byassee, *American Congregations at the Beginning of the 21st Century* (Durham, NC: National Congregations Study, 2009), accessed at: www.soc.duke.edu/natcong/.

11. This estimate was derived by applying the share of total congregational revenue coming from charitable contributions, as shown by the National Congregations Study, to the estimate of total contributions to religious organizations provided by *Giving USA*. With congregational revenue from giving estimated to be 85 percent of total revenue as of 2007 and giving to religion estimated at $101.3 billion in 2007, this yields an estimate of total religious income of $119 billion. The distribution of the balance of congregational revenue between fees and other income is also based on the National Congregation Survey. See: Chaves, "Religious Congregations" (2011); and *Giving USA 2009*, 212.

12. Some congregations, particularly the mega-churches, have also developed business operations, including shopping centers, property management, and food service. Chaves, "Religious Congregations" (2011); Diana B. Henriques and Andrew W. Lehren, "Megachurches Add Local Economy to Mission," *New York Times* (November 3, 2007), p. A1.

13. The estimate of religious congregation employment was drawn from Wing et al., *The Nonprofit Almanac: 2008*, 57, Table 2.13. Data on volunteer involvement in religious congregations were taken from U.S. Census Bureau, *Current Population Survey*, September Supplement for 2008, downloaded from: www.census.gov/cps/.

14. Lindner, *Yearbook of American and Canadian Churches 2010*, 15.

15. Chaves, "Religious Congregations" (2011); Ram A. Cnaan, *The Invisible Caring Hand: American Congregations and the Provision of Welfare* (New York: New York University Press, 1988).

16. Chaves, "Religious Congregations" (2011).

17. Chaves et al., *American Congregations at the Beginning of the 21st Century*, 12.

18. 1977 data from Virginia A. Hodgkinson et al., *Nonprofit Almanac 1996–1997: Dimensions of the Independent Sector* (San Francisco: Jossey Bass, 1996); 1996 data from Independent Sector, 1998, Preliminary estimates. *See also*: Lester M. Salamon, *America's Nonprofit Sector: A Primer,* 2nd ed. (New York: Foundation Center, 1999), 154.

19. Data on religious organization revenue computed by assuming charitable giving accounts for 85 percent of religious congregation revenue. Giving data from *Giving USA 2009*, 212. For origins of the estimate of overall nonprofit revenue growth, see Chapter 5, endnote 31.

20. John and Sylvia Ronsvalle, "The State of Church Giving Through 1991," *Yearbook of American and Canadian Churches 1994* (Nashville: Abingdon Press, 1994), 12.

21. Computed from data in *Giving USA 2009*, 212.

22. Kenneth B. Bedell, ed., *Yearbook of American and Canadian Churches 1993* (Nashville: Abingdon Press, 1993), 14–15; Kenneth B. Bedell, ed., *Yearbook of American and Canadian Churches 1997* (Nashville: Abingdon Press, 1997), 9.

23. Computed from data reported in Lindner, *Yearbook of American and Canadian Churches 2010*, 10.

24. U.S. Bureau of the Census, *Statistical Abstract of the United States, 2011* (Washington, DC: U.S. Government Printing Office, 2011), Table 75. All data on religious identity in this and the following two paragraphs draw on this source. Data on religious members are from Lindner, *Yearbook 2010*, 10–12.

25. For the purposes of this analysis, mainline Protestant congregations include those affiliated with the Methodist, Lutheran, Presbyterian, Episcopalian, and United Church of Christ denominations.

PART THREE

Looking to the Future

12

Trends and Challenges

As the previous chapters have made clear, the nonprofit sector remains a vital force in American society, enlivening American democracy and enriching national life in countless ways. This set of organizations helps to meet human needs, give expression to diverse values, foster social bonds, voice citizen concerns, hold government accountable, and generally mobilize private initiative in the pursuit of public purposes.

At the same time, as previous chapters have also made clear, America's nonprofit sector functions in a context of dynamic change. Many of the changes affecting this sector are strengthening it in important ways, but others pose significant risks.

The purpose of this chapter is to examine these changes and to identify the opportunities and threats they seem to hold for the nation's nonprofit sector in the years ahead. Such an analysis is not only important for the future of the American nonprofit sector, moreover. It also has implications for the evolution of private nonprofit, or "civil society," sectors elsewhere in the world—in the developed countries of Western Europe and Asia, in Central and Eastern Europe, and in the developing world.

Supportive Trends

As a first step in this direction, it may be useful to focus on a number of trends that seem to hold important promise for the nonprofit sector's future development. Four of these in particular seem especially noteworthy.

SOCIAL AND DEMOGRAPHIC DEVELOPMENTS

In the first place, nonprofit organizations are being affected by a number of demographic trends that are boosting the demand for the kinds of services that these organizations provide. Among the more salient of these trends are the following:

- **Aging of the population.** The country's population of seniors 75 years and older doubled between 1980 and 2008 on top of a doubling of the 65-and-older population between 1960 and 2000. This trend seems likely to continue, moreover, with the prospect that the over-75 population will grow by 77 percent between 2010 and 2030 while the overall population of the country will grow by only 20 percent.[1] This will boost the need for nursing home care, assisted living, and other elderly services, fields in which nonprofits have a considerable presence.

America's nonprofit sector enjoys a number of opportunities due to demographic developments increasing the need for its services, increased policy attention, and new philanthropic currents.

- **Expansion of the labor force participation rate of women.** The labor force participation rate for women jumped from less than 20 percent in 1960 to over 60 percent in 1998 and has been holding at that level since. Even more dramatically, the labor force participation rate for married women with children under the age of six rose from 18.6 percent in 1960 to 62 percent in 2009, and for single women with children under six it reached nearly 68 percent.[2] This naturally translates into increased demand for child care services, another significant arena of nonprofit activity.

- **Shifts in family structure.** Significant changes have also occurred in the American family structure, and these, too, have important implications for nonprofit agencies. In 1960, there was one divorce for every four marriages. By 1980, this figure had jumped to one divorce for every two marriages, and it has remained there into the new millennium. During this same period, the number of children involved in divorces increased from 463,000 in 1960 to more than 1 million throughout the 1980s and 1990s. Since divorce typically involves a certain amount of emotional trauma and often brings with it significant loss of economic status, this shift also translates into increased need for human services of the sort that many nonprofit agencies offer. Also contributing to this increased demand is the tremendous surge that has occurred in out-of-wedlock births. Between 1960 and 1980, the proportion of all births that were to unwed mothers increased from 5 percent to 18 percent, and by 1994 it had reached 33 percent. This represents an eight-fold increase in the number of out-of-wedlock births, from 224,000 in 1960 to 1.3 million in 1995, and to 1.7 million by 2007. The vast majority of these births (68 percent) are to white mothers, moreover.[3]

- **Substance abuse.** Changes have also occurred in the prevalence of substance abuse in American society. One reflection of this is the striking increase in the number of people receiving substance abuse treatment services over the past several decades. Thus, as recently as 1977, the number of people using such services stood at approximately 235,000. By 1995 it was over 1 million; and by 2009 it was close to 1.2 million.[4]

A recent spate of political and policy developments has substantially increased the visibility of nonprofit organizations.

- **Surge of immigration.** A significant expansion has also occurred in the number of people obtaining legal permanent resident status, from 3.3 million in the decade of the 1960s to 9.5 million in just the first nine years of the new millennium.[5]

Taken together, these and other sociodemographic changes have expanded the demand for many of the services that nonprofit organizations have traditionally provided, such as child day care, home health and nursing home care for the elderly, family counseling, foster care, relocation assistance, and substance abuse treatment and prevention. The demand for these services has spread well beyond the poor, moreover, and now encompasses middle-class households with resources to pay for them, a phenomenon that one analyst has called "the transformation of social services."[6] The pressure on the foster care system alone, for example, has ballooned as the number of children in foster care doubled between the early 1980s and the early 1990s, though the growth has subsided somewhat in the new millennium. At the same time, the welfare reform legislation enacted in 1996, with its stress on job readiness, created additional demand for the services that nonprofits typically offer.

GREATER VISIBILITY AND POLICY SALIENCE

Another factor working to the advantage of nonprofit organizations has been a recent spate of political and policy developments that has substantially increased the visibility of these organizations. This has included the neo-liberal ideology popularized by the Thatcher and Reagan regimes in the U.K. and the U.S. in the 1980s, with their anti-government rhetoric and emphasis on philanthropy and the private sector, including the private nonprofit sector, as a better vehicle than government for addressing human needs; the revival of these notions with the rise of the Tea Party movement in the United States in 2008 and beyond; the significant credibility that the concept of "civil society," of citizen self-organization, gained during the uprisings that brought down communism in Central Europe in the latter 1980s and again in the citizen movements challenging authoritarian regimes in the "Arab spring" of 2011; the recent emphasis on the importance of "social capital" in promoting democracy and economic growth and the linkage of social capital to the presence of associations; and the Obama administration's support for "social innovation" and the "social entrepreneurs" that promote it. Despite some evidence of declining confidence in nonprofit organizations, other evidence points to continued popular support for these organizations through charitable giving and volunteering.[7]

To cope with increased complexity, nonprofit management has had to become increasingly professional.

PROFESSIONALIZATION

Along with increased visibility and growing demand for their services, nonprofit organizations have become increasingly professionalized. No longer the preserve only of hearty volunteers, nonprofit organizations had become major employers by the late 1970s, and their attraction of paid staff has continued into the new century. Indeed, between the late 1970s and the mid-1990s, the paid staff of nonprofit organizations grew at an annual rate that was more than 70 percent higher than that of all non-agricultural employment.[8] This disparity in employment growth has not only continued but accelerated in the new millennium, as the U.S. economy continued its structural shift from manufacturing to services. Thus, nonprofit employment grew two and one-half times faster than overall nonfarm employment between 1998 and 2005, and it appears to have sustained this growth through much of the economic recession of 2008 and beyond.[9] Indeed, if the nonprofit sector were itself one of the 18 "industries" into which statisticians divide economies, as of 2007 it would be the fourth-largest such industry in the U.S. economy in terms of employment. In the process, many of these organizations have become quite complex institutions. Unable to sustain themselves from traditional charitable sources, these organizations have had to develop sophisticated funding strategies involving government grants and contracts, fees for service, and a variety of earned-income schemes. Even traditional charitable fundraising has grown enormously more complex, utilizing elaborate telemarketing, direct mail, and donor "planned giving" arrangements.

Not surprisingly, to cope with this increased complexity, nonprofit management has had to become increasingly professional. As one recent account has noted, "Although some nonprofit industries, such as education and health care, had been professionally managed for decades, by the end of the Reagan era, professionalization had penetrated every area in which nonprofits operated, including religion."[10] This process began, ironically enough, in the most voluntaristic component of the nonprofit field—that is, the charitable fundraising sphere. A veritable revolution has occurred in this arena of nonprofit action, as reflected in the emergence and growth of specialized fundraising organizations, such as the National Society of Fund Raisers (1960), now the Association of Fundraising Professionals (AFP); the Council for the Advancement and Support of Education (1974); the Association for Healthcare Philanthropy (1967); and the National Committee for Planned Giving (1988). Equally impressive has been the transformation in the technology of charitable giving through the development of such devices as workplace solicitation, telethons, direct mail campaigns, telephone solicitation, e-philanthropy, and a host of complex "planned giving" vehicles such as "charitable remainder trusts." Entire organizations have surfaced to manage this process of extracting funds, and for-profit businesses, such as Fidelity Investments, have also gotten into the act with their own charitable funds offering their investors an opportunity to manage their charitable resources through a nonprofit affiliated with the firm that handles their regular investments.[11]

Other evidence of the growing professionalization of the nonprofit field has included the construction of a set of sector-wide infrastructure institutions, such as Independent Sector, the Council on Foundations, the Association of Small Foundations, the Forum of Regional Associations of Grantmakers, and state nonprofit organizations; as well as the emergence of a nonprofit press (*The Chronicle of Philanthropy, The NonProfit Times, The Nonprofit Quarterly*). To meet the resulting demand for more professionalized staff, moreover, new nonprofit management training programs have been organized at universities throughout the country. As of 2009, 168 U.S. colleges or universities had graduate degree programs with a concentration in the management of nonprofit organizations, up from only 17 as recently as 1990.[12]

What was once a scattering of largely overlooked institutions has thus become a booming cottage industry attracting organizations, personnel, publications, services, conferences, web sites, head-hunting firms, consultants, rituals, and fads—all premised on the proposition that nonprofit organizations are distinctive institutions with enough commonalities, despite their many differences, to be studied, represented, serviced, and trained as a group. While this professionalization has its costs, as will be detailed below, it also brings with it the potential for improving the quality of nonprofit operations and attracting higher-quality personnel. This, in turn, can contribute to the sector's reputation for effectiveness and competence.

While the American nonprofit sector stands to benefit from a number of supportive trends, it also faces enormous challenges.

THE NEW PHILANTHROPY

Also working to the benefit of the nonprofit sector are a series of developments potentially affecting private philanthropy. These include:

- A widely anticipated *intergenerational transfer of wealth* between the Depression-era generation and the postwar baby boomers expected over the next forty years,[13] though the sharp drop in home prices beginning in 2008 and the rising cost of health care for the baby boom generation seem likely to take a large bite out of this rather optimistic scenario;

- The greater corporate willingness to engage in partnerships and collaborations with nonprofit organizations that has resulted from globalization and the resulting growing importance of corporate "reputational capital";[14]

- The dot-com phenomenon, which led to the accumulation of enormous fortunes in the hands of a small group of high-tech entrepreneurs, some of whom have turned their new-found wealth into charitable ventures;[15] and

- The emergence on the "frontiers of philanthropy" of a host of new actors and new tools for channeling private investment capital into support of social and environmental objectives.[16]

Together, these developments are injecting a substantial amount of new blood and new energy into the philanthropic field.

The economic crisis of 2008 and the economic recession it triggered have put considerable strain on the commercial revenues of nonprofits.

Major Challenges

While the American nonprofit sector stands to benefit from a number of supportive trends, however, it also faces enormous challenges. In part, these challenges grow out of limitations in the positive trends. Thus, for example, while the prospect of significant intergenerational wealth transfer and a changing corporate posture toward the voluntary sector offer much-needed relief, the extent of this relief is open to serious question. After all, charitable giving is not the only potential use of the new wealth, and investment managers have been hard at work devising more profitable alternatives. What is more, the projected inheritances may never materialize, or never materialize to the extent anticipated, if home values, the major anticipated source of this windfall, continue to be depressed, life expectancy continues to expand, and medical or nursing care costs absorb more than the anticipated share of the accumulation. Certainly the recent record of bequest giving offers little encouragement. Far from increasing, the level of such giving has actually declined in inflation-adjusted terms for most of the years since 2000, perhaps partly in response to changes in tax law that eliminated part of the tax incentives for such giving.[17] Similarly, the reorientation of corporate philanthropy has recently run headlong into the imperatives of corporate downsizing. In re-engineering the corporation, many corporate managements are re-engineering the corporate philanthropy function out of existence.

Under these circumstances, the pressures on the nation's nonprofit sector are likely to persist. More specifically, the nonprofit sector faces four rather serious challenges at the present time.

THE FISCAL CHALLENGE

In the first place, as the second decade of the twentieth century dawns, the nonprofit sector finds itself in the midst of a serious fiscal challenge reminiscent of the retrenchment era of the early 1980s. As we have seen, the nonprofit sector grew rather robustly during the period from 1997 to 2007. This growth was fueled in large part by an expansion of commercial income in the form of fees and charges for nonprofit services; the continued expansion of government support, albeit at a slightly less robust rate than previously; and a surprising expansion of private charitable support. By the end of this period, however, the basic structure of nonprofit finance remained fairly close to what it has been for the past several decades, with most (52 percent) of the revenue coming from fees and charges; another sizable proportion (38 percent) from government grants, contracts, and payments; and the remaining sliver (10 percent) from private philanthropy.

For a variety of reasons, however, this fiscal structure is now open to serious strains. For one thing, the economic crisis of 2008 and the economic recession it triggered have put considerable strain on the commercial revenues of nonprofit organizations, not to mention their revenues from charitable giving. Even health care has begun to feel the strain, as consumers delay or avoid medical treatment to conserve resources and avoid escalating co-pays.[18] Moreover, although the Economic Recovery Program passed by Congress in early 2009 helped to buffer many human service nonprofits from the early effects of the economic recession, a shift in the country's political climate has all but slammed the door on additional anti-recessionary assistance. More seriously, that same shift in political climate has made it increasingly clear that government's past role as a major source of nonprofit revenue is likely to suffer a serious shock as efforts are launched to pare the federal deficit bequeathed by the significant tax cuts for wealthy Americans enacted in 2001, the costly wars in Afghanistan and Iraq, and the efforts to combat the recession. With powerful political forces insisting that deficit reduction proceed entirely, or at least chiefly, through spending cuts as opposed to revenue increases, the stage is set for another extended period of retrenchment focusing on precisely the public programs of most concern to nonprofit organizations. Already, serious proposals are circulating to radically transform and limit the growth of Medicare and Medicaid, two of the major sources of federal support to nonprofit organizations across a broad front, from hospitals and home health providers to assisted living facilities, providers of day care, and supportive services for the developmentally disabled, with further cuts pending in a wide variety of other programs providing crucial assistance to nonprofit organizations.[19] With state and local governments similarly strapped, the prospects for continued growth in nonprofit revenue from government sources at anything like recent rates thus appear dim.

Nonprofits are increasingly losing market share to for-profit firms in a wide assortment of fields.

THE COMPETITION CHALLENGE

In addition to a fiscal challenge, nonprofit America also continues to face a serious competition challenge. This, too, is not a wholly new development. Thus, as previous chapters have shown, between 1982 and 1997, the nonprofit share of day care jobs dropped from 52 to 38 percent, a decline of some 27 percent in market share. Similarly sharp declines in the relative nonprofit share occurred among rehabilitation hospitals (down 50 percent), home health agencies (down 48 percent), health maintenance organizations (down 60 percent), kidney dialysis centers (down 45 percent), hospices (down 15 percent), and mental health clinics (down 11 percent). In many of these fields the absolute number of nonprofit facilities continued to grow, but the for-profit growth outpaced it. And in at least one crucial field—acute care hospitals—while the nonprofit *share* increased slightly, a significant reduction occurred in the *absolute number* of nonprofit (as well as public) facilities, so that the for-profit share of the total increased even more.

This trend has continued in more recent years, moreover. Thus, as Table 12.1 reveals, between 1997 and 2007 the nonprofit sector continued to lose ground to for-profit providers in terms of its share of employment in the fields of individual and family services (down 23 percent), community care facilities for the elderly (down 20 percent), home health care (down 19 percent), specialty hospitals (down 13 percent), outpatient care facilities (down 8 percent), nursing care facilities (down 3 percent), and child day care (down 2 percent).[20]

TABLE 12.1: Change in Nonprofit Share of Employment, Selected Fields, 1997–2007

Field	Change in Nonprofit Share
Individual and Family Services	-23%
Community Care Facilities for the Elderly	-20%
Home Health Care Facilities	-19%
Specialty Hospitals (Other Than Psychiatric)	-13%
Outpatient Care Facilities	-8%
Nursing Care Facilities	-3%
Other Residential Care Facilities	-3%
Child Day Care	-2%

Source: U.S. Census Bureau, *Economic Census, 1997 and 2007.*

The range of for-profit firms competing with nonprofits has grown increasingly broad, moreover. For example, the recent welfare reform legislation, which seeks to move large numbers of welfare recipients from welfare dependence to employment, attracted defense contractors like Lockheed Martin into the social welfare field. What these firms offered is not the knowledge of human services but the information-processing technology and contract management skills they gained from serving as master contractors on huge military system projects, which have become the skills now needed to manage the subcontracting systems required to prepare welfare recipients for work.[21] Similarly, as we have seen, for-profits have recently made substantial inroads in the field of higher education. Between 1980 and 2005, while enrollment in public and nonprofit higher education institutions each grew by roughly 37 percent, enrollments in for-profit higher education institutions surged by 800 percent—from just over 110,000 to more than 1 million students.[22] Even the sacrosanct field of charitable fundraising has recently experienced a significant for-profit incursion in the form of financial service firms such as Fidelity and Merrill Lynch. By 2000, the Fidelity Charitable Gift Fund had attracted more assets than the nation's largest community foundation and distributed three times as much in grants.[23]

What accounts for this striking and widespread challenge to nonprofit market share? Broadly speaking, three factors seem to be at work. In the first place, the very same social and demographic trends that are expanding the demand for nonprofit services are creating important markets for for-profit competitors. By broadening the market for social, health, and related services well beyond the disadvantaged, these trends have opened opportunities to earn fees from the users of these services or from the insurance companies that reimburse providers on their behalf. As we have seen, nonprofits, constrained by the limited availability of philanthropic support and unnerved by the uncertainties surrounding government support, have turned massively to such user fees, with the result that such fees have accounted for over half of the substantial revenue growth the nonprofit sector has enjoyed over the recent past. But such fees have also enticed many for-profit firms into lines of "business" that nonprofits once had mostly to themselves.

A second factor affecting the striking expansion of for-profit competition in traditional nonprofit fields of activity has been a significant shift in the forms of government support. With the ascendance of conservative political elements in the 1980s and beyond, conscious efforts were launched through Executive Office Circulars and other vehicles to encourage government program managers to promote for-profit involvement in government contract work, including that for human services, under the banner of "privatization."[24] More significantly, so-called "producer-side subsidies" such as grants and contracts that delivered aid directly to the providers of services (for example, day care centers and drug abuse centers) were replaced by forms of assistance such as vouchers and tax expenditures that channel aid to the consumers of services instead, thus requiring nonprofits to compete for clients in the marketplace, where for-profits have traditionally had the edge.[25] Already by 1980, the majority (53 percent) of federal assistance to nonprofit organizations took the form of such consumer subsidies, much of it through the Medicare and Medicaid programs. By 1986 this stood at 70 percent, and it continued to rise into the 1990s.[26]

Nonprofits are at a systematic competitive disadvantage in competing with for-profits because of the uneven playing field they face in accessing investment capital.

In part, this shift toward consumer subsidies resulted from the concentration of the budget cuts of the 1980s on the so-called discretionary spending programs, which tended to be producer-side grants and contracts, while Medicare and Medicaid—both of them consumer-side subsidies—continued to grow. In part also, however, the shift toward consumer-side subsidies reflected the ascendance of conservative political forces that favored forms of assistance that maximized consumer choice in the marketplace. The price of securing conservative support for new or expanded programs of relevance to nonprofit organizations in the late 1980s and early 1990s, therefore, was to make them vouchers or tax expenditures. The new Child Care and Development Block Grant enacted in 1990 and then reauthorized and expanded as part of the welfare reform legislation in 1996, for example, specifically gave states the option to use the $5 billion in federal funds provided for day care to finance voucher payments to eligible families rather than grants or contracts to day care providers, and most states exercised this option. As of 1998, therefore, well over 80 percent of the children receiving day care assistance under this program were receiving it through voucher certificates, and an additional $2 billion in federal day care subsidies was delivered through a special child care tax credit.[27] Nearly $7 billion was thus provided in new consumer-side day-care subsidies, much more than the $2.8 billion allocated for producer-side subsidies to social service providers for day care and all other forms of social services under the federal government's Social Services Block Grant. What is more, by 2009, a decade later, the value of the day tax subsidy had grown from $2 billion to $4.3 billion.[28] Nonprofit day care providers, like their counterparts in other fields, have thus been thrown increasingly into the private market to secure even public funding for their activities, and not surprisingly, they have found increasing numbers of for-profit providers ready to compete with them.

> ### *Like government agencies, nonprofits are facing new accountability demands and challenges to the legitimacy of the special tax and other advantages they enjoy.*

Finally, and perhaps most decisively, one of the major reasons nonprofits have lost market share to for-profits in these expanding markets is that nonprofits are at a systematic competitive disadvantage, particularly where new government funding streams create rapid expansions of effective demand. This is so because of the uneven playing field nonprofits confront when it comes to accessing the investment capital required to establish new facilities and new operations in response to rapid surges in demand. Because they are prohibited from distributing profits to their "owners," and indeed are not allowed to have "owners" in the market sense of the word, nonprofits lack access to the "free" capital that for-profit businesses can generate merely by issuing and selling stock. Nonprofits can therefore access capital only by borrowing it, typically from the most expensive sources—commercial banks.[29] When surges in demand occur, such as accompanied the decision by the Medicare program to make home health care a reimbursable expense in 1980 as a way to reduce the spiraling cost of hospital care, it was the for-profit providers who were in the best position to respond by floating IPOs (initial public offerings) and generating the capital to build thousands of new facilities. And this pattern has been repeated in numerous other spheres. While there have been recent efforts to attract private investment capital into "social enterprises" and other social-purpose organizations and to entice foundations to function like "philanthropic banks" by leveraging their assets to incentivize such flows of private investment capital into nonprofit and for-profit social ventures, such efforts remain on the "frontiers" of philanthropic and private investment practice and have yet to be fully mainstreamed.[30]

THE EFFECTIVENESS CHALLENGE

In addition to the fiscal and competition challenges confronting the nonprofit sector at the present time is a third challenge, a veritable crisis of effectiveness.

Because they do not meet a formal "market test," nonprofits are always vulnerable to charges of inefficiency and ineffectiveness. However, the scope and severity of these charges have grown massively in recent years. In fact, the competence of the nonprofit sector has been challenged on at least four different grounds.

Programmatic Opposition. In the first place, nonprofit organizations, particularly in the human services field, have been implicated in the general assault on public social programs that has animated national political debate for close to three decades now. Despite considerable contrary evidence,[31] the persistence of poverty, the continuation of serious urban crime, the epidemic of teenage pregnancy, and the persistence of welfare dependency have been taken as evidence that these programs do not work. The resulting open season on government social programs has caught significant components of the nonprofit sector in the crossfire, particularly since the sector has been involved in administering many of the discredited programs.

Worse than that, the very motives of the nonprofit agencies have been called into question. Involvement in government programs "changes charities' incentives," charges one recent critique, "giving them reasons to keep caseloads up instead of getting them down by successfully turning around people's lives."[32] Nonprofits thus stand accused not only of being ineffective, but also of preferring not to solve the problems they are purportedly addressing.

Reconceptualization of Social Assistance. Underlying this critique of public social programs is a profound rethinking of the causes of poverty and of the interventions likely to reduce it. The central change here involves a loss of faith in the traditional premise of professional social work, with its emphasis on casework and individualized services as the cure for poverty and distress. During the 1960s, this precept was translated into public policy through the 1962 amendments to the Social Security Act and, later, through portions of the Economic Opportunity Act of 1964, both of which made federal resources available to purchase social services for poor people in the hope that this would allow them to escape the "culture of poverty" in which they were enmeshed.

A massive mismatch has opened between the sector's actual operations and popular conceptions of what it is supposed to be like.

This "services strategy" was subsequently challenged by critics on both the right and the left. Those on the right have argued that the growth of supportive services and income assistance for the poor ultimately proved counterproductive because they created disincentives to work and undermined fundamental values of self-reliance.[33] Those on the left, by contrast, point to the structural shifts in the economy that have eliminated much of the market for blue-collar labor, and not a lack of services, as the real causes of poverty, unemployment, and the social maladies that flow from them. Both sides seem to agree, however, that the traditional skills of the nonprofit human services sector have become increasingly irrelevant to the problems facing the poor. More important than social services in the new paradigm is job-readiness, and ultimately a job. Under these circumstances, the employer rather than the social worker becomes the pivot of social policy. While private nonprofit organizations may still play a role in the alleviation of poverty, the real action has shifted to the business community, the educational system, and, in the conservative view, the faith community. This is clearly reflected in the welfare reform law of 1996, which ended the entitlement to assistance and placed much heavier emphasis on employment as a condition of assistance. It also advantaged so-called "faith-based initiatives" as vehicles for helping individuals gain the life skills and moral backbone thought to be needed to succeed in the workplace, a strategy that gained presidential endorsement with the election of George W. Bush in 2000. This jobs focus also lies behind the recent enthusiasm for "social enterprises," which, unlike standard human service agencies, utilize the market to pursue social objectives. All of this threatens to push the nonprofit sector more to the periphery of social problem solving, at least as far as the poor are concerned.

The Accountability Movement. Complicating matters further is the fact that nonprofit organizations generally lack meaningful bases for demonstrating the value of what they do. Indeed, nonprofit organizations have often resisted demands for greater accountability on grounds that responding to such demands might interfere with the independence that gives the sector its special character. Instead, nonprofits have tended to point to their not-for-profit status as *ipso facto* evidence of their trustworthiness and effectiveness.

Increasingly, however, these implicit claims by nonprofit providers have been subjected to serious challenge as a result not only of a number of recent scandals, but also of growing questions about the basic efficiency and effectiveness of nonprofit agencies. "Unlike publicly traded companies," management expert Regina Herzlinger has thus noted, "the performance of nonprofits and governments is shrouded behind a veil of secrecy that is lifted only when blatant disasters occur."[34] This is problematic, she argues, because nonprofit organizations generally lack the three basic accountability mechanisms of business: the self-interest of owners, competition, and the ultimate bottom-line measure of profitability. This has prompted calls on the part of even advocates of the sector for more formalized mechanisms for holding nonprofit organizations accountable for the pursuit of their charitable missions, and continuing suggestions from political leaders that the nonprofit sector is riddled with bad apples and in serious need of additional regulation.[35]

How well the nonprofit sector will be able to take advantage of opportunities and fend off perils will depend on how well prepared it is and how well prepared it makes those on whom it relies.

THE LEGITIMACY CHALLENGE

All of this, finally, has led to a fourth challenge for the nonprofit sector, a much more serious and profound crisis of legitimacy that is questioning the whole concept of the nonprofit sector. Ironically, the nonprofit sector's success in adjusting to the realities of post-war, and then post-Reagan, American society may be costing it the support of significant elements of the American public as a massive mismatch has opened between the sector's actual operations and popular conceptions of what it is supposed to be like, conceptions that the sector itself has helped to promote. While opinions may differ about whether public trust in the nonprofit sector has weakened or remained constant, there is considerable evidence that the image of the nonprofit sector in the public mind differs widely from the nonprofit sector that actually exists.

In its public persona, the nonprofit sector is still perceived through a comforting nineteenth-century prism that pictures small voluntary groups ministering to the needy and downtrodden and relying mostly on charitable donations and the time of well-meaning volunteers. In reality, however, the actual operations of the nonprofit sector have become far more complex. Thus, for example, instead of private philanthropy, fees and service charges are now the sector's principal source of support, with government a close second, as we have seen. Yet neither the commercial foundation of nonprofit finances nor the sector's complex relationships with government have been fully integrated into the popular image of how this sector functions. As a consequence, the sector is vulnerable to perennial criticism for chief executive salaries that CEOs of much less complex for-profit companies would view with scorn. Even the nonprofit sector's involvement in advocacy has been called into question as a consequence. Having joined with government to respond to public needs, nonprofit organizations are now in the uncomfortable position of appearing to advocate not on behalf of the clients and communities they serve, but in their own self-interest, for the budgets and programs that support their own operations, a point that conservative critics of government spending have made a particular point of attack.

As nonprofits have moved wisely to professionalize their operations, they have found themselves attacked by critics hankering for a return to the simple virtues of self-help, faith-based charity, or other community-based approaches, and this critique arises from the left and not just from the conservative side of the political spectrum. The nonprofit sector stands accused from this perspective of becoming a principal locus for the "overprofessionalization" of societal problem solving. According to this line of thinking, the professionalization of social concerns, by redefining basic human needs as "problems" that only professionals can resolve, has alienated people from the helping relationships they could establish with their neighbors and kin. "Through the propagation of belief in authoritative expertise," Northwestern University Professor John McKnight thus notes, "professionals cut through the social fabric of community and sow clienthood where citizenship once grew."[36]

Taking advantage of the resulting questioning, local governments have been increasingly emboldened to challenge the tax exemptions of nonprofit organizations. Such challenges have surfaced vigorously in Pennsylvania, New York, New Hampshire, Oregon, Maine, Wisconsin, Colorado, and, more recently, Massachusetts and Illinois.[37] A recent survey showed, in fact, that among one sample of mostly mid-sized and large nonprofits operating in the fields of social services, community development, and arts and culture, a striking 63 percent reported paying some kind of tax, payment in lieu of taxes, or other fee to state or local government.[38]

More recently, congressional critics brought the same questioning to one of the other fundamental functions of the voluntary sector—its advocacy and representational function. Under the so-called Istook Amendment, named after its congressional sponsor, nonprofit organizations receiving federal grants could not use more than 5 percent of their total revenues, including their private revenues, for a broad range of advocacy activities. This would significantly broaden existing restrictions on nonprofit lobbying and advocacy. Though ultimately defeated, this amendment evidences the considerable questioning of nonprofit activity that has surfaced in relatively recent years.

Nonprofits have three options: continued drift, shifting more energies and resources to social enterprises, or pursuing a proactive strategy of renewal and reinvigoration.

The Road Ahead: Three Possible Futures

Whether the supportive trends or the significant challenges facing the nonprofit sector at the present time will prevail is difficult to determine with any precision. To a considerable extent, the answer to this question will depend on forces outside the sector's control—the shifting realities of political life, the resulting patterns of government policy, and broader economic trends. Nevertheless, how well the sector will be able to take advantage of the opportunities and fend off the perils will depend also on how well prepared it is, and how well prepared it makes those on whom it relies.

From the evidence at hand, it appears that this preparation is far from adequate. Unfortunately, the nonprofit sector has yet to develop a meaningful narrative that can square its current operations with the deeply held public convictions about how it is supposed to operate. Worse than that, some of the sector's own messaging, such as its constant celebration of giving and volunteering to the exclusion of its major sources of actual support, whether intentionally or inadvertently, helps perpetuate an image that is increasingly at odds with the known facts. Under these circumstances, any of three possible scenarios is equally likely.

The challenges facing the nonprofit sector at the present time can be seen as an opportunity for renewal, for rethinking the nonprofit sector's role and operations in light of contemporary realities.

CELEBRATION AND DRIFT: THE STATUS QUO OPTION

In the first place, the nonprofit sector can continue its historic posture of self-celebration and drift—emphasizing the virtues of charitable giving and volunteering while drifting toward ever greater reliance on commercial, or quasi-commercial, sources of support. Given the obvious strength of nonprofit organizations in a number of spheres, the extensive reliance placed upon them by governments in crucial policy arenas, and the growing capability of nonprofit managers to balance the competing pressures they are facing, it seems likely that this scenario could sustain the sector for some time to come. However, it is equally likely that a policy of drift will cause nonprofits to lose more of their market share in a wide assortment of fields, surrender more of their mission-critical functions such as advocacy and community organizing that for-profit competitors do not need to support, and see the *raison d'être* for many of their special advantages, such as tax exemption, slip away.

THE SOCIAL ENTERPRISE OPTION

A second option, especially attractive to younger activists and the socially conscious entrepreneurs who have emerged from the dot-com industry, is to give up on the nonprofit sector as it now exists and work toward the creation of a self-consciously new "social enterprise" or "fourth" sector that explicitly merges social purpose with business methods and taps into the much larger resources available through socially focused private investment capital. Hundreds of such "social enterprises" have surfaced in recent years, both in the United States and around the world. They include entities such as New Door Ventures in San Francisco, which operates two social ventures offering at-risk youth job-readiness skills through actual employment in the organization's ventures; DC Central Kitchen, which turns leftover food into millions of meals for thousands of at-risk individuals; and Pioneer Human Services, a $55 million human service agency in Seattle that improves the life chances of ex-offenders and drug addicts by engaging them in a variety of business ventures, such as a metal fabrication shop that markets its products to Boeing. Supporting this new wave of social-purpose businesses has emerged a sizable infrastructure of capacity builders like New Profit and Community Wealth Ventures as well as a growing number of investment funds and vehicles.[39] Already, one portion of this "fourth sector," composed of micro-enterprises and the "micro-finance institutions" that support them, is estimated to have a global scale of $75 to $150 billion with prospects of growing into a much broader "micro-financial services" industry on a global scale.[40] Another branch is incubating a host of so-called "bottom of the pyramid" lines of business that design products and distribution channels that appeal to people at the bottom of the economic pyramid who need a variety of products but often pay a premium price for them because of inadequate or inappropriate packaging or distribution systems.[41] Through these and other forms, a considerable portion of the new energy in the social purpose space is going into the promotion of this type of entity, which many see as a more viable, long-term, sustainable approach to solving problems of poverty, ill health, and environmental degradation than the traditional nonprofit sector.

THE RENEWAL OPTION

Finally, a third possible path of nonprofit evolution might be characterized as the "renewal option." The key to this approach is to see the challenges facing the nonprofit sector at the present time not as an excuse for retreat into some pretended golden age of nonprofit independence or a time for continued drift toward greater commercialization, but rather as an opportunity for *renewal*, for rethinking the nonprofit sector's role and operations in light of contemporary realities, and for achieving a new consensus—a new settlement—regarding the functions of these organizations; the relationships they have with citizens, with government, and with business; and the way they will operate in the years ahead.

At the center of such an undertaking must be a reconceptualization of the sector's "value proposition," its distinctive contributions to American society.[42] To many Americans, the value of the nonprofit sector has come to be confined to its service functions. While these functions are important, they hardly exhaust the value that Americans derive from this set of institutions. Re-establishing the other contributions this set of institutions makes, and doing so in a form that can be easily understood, may be pivotal to the sector's ability to retain its special place in American life.

What is needed is a realistic effort to acquaint the public with the broader mission of nonprofit organizations in a modern democracy.

Equally important will be a forthright acknowledgment—indeed celebration—of the nonprofit sector's important role as a "partner in public service,"[43] as the delivery system for a wide variety of publicly funded services that have expanded opportunities and the quality of life for millions of citizens, but an acknowledgment as well of the need for making the resulting partnerships work more effectively. As we have seen, government has emerged as the second most important source of nonprofit revenue, outdistancing philanthropy by a ratio of nearly 4 to 1. Yet the nonprofit sector's relationship with government remains suspect in the minds of many and poorly understood among most of the rest. More significantly, it remains in significant need of restructuring and reconstructions. As a declaration by leaders representing over 100,000 nonprofit organizations recently noted, "the relationships between government and the nonprofit sector have evolved in ad hoc fashion, with too little attention to their operational inefficiencies or to their tendency to put valued characteristics of the citizen sector at risk."[44] Other countries have dealt with these problems by forging "compacts" between government and nonprofit-sector organizations in order to make the collaborations between these two sectors that have become so central to modern public problem solving operate better for both sides. While such overarching policy prescriptions are difficult to establish in America's fragmented political system, it seems clear that some more explicit recognition is needed that this partnership is here to stay, that it offers enormous advantages to both government and nonprofits and to the citizens they both serve, but that significant improvements are needed to allow it to achieve the promise of which it is capable. Particularly needed is a grand bargain under which nonprofits would acknowledge the government need for stronger and more reliable performance reporting on the part of nonprofits, and governments would acknowledge more explicitly the need to protect the important mission-critical functions of nonprofits, such as advocacy and community organizing, in setting reimbursement rates on government vouchers and contracts.

A serious renewal strategy must also address the perennial problem of nonprofit finance. Of special importance here is solving the problem of nonprofit access to investment capital given the uneven playing field nonprofits confront in this arena and the resulting persistent nonprofit loss of market share in fields that they pioneer. Government tax credits for private investment in nonprofit capital projects and a greater willingness of foundations to function as "philanthropic banks" offering loans and loan guarantees that can help leverage private investment capital at premium rates are just some of the steps that might be needed here.

Finally, all of this will require a major effort at public education. What is needed here, however, is not another celebration of private giving and volunteering, important though these are, but a realistic effort to acquaint the public with the broader mission of nonprofit organizations in a modern democracy, and particularly to the modern reality of collaborative public problem solving, of nonprofit organizations as crucial links working collaboratively with government and the business sector to solve public problems. This may be a complex message to convey, but it is the one that best reflects the current realities, and perhaps the best hope for the nonprofit sector's future.

Conclusion and Implications

The building of sustainable nonprofit, or civil society, sectors has been a focus of immense concern in many parts of the world in recent years, from the newly emerging democracies of Central and Eastern Europe to the post-colonial regions of Africa, Asia, and Latin America. Taken for granted in these deliberations, however, has been the assumption that such a sector is already securely in place in much of the developed world, and certainly in the United States.

What the discussion here has made clear, however, is that the survival and prosperity of nonprofit institutions is not only at issue in the emerging democracies of the East and South; it is also very much in question in mature market economies such as the United States. Indeed, the very maturation and growth of nonprofit institutions may paradoxically pose challenges to their continued viability and support. Certainly in the United States, where a somewhat naïve myth of voluntarism has long enveloped the nonprofit sector, recent years have witnessed a steady broadening of the gap between what nonprofit organizations have had to do to prosper and grow and what popular mythologies have expected them to do to retain public support. The upshot has been a crisis of legitimacy for America's nonprofit sector that has manifested itself in growing demands for greater accountability, challenges to tax-exempt status, questioning of the sector's advocacy role, and a growing unease about the pay and perquisites of significant types of nonprofit organizations.

What this suggests is that the nonprofit sector is an inherently fragile organism, even in societies like the United States where commitment to this type of organization is an integral part of the national heritage. More than that, the role and character of these organizations can no more be frozen in time than those of other types of institutions: they must evolve in response to new circumstances and adapt to new opportunities and needs.

Those committed to the sustenance of a sphere of action outside the market and the state, whether in the United States or elsewhere, can therefore not afford to take the survival of this set of institutions for granted. To the contrary, they must continuously re-examine this sector in the light of broader societal trends and reposition it as needed to keep it vital as conditions change.

ENDNOTES

1. U.S. Bureau of the Census, *Statistical Abstract of the United States 2011* (Washington, DC: U.S. Government Printing Office, 2011), Table 8. Accessed at www.census.gov/compendia/statab/. (Cited hereafter as *U.S. Statistical Abstract, 2011*.)

2. U.S. Bureau of the Census, *Statistical Abstract of the United States 2000* (Washington, DC: U.S. Government Printing Office, 2000), 408–9; *U.S. Statistical Abstract 2011*, 385, Table 598.

3. *U.S. Statistical Abstract 2000*, 71; *U.S. Statistical Abstract 2011*, 96, Table 129; 68, Table 85.

4. U.S. Bureau of the Census, *Statistical Abstract of the United States 1983* (Washington, DC: U.S. Government Printing Office, 1983), 124, Table 197; *U.S. Statistical Abstract 2011*, 133, Table 202.

5. *U.S. Statistical Abstract 2011*, 76, Table 43.

6. Neil Gilbert, "The Transformation of Social Services," *Social Services Review*, 51:4 (December 1977): 624–641.

7. On the Reagan Administration's approach to nonprofits and philanthropy, see: Lester M. Salamon, "Nonprofit Organizations: The Lost Opportunity," in *The Reagan Record*, ed. John L. Palmer and Isabel V. Sawhill (Cambridge: Ballinger, 1984), 261–286. For a discussion of

the competing evidence on public confidence in nonprofit organizations, see: Michael O'Neill, "Public Confidence in Charitable Nonprofits," *Nonprofit and Voluntary Sector Quarterly*, 38:2 (April 2009): 237–269. For a statement of the importance of social capital and the nonprofit sector contribution to it, see: See: Robert Putnam, *Making Democracy Work: Civic Traditions in Modern Italy* (Princeton: Princeton University Press, 1993).

8. The paid employment of public-benefit nonprofit organizations grew at an annual average rate of 3.3 percent between 1977 and 1994, compared to 1.9 percent for all nonagricultural employment. Bureau of Labor Statistics data as reported in Hodgkinson, *Nonprofit Almanac 1996*, 129.

9. Nonprofit employment grew by 16.4 percent between 1995 and 2008 while total nonfarm employment grew by only 6.2 percent. Wing et al., *The Nonprofit Almanac 2008* (Washington, DC: The Urban Institute Press, 2008), 20, Table 1.8. Evidence on 21 states across the country indicates that nonprofit employment actually grew by an average of 2.5 percent per year between the second quarter of 2007 and the second quarter of 2009, the worst part of the recent recession. By contrast, for-profit employment in these states fell during this same period by an average of 3.3 percent per year. And this pattern held for every single state examined. See: Lester M. Salamon and S. Wojciech Sokolowski, "Nonprofits and Recession: Evidence from 21 States," Nonprofit Employment Data Project Bulletin (Baltimore: Johns Hopkins Center for Civil Society Studies, 2010).

10. Peter Dobkin Hall, "Historical Perspectives on Nonprofit Organizations," in *The Jossey-Bass Handbook of Nonprofit Leadership and Management*, ed. Robert D. Herman (San Francisco: Jossey-Bass Publishers, 1994), 28.

11. For an analysis of these corporate-initiated charitable funds, see: Rick Cohen, "Corporate-Initiated Charitable Funds," in *New Frontiers of Philanthropy: A Guide to the New Tools* and *New Actors that are Reshaping Global Philanthropy and Social Investing*, ed. Lester M. Salamon (San Francisco: Jossey-Bass Publishers, 2012).

12. Roseanne Mirabella, "Nonprofit Management Education: Current Offerings in University-Based Programs," accessed at: academic.shu.edu/npo/, May 14, 2011. *See also*: Roseanne Mirabella, "University-Based Educational Programs in Nonprofit Management and Philanthropic Studies: A 10-Year Review and Projections of Future Trend." *Nonprofit and Voluntary Sector Quarterly* 36:4 supplement (2007), 11S–27S.

13. John J. Havens and Paul G. Schervish, "Millionaires and the Millennium: New Estimates of the Forthcoming Wealth Transfer and the Prospects for a Golden Age of Philanthropy" (Boston: Boston College Social Welfare Research Institute, 1999).

14. Craig Smith, "The New Corporate Philanthropy," *Harvard Business Review* 72:1 (May/June 1994): 105–16; Jane Nelson, *Business as Partners in Development: Creating Wealth for Countries, Companies, and Communities* (London: Prince of Wales Business Leaders Forum, 1996); Lester M. Salamon, *Rethinking Corporate Social Engagement: Lessons from Latin America* (Sterling, VA: Kumarian Press, 2010).

15. Matthew Bishop and Michael Green, *Philanthrocapitalism: How the Rich Can Save the World* (New York: Bloomsbury Press, 2008).

16. See, for example: Steven Godeke and Doug Bauer, *Philanthropy's New Passing Gear: Mission-Related Investing—A Policy and Implementation Guide for Foundation Trustees* (New York: Rockefeller Philanthropy Advisors, 2008); David Wood and Belinda Hoff, *Handbook on Responsible Investment Across Asset Classes* (Boston: Institute for Responsible Investment, n.d. [2008]) and Salamon, *New Frontiers of Philanthropy*.

17. Bequest giving, adjusted for inflation, was 3 percent below its 2000 level as of 2007, the year before the recession, and dropped another 6.3 percent in 2008. *Giving USA 2009*, 211.

18. See, for example, Reed Abelson, "Health Insurers Profit as Many Postpone Care," *New York Times* (May 14, 2011), p. A1.

19. "Federal Budget (2011 and 2012)—Obama and Ryan Budget Plans," *New York Times* (May 5, 2011), topics.nytimes.com/top/reference/timestopics/subjects/f/federal_budget_us/index.html?scp=3&sq=U.S.%20Budget&st=cse.

20. U.S. Bureau of the Census, *Economic Census,* 1997 and 2007.

21. In what has become a frequent pattern, Lockheed Martin exited the welfare reform management arena in 2001, selling its IMS affiliate to Affiliated Computer Services, Inc. as part of a corporate realignment strategy to divest non-core businesses, but problems with its welfare reform business in Florida and Kansas likely played a role. See: Robert B. Denhardt and Janet V. Denhardt, *Public Administration: An Action Orientation*, 6th ed. (Belmont, CA: Thomson Wadsworth, 2009), 113.

22. U.S. Department of Education, *Digest of Education Statistics 2007* (Washington, DC: U.S. Government Printing Office, 2007).

23. *Giving USA 2001*, 53.

24. Donald Kettl, *Shared Power: Public Governance and Private Markets* (Washington, DC: The Brookings Institution Press, 1993).

25. For a discussion of these different forms of assistance and their consequences, see: Lester M. Salamon, "The New Governance and the Tools of Public Action: An Introduction," in *The Tools of Government: A Guide to the New Governance*, ed. Lester M. Salamon (New York: Oxford University Press, 2002), 1–47.

26. Lester M. Salamon, *Partners in Public Service: Government-Nonprofit Relations in the Modern Welfare State* (Baltimore: Johns Hopkins University Press, 1995), 208.

27. U.S. Congress, Committee on Ways and Means, *2000 Green Book: Background Material and Data on Programs within the Jurisdiction of the Committee on Ways and Means*, 106th Congress, 2d Session (October 6, 2000), 912, 923.

28. U.S. Office of Management and Budget, *Special Analysis, Budget of the United States Government, Fiscal Year 2011* (Washington, DC: Government Printing Office, 2010), 217.

29. For a discussion of the limited avenues nonprofits have available for generating capital, see: Lester M. Salamon and Stephanie L. Geller, "Investment Capital: The New Challenge for American Nonprofits," *Communiqué No. 5*, Johns Hopkins Nonprofit Listening Post Project (Baltimore: Johns Hopkins Center for Civil Society Studies, 2006).

30. For one recent attempt to give such ideas greater traction and visibility, see: Salamon, *New Frontiers of Philanthropy.*

31. See, for example: Lisbeth Schorr, *Within Our Reach: Breaking the Cycle of Disadvantage* (New York: Anchor Books, 1988).

32. Kimberly Dennis, "Charities on the Dole," *Policy Review: The Journal of American Citizenship* 76:5 (1996), 76.

33. See, for example, Charles Murray, *Losing Ground: American Social Policy, 1950–1980* (New York: Basic Books, 1984).

34. Regina Herzlinger, "Can Public Trust in Nonprofits and Governments Be Restored? " *Harvard Business Review 74* (March/April, 1996), 96.

35. Joel Fleishman, "To Merit and Preserve the Public's Trust in Not-For-Profit Organizations: The Urgent Need for New Strategies for Regulatory Reform," in *The Future of Philanthropy in a Changing America*, ed. Charles Clotfelter and Thomas Ehrlich (Bloomington: Indiana University Press, 1999), 172–197. For a recent Congressional challenge to the accountability features of nonprofits, see: U.S. Senate Finance Committee, "Staff Document on Regulation on Tax-Exempt Organizations" (June 22, 2004).

36. John McKnight, *The Careless Society: Community and its Counterfeits* (New York: Basic Books, 1995).

37. Michael Cooper, "Squeezed Cities Seek Some Relief from Nonprofits," *New York Times*, May 12, 2011, A1

38. Lester M. Salamon, Stephanie L. Geller, and S. Wojciech Sokolowski, "Taxing the Tax-Exempt Sector: A Growing Danger for Nonprofit Organizations," *Communique No. 21*, Johns Hopkins Nonprofit Listening Post Project (Baltimore: Johns Hopkins Center for Civil Society Studies, 2011).

39. For other examples of social ventures, see: www.community-wealth.org/strategies/panel/social/models.html. For a discussion of the broader array of financial instruments and institutions supporting this development, see: Salamon, *New Frontiers of Philanthropy*. For a conceptualization of this development as a "fourth sector," see: Heerad Sabeti and the Fourth Sector Network Concept Working Group, "The Emerging Fourth Sector," Executive Summary (Washington, DC: The Aspen Institute, 2009).

40. Sam Daley-Harris, *State of the Microcredit Summit Campaign Report* (Washington, DC: Microcredit Summit Campaign, 2009), 3.

41. See: C.K. Prahalad, *The Fortune at the Bottom of the Pyramid: Eradicating Poverty through Profits* (Philadelphia: Wharton School Publishing, 2004).

42. As John Gardner put it in his influential book on self-renewal, "Anyone concerned about the continuous renewal of society must be concerned for the renewal of that society's values and beliefs." John Gardner, *Self-Renewal: The Individual and the Innovative Society*, Revised edition (New York: W. W. Norton, 1981), 115.

43. This term is drawn from the title of Salamon, *Partners in Public Service* (1995).

44. "Forward Together: Empowering America's Citizen Sector for the Change We Need" (March 20, 2009), accessed at: www.jhu.edu/listeningpost/forward/.

13

Conclusions

Perhaps the central conclusion that flows from the foregoing chapters is that private nonprofit organizations continue to play a significant role in American society despite the expanded role of government over the past half-century or more. This runs counter to much conventional wisdom, which has viewed this expansion of government action as fundamentally hostile to the preservation of a vibrant private nonprofit sector. In fact, however, as we have seen, the growth of government activity in the American context has done at least as much to strengthen the nonprofit sector as to threaten it, and probably far more so. Because of American hostility to centralized government bureaucracies and the presence of significant nonprofit providers in many of the fields that government has entered, we have tended to rely heavily on nonprofit organizations to deliver even publicly funded services—in health, in education, in social services, and even in arts and culture. Consequently, the growth of government has helped to expand the nonprofit role, not limit or eliminate it, and as a result nonprofit organizations retain a significant foothold in virtually every sphere of human service.

This situation poses a serious challenge to the traditional terms and concepts commonly used to depict our social welfare system. Although government provides most of the funds in many of the key social welfare fields, private institutions deliver most of the services. Does this make the system public or private? Unfortunately, we do not even have the words to portray the situation. In some fields, such as hospital care, nonprofit organizations clearly play the largest role. In others, such as nursing home care, for-profit institutions are the major providers. Does this make the system mostly philanthropic or mostly commercial? Like the elephant examined by three blind men in the ancient tale, the American social welfare system appears to be a different beast depending on who touches it and where. It is, in fact, not a single system at all—whether governmental, nonprofit, or for-profit—but a blended system engaging a variety of actors that work together, in varying degrees of tension and cooperation, to address our common problems. As long-time nonprofit leader Brian O'Connell once put it, we have tended to make a "mesh" of things in this country. More generally, the "marble cake" analogy that political scientist Morton Grodzins coined to depict America's actual system of federal, state, and local government relationships applies equally to the relationships between the public and nonprofit sectors at all levels.[1] Instead of neatly demarcated spheres, public and private roles are intermixed in a dazzling array of swirls, each with its own contours and mixture of sectoral responsibilities.

The growth of government activity in the American context has done at least as much to strengthen the nonprofit sector as to threaten it, and probably far more so.

But even this concept has limitations, because nonprofit organizations are not only partners in public service, assisting government in the delivery of publicly financed services, but also—and importantly—often in the position of criticizing and prodding government rather than simply cooperating with it to carry out public objectives. Indeed, as we have seen, far from only providers of services, these organizations have a variety of other critical functions as well: we rely on them to give expression to diverse cultural values, facilitate citizen engagement in the policy process, build community, embody important national norms, and help us satisfy our spiritual needs.

While the "mixed" character of the American social welfare system makes it more difficult to comprehend and explain, it may also make it stronger and more capable of change. In a sense, Americans have surrendered the comprehensiveness and coherence of the social welfare systems of many European countries for the pluralism and adaptability of a much looser and more diverse system of mixed public and private care. In doing so, however, we have also taken on an added challenge of analysis and education to make our complex system comprehensible to our own citizenry and government officials as well as to those abroad interested in comprehending its lessons.

Unfortunately, ideological stereotypes and political rhetoric have kept us from meeting this challenge very effectively. As a consequence, the nonprofit sector remains shrouded in myths and barely perceptible to large portions of the American public. This is problematic not only because of the vital place these organizations continue to occupy in our national life, but also because of the serious risks they confront at the present time, risks arising from shifts in government policy, increased competition from for-profit providers, and a growing questioning of the contribution these organizations make. Penetrating the myths and improving understanding of this important set of institutions has thus become a matter of special urgency. If this primer has helped to contribute to such understanding, it will have served its purpose well.

ENDNOTE

1. Morton Grodzins, *The American System: A New View of Government in the United States*, ed. Daniel Elazar (Chicago: Rand-McNally, 1966).

References

Abelson, Reed. "Health Insurers Profit As Many Postpone Care." *New York Times*, May 14, 2011.

American Hospital Association. *Hospital Statistics*. Chicago: American Hospital Association, various years.

Ascoli, Ugo, and Costanzo Ranci, editors. *Dilemmas of the Welfare Mix: The New Structure of Welfare in an Era of Privatization*. London: Kluwer Academic/Plenum Publishers, 2002.

Baltimore City Department of Planning. *Baltimore City's Community Association Directory* (1991).

Bass, Gary D., David F. Arons, Kay Guinane, and Mathew F. Carter, with Susan Rees. *Seen but Not Heard: Strengthening Nonprofit Advocacy*. Washington, DC: The Aspen Institute, 2007.

Baumgartner, Frank R., and Beth L. Leech. "Interest Niches and Policy Bandwagons." *Journal of Politics* 63 (November 2001): 1191–1213.

Baxter, Christie I. *Program-Related Investments: A Technical Manual for Foundations*. New York: John Wiley and Sons, 1997.

Bedell, Kenneth B., editor. *Yearbook of American and Canadian Churches 1993*. Nashville: Abingdon Press, 1993.

Bedell, Kenneth B., editor. *Yearbook of American and Canadian Churches 1994*. Nashville: Abingdon Press, 1994.

Bedell, Kenneth B., editor. *Yearbook of American and Canadian Churches 1997*. Nashville: Abingdon Press, 1997.

Bell, Judith E. "Saving their Assets: How to Stop the Plunder at Blue Cross and Other Nonprofits." *The American Prospect* (May–June, 1996), 60–66.

Ben-Ner, Avner, and Theresa van Hoomissen. "Nonprofit Organizations in the Mixed Economy: A Demand and Supply Analysis." In *The Nonprofit Sector in the Mixed Economy*, edited by Avner Ben-Ner and Benedeto Gui. Ann Arbor: The University of Michigan Press, 1993.

Berry, Jeffrey M. "Citizen Groups and the Changing Nature of Interest Groups in America." *Annals of the American Academy of Political Science* 528 (July 1993): 30–41.

Berry, Jeffrey M. *Lobbying for the People: The Political Behavior of Public Interest Groups*. Princeton: Princeton University Press, 1977.

Berry, Jeffrey M. *The New Liberalism: The Rising Power of Citizen Groups*. Washington, DC: Brookings Institution Press, 1999.

Bishop, Matthew, and Michael Green. *Philanthrocapitalism: How the Rich Can Save the World*. New York: Bloomsbury Press, 2008.

Bixby, Ann Kallman. "Public Social Welfare Expenditures, Fiscal Years 1965–87." *Social Security Bulletin* 53:2 (February 1990): 10–26.

Bixby, Ann Kallman. "Public Social Welfare Expenditures, Fiscal Year 1994." *Social Security Bulletin* 60:3 (1997), 40.

Bixby, Ann Kallman. "Social Welfare Expenditures, 1963–83." *Social Security Bulletin* 49:2 (February 1986): 12–21.

Board of Governors of the Federal Reserve System. Federal Reserve Statistical Release Z.1, Flow of Funds Accounts of the U.S., Washington, DC, 2009. Accessed at: www.federalreserve.gov/releases/Z1/20090312.

Boris, Elizabeth T. "Nonprofit Organizations in a Democracy." In Nonprofits and Government: *Collaboration and Conflict*, edited by Elizabeth T. Boris and C. Eugene Steurle, 1–36. Washington: Urban Institute Press, 2006.

Bratton, Michael. "Review: Beyond the State: Civil Society and Associational Life in Africa." *World Politics* 41:3 (1989).

Brilliant, Eleanor. *The United Way: Dilemmas of Organized Charity*. New York: Columbia University Press, 1991.

Brody, Evelyn, editor. *Property-Tax Exemption for Charities: Mapping the Battlefield*. Washington, DC: The Urban Institute Press, 2002.

Center for Education Reform. *Annual Survey of Charter Schools 2008*. Washington, DC: Center for Education Reform, 2008.

Chaves, Mark. "Religious Congregations." In *The State of Nonprofit America*, 2nd Edition, edited by Lester M. Salamon. Washington, DC: Brookings Institution Press, 2012.

Chaves, Mark, Shawna Anderson, and Jason Byassee. *American Congregations at the Beginning of the 21st Century*. Durham, NC: National Congregations Study, 2009.

Cnaan, Ram A. *The Invisible Caring Hand: American Congregations and the Provision of Welfare.* New York: New York University Press, 1988.

Cobb, Nina Kressner. *Looking Ahead: Private Sector Giving to the Arts and the Humanities.* Washington, DC: President's Committee on the Arts and the Humanities, n.d. [1977].

Cohen, Rick. "Corporate-Initiated Charitable Funds." In *New Frontiers of Philanthropy: A Guide to the New Tools and New Actors that are Reshaping Global Philanthropy and Social Investing,* edited by Lester M. Salamon. San Francisco: Jossey-Bass Publishers, 2012.

Coleman, James S. *Foundations of Social Theory.* Cambridge, MA: Harvard University Press, 1990.

Commission on Private Philanthropy and Public Needs. *Giving in America: Toward a Stronger Voluntary Sector.* Washington, DC: Commission on Private Philanthropy and Public Needs, 1975.

Cooch, Sarah, and Mark Kramer. *Compounding Impact: Missing Investing by U.S. Foundations.* Boston: FSG Social Impact Advisors, 2007.

Cooper, Michael. "Squeezed Cities Seek Some Relief from Nonprofits." *New York Times,* May 12, 2011.

Corporation for National and Community Service, Office of Research and Policy Development. *Volunteering in America 2010: National, State, and City Information.* Issue Brief. Washington, DC: Corporation for National and Community Service, June 2010.

Coughlin, Teresa A., Leighton Ku, and John Holahan. *Medicaid Since 1980: Costs, Coverage, and the Shifting Alliance between the Federal Government and the States.* Washington: The Urban Institute Press, 1994.

Council for Aid to Education. *1996 Voluntary Support of Education.* Prepared by David Morgan. New York: Council for Aid to Education, 1997.

Daley-Harris, Sam. *State of the Microcredit Summit Campaign Report.* Washington, DC: Microcredit Summit Campaign, 2009.

DeFourny, Jacques, Patrick Develtere, and Bénédicte Fonteneau. "L'économie sociale au Nord et au Sud." *New Social Practices* 13:2 (December 2000): 216–219.

Denhardt, Robert B., and Janet V. Denhardt. *Public Administration: An Action Orientation,* 6th Edition. Belmont, CA: Thomson Wadsworth, 2009.

Dennis, Kimberly. "Charities on the Dole." *Policy Review: The Journal of American Citizenship* 76:5 (1996).

de Tocqueville, Alexis. *Democracy in America: The Henry Reeve Text, Vol. II.* New York: Vintage Books, 1945 [1835].

DiMaggio, Paul. "Nonprofit Organizations in the Production and Distribution of Culture." In *The Nonprofit Sector: A Research Handbook,* edited by Walter Powell, 195–220. New Haven: Yale University Press, 1987.

Dighe, Atul. "Demographic and Technological Imperatives." In *The State of Nonprofit America*, 2nd Edition, edited by Lester M. Salamon. Washington: Brookings Institution Press, 2012.

Erickson, David. *The Housing Policy Revolution: Networks and Neighborhoods*. Washington, DC: Urban Institute Press, 2009.

"Federal Budget (2011 and 2012)—Obama and Ryan Budget Plans." *New York Times*, May 5, 2011. Accessed at: topics.nytimes.com/top/reference/timestopics/subjects/f/federal_budget_us/index.html?scp=3&sq=U.S.%20Budget&st=cse.

Fetter, Frank. "The Subsidizing of Private Charities." *American Journal of Sociology* (1901–2): 359–85.

Fidelity Charitable Gift Fund. *Annual Report, 2008*. Cincinnati: Fidelity Charitable Gift Fund, 2008.

"Fixing D.C.'s Schools: The Charter Experiment," *A Washington Post Investigation*. Available at: www.washingtonpost.com/wp-srv/metro/specials/charter/.

Fleishman, Joel. "To Merit and Preserve the Public's Trust in Not-for-Profit Organizations: The Urgent Need for New Strategies for Regulatory Reform." In *The Future of Philanthropy in a Changing America*, edited by Charles Clotfelter and Thomas Ehrlich, 172–197. Bloomington: Indiana University Press, 1999.

Foundation Center. *Foundation Yearbook*, 2009. New York: The Foundation Center, 2009.

Gardner, John. *Self-Renewal: The Individual and the Innovative Society*, Revised Edition. New York: W.W. Norton, 1981.

Garr, Robin. *Reinvesting in America: The Grassroots Movements That Are Feeding the Hungry, Housing the Homeless, and Putting Americans Back to Work*. Reading, MA: Addison-Wesley, 1995.

Gidron, Benjamin, Ralph Kramer, and Lester M. Salamon, editors. Government and the Third Sector: *Emerging Relationships in Welfare States*. San Francisco: Jossey-Bass, 1992.

Gilbert, Neil. "The Transformation of Social Services." *Social Services Review* 51:4 (December 1977): 624–641.

Giving USA 1997. Researched and written at The Center on Philanthropy at Indiana University. Bloomington, IN: Giving USA Foundation, 1997.

Giving USA 2009. Researched and written at The Center on Philanthropy at Indiana University. Bloomington, IN: Giving USA Foundation, 2009.

Godeke, Steven, and Doug Bauer. *Philanthropy's New Passing Gear: Mission-Related Investing—A Policy and Implementation Guide for Foundation Trustees*. New York: Rockefeller Philanthropy Advisors, 2008.

Gray, Bradford H. *The Rise and Decline of the HMO: A Chapter in U.S. Health-Policy History*. Washington, DC: The Urban Institute, 2006.

Gray, Bradford H., and Mark Schlesinger. "Health." In *The State of Nonprofit America*, edited by Lester M. Salamon, 65–106. Washington, DC: The Brookings Institution Press, 2002.

Grodzins, Morton. *The American System: A New View of Government in the United States*, edited by Daniel Elazar. Chicago: Rand-McNally, 1966.

Grønbjerg, Kirsten A., Helen Liu, and Thomas Pollak. "Incorporated but not IRS-Registered: Exploring the (Dark) Grey Fringes of the Nonprofit Universe." *Nonprofit and Voluntary Sector Quarterly* 39:3 (September 2009).

Grønbjerg, Kirsten, and Sheila Nelson. "Mapping Small Religious Nonprofit Organizations: An Illinois Profile." *Nonprofit and Voluntary Sector Quarterly* 27:1 (March 1998): 13–31.

Hacker, Jacob S., and Paul Pierson. *Winner-Take-All Politics: How Washington Made the Rich Richer—and Turned Its Back on the Middle Class*. New York: Simon and Schuster, 2010.

Hadaway, C. Kirk, and Penny Long Marler. "How Many Americans Attend Worship Each Week? An Alternative Approach to Measurement." *Journal for the Scientific Study of Religion* 44:3 (2005): 307–322.

Hall, Peter Dobkin. "Historical Perspectives on Nonprofit Organizations." In *The Jossey-Bass Handbook of Nonprofit Leadership and Management*, edited by Robert D. Herman, 3–43. San Francisco: Jossey-Bass, 1994.

Hansmann, Henry. "The Role of Nonprofit Enterprise." *Yale Law Journal* 89 (1990): 835–901.

Hastings, Andrew W. "Donor Advised Fund Market: An analysis of the overall market and trends by National Philanthropic Trust." Jenkintown, PA: National Philanthropic Trust, November 2008.

Havens, John J., and Paul G. Schervish. "Millionaires and the Millennium: New Estimates of the Forthcoming Wealth Transfer and the Prospects for a Golden Age of Philanthropy." Boston: Boston College Social Welfare Research Institute, 1999.

Henriques, Diana B., and Andrew W. Lehren. "Megachurches Add Local Economy to Mission." *New York Times*, November 3, 2007.

Herzlinger, Regina. "Can Public Trust in Nonprofits and Governments Be Restored?" *Harvard Business Review* 74 (March/April, 1996): 96–107.

Hodgkinson, Virginia A., and Murray S. Weitzman, with John A. Abrahams, Eric A. Crutchfield, and David R. Stevenson. *Nonprofit Almanac 1996–1997: Dimensions of the Independent Sector*. San Francisco: Jossey Bass, 1996.

Hopkins, Bruce R. *The Law of Tax-Exempt Organizations*, 5th Edition. New York: John Wiley and Sons, 1987.

Hopkins, Bruce R. *The Law of Tax-Exempt Organizations*, 6th Edition. New York: John Wiley and Sons, 1992.

Hopkins, Bruce R. *The Law of Tax-Exempt Organizations*, 9th Edition. New York: John Wiley and Sons, 2007.

Hrywna, Mark. "The L3C Status: Groups Explore Structure that Limits Liability for Program-related Investing." *The NonProfit Times*, September 1, 2009. Accessed at: www.nptimes.com/09Sep/npt-090901-3.html.

Independent Sector. *America's Nonprofit Sector in Brief.* Washington, DC: Independent Sector, 1998.

Institute of Museum and Library Services, *Public Library Survey*. Accessed at: harvester.census.gov/imls/data/pls/index.asp#fy2008KsInfo.

James, Estelle. "The Nonprofit Sector in Comparative Perspective." In *The Nonprofit Sector: A Research Handbook*, edited by Walter W. Powell, 397–415. New Haven: Yale University Press, 1987.

Jones, Chris. "Monster or Mainstay?" *American Theatre* (March 1996).

Kaiser Permanente, *Annual Report: 2009*. Accessed at: xnet.kp.org/newscenter/annualreport/by_the_numbers.html.

Kendall, Jeremy, and Martin Knapp. "The United Kingdom." In *Defining the Nonprofit Sector: A Cross-National Analysis*, edited by Lester M. Salamon and Helmut K. Anheier, 249–279. Manchester, U.K.: Manchester University Press, 1996.

Kettl, Donald. *Shared Power: Public Governance and Private Markets*. Washington, DC: The Brookings Institution Press, 1993.

Kramer, Ralph M. *Voluntary Agencies in the Welfare State*. Berkeley: University of California Press, 1981.

Kramer, Ralph M. "Voluntary Agencies and the Personal Social Services." In *The Nonprofit Sector: A Research Handbook*, edited by Walter W. Powell, 240–257. New Haven: Yale University Press, 1987.

Krashinsky, Michael. "Stakeholder Theories of the Nonprofit Sector: One Cut at the Economic Literature." *Voluntas* 8:2 (1997): 149–161.

Levitan, Sar, and Robert Taggart. *The Promise of Greatness*. Cambridge: Harvard University Press, 1976.

Lindner, Eileen W., editor. *Yearbook of American and Canadian Churches*, 2010 edition. Prepared for the National Council of the Churches of Christ. Nashville: Abingdon Press, 2010.

Lipton, Eric. "Billionaire Brothers' Money Plays Role in Wisconsin Budget Dispute." *New York Times*, February 22, 2011.

Mayes, Rick. "The Origins, Development, and Passage of Medicare's Revolutionary Prospective Payment System." *Journal of the History of Medicine and Allied Sciences* 62:1 (January 2007): 21–55.

McKnight, John. *The Careless Society: Community and Its Counterfeits*. New York: Basic Books, 1995.

Mirabella, Roseanne. "Nonprofit Management Education: Current Offerings in University-Based Programs," Accessed at: http://academic.shu.edu/npo/, May 14, 2011.

Mirabella, Roseanne. "University-Based Educational Programs in Nonprofit Management and Philanthropic Studies: A 10-Year Review and Projections of Future Trends." *Nonprofit and Voluntary Sector Quarterly* 36:4 supplement (2007): 11S–27S.

Monzon, José Luis, and Rafael Chaves. "The European Social Economy: Concept and Dimensions of the Third Sector." *Annals of Public and Cooperative Economics* 79:3–4 (2008): 549–577.

Murray, Charles. *Losing Ground: American Social Policy, 1950–1980*. New York: Basic Books, 1984.

Nash, Matthew T. A. "Social Entrepreneurship and Social Enterprise." In *The Jossey-Bass Handbook of Nonprofit Leadership and Management*, edited by David O. Renz, 262–298. San Francisco: Jossey-Bass, 2010.

Nelson, Jane. *Business as Partners in Development: Creating Wealth for Countries, Companies, and Communities*. London: Prince of Wales Business Leaders Forum, 1996.

Nichols, Alex. "Introduction." In *Social Entrepreneurship: New Models of Sustainable Social Change*, edited by Alex Nichols, 1–36. Oxford, UK: Oxford University Press, 2006.

Nichols, Alex, editor. *Social Entrepreneurship: New Models of Sustainable Social Change*. Oxford, UK: Oxford University Press, 2006.

Nielsen, Waldemar. *The Endangered Sector*. New York: Columbia University Press, 1979.

Nyssens, Marthe, editor. *Social Enterprise: At the Crossroads of Market, Public Policies, and Civil Society*. London: Routledge, 2006.

O'Connell, Brian. *People Power: Service, Advocacy, Empowerment*. New York: The Foundation Center, 1994.

O'Neill, Michael. "Public Confidence in Charitable Nonprofits." *Nonprofit and Voluntary Sector Quarterly* 38:2 (April 2009): 237–269.

O'Neill, Michael. *The Third America: The Emergence of the Nonprofit Sector in the United States*. San Francisco: Jossey-Bass Publishers, 1989.

Powell, Walter W., editor. *The Nonprofit Sector: A Research Handbook*. New Haven: Yale University Press, 1987.

Prahalad, C.K. *The Fortune at the Bottom of the Pyramid: Eradicating Poverty Through Profits*. Philadelphia: Wharton School Publishing, 2004.

Putnam, Robert. *Making Democracy Work: Civic Traditions in Modern Italy*. Princeton: Princeton University Press, 1993.

Reagan, Ronald. *Papers of the President of the United States: President Ronald Reagan*, Speech of September 24, 1981. Accessed at: www.reagan.utexas.edu/archives/speeches/1981/92481d.htm.

Ronsvalle, John and Sylvia. "The State of Church Giving Through 1991." In *Yearbook of American and Canadian Churches 1994*, edited by Kenneth B. Bedell, 12–15. Nashville: Abingdon Press, 1994.

Rosner, David. "Gaining Control: Reform, Reimbursement, and Politics in New York's Community Hospitals, 1890–1915." *American Journal of Public Health* 790 (1980): 533–542.

Rothman, David. *The Discovery of the Asylum: Social Order and Disorder in the New Republic*. Boston: Little, Brown, 1971.

Sabeti, Heerad, and the Fourth Sector Network Concept Working Group, "The Emerging Fourth Sector," Executive Summary. Washington, DC: The Aspen Institute, 2009.

Salamon, Lester M. *America's Nonprofit Sector: A Primer*, 2nd Edition. New York: Foundation Center, 1999.

Salamon, Lester M. "The Marketization of Welfare: Changing Nonprofit and For-Profit Roles in the American Welfare State." *Social Service Review* 67:1 (March 1993): 17–39.

Salamon, Lester M. "The New Governance and the Tools of Public Action: An Introduction." In *The Tools of Government: A Guide to the New Governance*, edited by Lester M. Salamon, 1–47. New York: Oxford University Press, 2002.

Salamon, Lester M., editor. *New Frontiers of Philanthropy: A Guide to the New Tools and New Actors that are Reshaping Global Philanthropy and Social Investing*. San Francisco: Jossey-Bass Publishers, 2012.

Salamon, Lester M. "Nonprofit Organizations: The Lost Opportunity." In *The Reagan Record*, edited by John L. Palmer and Isabel V. Sawhill, 261–286. Cambridge: Ballinger Publishing Company, 1984.

Salamon, Lester M. "Of Market Failure, Voluntary Failure, and Third-Party Government: Toward a Theory of Government-Nonprofit Relations in the Modern Welfare State." *Journal of Voluntary Action Research* 16:1–2 (1987): 29–49 [Reprinted in: Lester M. Salamon. *Partners in Public Service: Government-Nonprofit Relations in the Modern Welfare State*. Baltimore: Johns Hopkins University Press, 1995].

Salamon, Lester M. *Partners in Public Service: Government-Nonprofit Relations in the Modern Welfare State*. Baltimore: Johns Hopkins University Press, 1995.

Salamon, Lester M. "Putting Civil Society on the Economic Map of the World." *Annals of Public and Cooperative Economics* 81:2 (Summer 2010): 167–210.

Salamon, Lester M. *The Resilient Sector*. Washington, DC: The Brookings Institution Press, 2003.

Salamon, Lester M. *Rethinking Corporate Social Engagement: Lessons from Latin America*. Sterling, VA: Kumarian Press, 2010.

Salamon, Lester M. "Rethinking Public Management: Third-Party Government and the Changing Forms of Government Action." *Public Policy* 29 (1981): 255–275.

Salamon, Lester M. "The Rise of the Nonprofit Sector." *Foreign Affairs*, 73:4 (July/August 1994): 109–122.

Salamon, Lester M., editor. *The State of Nonprofit America*. Washington, DC: Brookings Institution Press, 2002.

Salamon, Lester M., editor. *The State of Nonprofit America*. 2nd Edition. Washington, DC: Brookings Institution Press, 2012.

Salamon, Lester M., editor. *The Tools of Government: A Guide to the New Governance*. New York: Oxford University Press, 2002.

Salamon, Lester M. "The Voluntary Sector and the Future of the Welfare State." *Nonprofit and Voluntary Sector Quarterly* 18:1 (Spring 1989): 16–39.

Salamon, Lester M. *Welfare: The Elusive Consensus—Where We Are, How We Got Here, and What's Ahead*. New York: Praeger Publishers, 1977.

Salamon, Lester M., and Alan J. Abramson. *The Federal Budget and the Nonprofit Sector*. Washington, DC: The Urban Institute Press, 1982.

Salamon, Lester M., and Alan J. Abramson. "The Nonprofit Sector." In *The Reagan Experiment*, edited by John L. Palmer and Isabel Sawhill, 219–243. Washington, DC: The Urban Institute Press, 1982.

Salamon, Lester M., David M. Altschuler, and Jaana Myllyluoma. *More Than Just Charity: The Baltimore Area Nonprofit Sector in a Time of Change*. Baltimore: The Johns Hopkins Institute for Policy Studies, 1990.

Salamon, Lester M., and Helmut K. Anheier. *Defining the Nonprofit Sector: A Cross-National Analysis*. Manchester, U.K.: Manchester University Press, 1996.

Salamon, Lester M., and Helmut K. Anheier. "In Search of the Nonprofit Sector: The Problem of Definition." *Voluntas* 3:2 (1992): 125–151.

Salamon, Lester M., and Stephanie L. Geller. "Investment Capital: The New Challenge for American Nonprofits." *Communiqué No. 5*, Johns Hopkins Nonprofit Listening Post Project. Baltimore: Johns Hopkins Center for Civil Society Studies, 2006.

Salamon, Lester M., and Stephanie L. Geller. "Nonprofit America: A Force for Democracy?" *Communiqué No. 9*, Johns Hopkins Nonprofit Listening Post Project . Baltimore: Johns Hopkins Center for Civil Society Studies, 2008.

Salamon, Lester M., Stephanie L. Geller, and S. Wojciech Sokolowski. "Taxing the Tax-Exempt Sector: A Growing Danger for Nonprofit Organizations." *Communique No. 21*,

Johns Hopkins Nonprofit Listening Post Project. Baltimore: Johns Hopkins Center for Civil Society Studies, 2011.

Salamon, Lester M., S. Wojciech Sokolowsi, and Associates. *Global Civil Society: Dimensions of the Nonprofit Sector*, Volume II. Bloomfield, CT: Kumarian Press, 2004.

Salamon, Lester M., S. Wojciech Sokolowsi, and Associates. *Global Civil Society: Dimensions of the Nonprofit Sector, Volume III*. Sterling, VA: Kumarian Press, 2011.

Salamon, Lester M., and S. Wojciech Sokolowski. "Nonprofits and Recession: Evidence from 21 States." Nonprofit Employment Data Project Bulletin. Baltimore: Johns Hopkins Center for Civil Society Studies, 2010.

Samuels, Steven, and Alisha Tonsic. *Theater Facts 1995*. New York: Theater Communications Group, 1996.

Schlozman, Kay Lehman, and John T. Tierney. *Organized Interests and American Democracy*. New York: Harper and Row, 1986.

Schorr, Lisbeth. *Within Our Reach: Breaking the Cycle of Disadvantage*. New York: Anchor Books, 1988.

Sirianni, Carmen, and Lewis Friedland. *Civic Innovation in America: Community Empowerment, Public Policy, and the Movement for Civic Renewal*. Berkeley: University of California Press, 2001.

Skocpol, Theda. *Social Policy in the United States: Future Possibilities in Historical Perspective*. Princeton: Princeton University Press, 1995.

Smith, Craig. "The New Corporate Philanthropy." *Harvard Business Review* 72:1 (May/June 1994): 105–116.

Smith, David Horton. "The Rest of the Nonprofit Sector: Grassroots Associations as the Dark Matter Ignored in Prevailing 'Flat Earth' Maps of the Sector." *Nonprofit and Voluntary Sector Quarterly* 26:2 (June 1997): 114–131.

Smith, Steven R., and Michael Lipsky. *Nonprofits For Hire: The Welfare State in the Age of Contracting*. Cambridge: Harvard University Press, 1993.

Stevens, Rosemary. *In Sickness and in Wealth: American Hospitals in the Twentieth Century*. New York: Basic Books, 1997.

Stevens, Rosemary. "A Poor Sort of Memory: Voluntary Hospitals and Government Before the Depression." *Milbank Fund Quarterly/Health and Society* 60:4 (1982): 551–584.

Stoddard, Abby. "International Assistance." In *The State of Nonprofit America*, 2nd Edition, edited by Lester M. Salamon. Washington DC: Brookings Institution Press, 2012.

Strahan, Genevieve W. "An Overview of Nursing Homes and their Current Residents: Data from the 1995 National Nursing Home Survey." *Advance Data* 280 (January 28, 1997).

Sundquist, James L., and David W. Davis. *Making Federalism Work*. Washington, DC: The Brookings Institution, 1969.

Sunstein, Cass. *After the Rights Revolution: Reconceiving the Regulatory State*. Cambridge: Harvard University Press, 1990.

United Nations Statistics Division. *Handbook on Nonprofit Institutions in the System of National Accounts*. New York: United Nations, 2003.

Urice, John. "The Future of the State Arts Agency Movement in the 1990s: Decline and Effect." *The Journal of Arts Management, Law, and Society* 22:1 (Spring 1992).

U.S. Agency for International Development. *2009 Volag Report of Voluntary Agencies*. Washington, DC: U.S. Agency for International Development, 2009.

U.S. Agency for International Development. *Voluntary Foreign Aid Programs*, various years. Washington, DC: U.S. Agency for International Development, various years.

U.S. Agency for International Development. Advisory Committee on Voluntary Foreign Aid. *An Assessment of the State of the USAID/PVO Partnership*. Washington, DC: Advisory Committee on Voluntary Foreign Aid, June 1997.

U.S. Bureau of the Census. *Service Annual Survey 1996*. Washington, DC: U.S. Government Printing Office, 1998.

U.S.Bureau of the Census. *Census of Government 2007*. Accessed at: harvester.census.gov/datadissem/Results.aspx.

U.S. Bureau of the Census. *Census of Service Industries*, various years. Washington, DC: U.S. Government Printing Office, various years.

U.S. Bureau of the Census. *Current Population Survey*, September Supplement, 2010. Accessed at: www.census.gov/cps/.

U.S. Bureau of the Census. *Economic Census*. Washington, DC: U.S. Government Printing Office, various years (1977, 1997, 2002, 2007).

U.S. Bureau of the Census. *Service Annual Survey 2006*. Washington, DC: U.S. Government Printing Office, 2008.

U.S. Bureau of the Census. *Statistical Abstract of the United States*, various years. Washington, DC: U.S. Government Printing Office, various years.

U.S. Bureau of Economic Analysis, Economic Accounts. "Current-dollar and 'Real' GDP levels 1929–2008." Accessed at: www.bea.gov/national/index.htm#gdp.

U.S. Bureau of Economic Analysis. *National Income and Product Accounts*, various tables. Accessed at: http://www.bea.gov/national/nipaweb/SelectTable.asp?Selected=N.

U.S. Bureau of Labor Statistics. "Volunteering in the United States—2010" (January 26, 2011). Accessed at: www.bls.gov/news.release/pdf/volun.pdf.

U.S. Congress, Committee on Ways and Means. *2000 Green Book: Background Materials and Data on Programs within the Jurisdiction of the Committee on Ways and Means.* Washington, DC: 106th Congress, 2nd Session, October 6, 2000.

U.S. Council of Economic Advisors, *Economic Report of the President,* 1998. Washington, DC: U.S. Government Printing Office, 1998.

U.S. Council of Economic Advisors, *Economic Report of the President,* 2009. Washington, DC: U.S. Government Printing Office, 2009.

U.S. Department of Education, Center for Education Statistics. *Digest of Education Statistics,* various years. Washington, DC: U.S. Government Printing Office, various years.

U.S. Department of Health and Human Services. "A Brief History of the AFDC Program." Accessed at: aspe.hhs.gov/hsp/afdc/baseline/1history.pdf.

U.S. Department of Health and Human Services, Centers for Medicare and Medicaid Services. *National Health Expenditure Data,* 2008. Accessed at: www.cms.gov/ NationalHealthExpendData/downloads/tables.pdf.

U.S. Department of Health and Human Services, Health Care Financing Administration. "National Health Expenditures, 1987." *Health Care Financing Review* 10:2 (Winter 1988).

U.S. Department of Health and Human Services, Health Care Financing Administration. "National Health Expenditures, 1995." *Health Care Financing Review* 18:1 (Fall 1996).

U.S. Department of Health and Human Services, Health Care Financing Administration. "National Health Expenditures, 1997," *Health Care Financing Review* 20:2 (1998).

U.S. Department of Health and Human Services, Public Health Service. *Surgeon General's Workshop on Self-Help and Public Health.* Washington, DC: U.S. Government Printing Office, 1988.

U.S. Department of Labor, Bureau of Labor Statistics. *Quarterly Census of Employment and Wages, 2005.* Washington, DC: U.S. Government Printing Office, 2005.

U.S. Internal Revenue Service. *Exempt Organization Master File.* Accessed at: www.irs.gov/ taxstats/charitablestats/article/0,,id=97186,00.html.

U.S. Internal Revenue Service. *Statistics of Income* Form 990 and 990 PF Date Files. Accessed at: www.irs.gov/taxstats/charitablestats/ and www.irs.gov/pub/irs-soi/07pf01ta.xls.

U.S. Office of Management and Budget. *Budget of the United States Government, Fiscal Year 2012.* Washington, DC: U.S. Government Printing Office, 2011.

U.S. Office of Management and Budget. *Special Analysis, Budget of the United States Government, Fiscal Year 2011.* Washington, DC: U.S. Government Printing Office, 2010.

U.S. Senate Finance Committee. "Staff Document on Regulation on Tax-Exempt Organizations." June 22, 2004 (unpublished).

Vogel, David. *Fluctuating Fortunes: The Political Power of Business in America.* New York: Basic Books, 1989.

Warner, Amos G. *American Charities: A Study in Philanthropy and Economics.* New York: Thomas Y. Crowell, 1894.

The Washington Post Company. Annual Report, 2007 and 2009. Accessed at: www. washpostco.com/phoenix.zhtml?c=62487&p=irol-reportsAnnualArch.

Weisbrod, Burton. *The Voluntary Nonprofit Sector.* Lexington, MA: Lexington Books, 1978.

Whitehead, John S. *The Separation of College and State: Columbia, Dartmouth, Harvard and Yale, 1776–1876.* New Haven, CT: Yale University Press, 1973.

Wing, Kennard T., Thomas H. Pollack, and Amy Blackwood. *The Nonprofit Almanac: 2008.* Washington, DC: The Urban Institute Press, 2008.

Wood, David, and Belinda Hoff. *Handbook on Responsible Investment Across Asset Classes.* Boston: Institute for Responsible Investment, n.d. [2008].

Wolch, Jennifer. *The Shadow State.* New York: The Foundation Center, 1990.

Young, Dennis R., and Lester M. Salamon. "Commercialization, Social Ventures, and For-Profit Competition." In *The State of Nonprofit America*, edited by Lester M. Salamon, 243–446. Washington, DC: Brookings Institution Press, 2002.

Index